# NOTES ON WESLEY'S
# FORTY-FOUR SERMONS

# NOTES ON WESLEY'S
# FORTY-FOUR SERMONS

BY
## JOHN LAWSON
M.A., B.D. (Cantab.), B.Sc. (Agriculture) (Lond.)

WIPF & STOCK · Eugene, Oregon

Wipf and Stock Publishers
199 W 8th Ave, Suite 3
Eugene, OR 97401

Notes on Wesley's Forty-Four Sermons
By Lawson, John
Copyright©1952 Epworth Press
ISBN 13: 978-1-60899-119-8
Publication date 9/30/2009
Previously published by Epworth Press, 1952


Copyright © Epworth Press 1952
First English edition 1952 by Epworth Press
This edition published by arrangement with Epworth Press

DEDICATED

IN AFFECTION AND RESPECT

TO MY FATHER-IN-LAW

PERCY A. IZZETT

HONOURED IN THE COMPANY OF METHODIST LOCAL PREACHERS

# PREFACE

It is a remarkable thing that a book of this nature was not written years ago. This continued lack clearly reflects an assumption on the part of bygone generations of Methodists that the meaning of Wesley's Sermons is self-evident to those beginners at theology who have been accustomed to read them. His work as a tutor in the correspondence courses so admirably organized by the Methodist Connexional Local Preachers' Department soon opened the eyes of the present writer to the error of this assumption, and so inspired this little book. It is designed primarily for the use of young Local Preachers as they take up the study of the Methodist Standard Sermons for the first time, but it is hoped that it will also serve to introduce the Methodist people in general to this part of our great heritage.

The student of Methodism will ask: 'What is the relation of this small volume to Dr. E. H. Sugden's great work, *The Standard Sermons of John Wesley, Annotated* (Epworth Press, 1921, 2 vols.)?' In answer it may be said that Sugden is the book for the careful student of Methodist history. This is for the beginner in theology and preaching. Sugden is admirable and indispensable as a mine of information regarding the historical background to the Sermons, comparison of statements therein to other statements in Wesley and in early Methodist writings, evidence as to the development of Wesley's own thought and of Methodist theology, etc. It is, however, largely assumed that the reader will have a competent background of Christian theology, and also will be able to appreciate a proposition when stated by Wesley in eighteenth-century diction, and in terms of eighteenth-century controversy. The present writer has, for the sake of the beginner, tried to avoid both these assumptions, even at the risk of explaining what to some may appear the obvious. To these explanations has been added a digest of the more important and interesting historical information from Sugden.

The author would wish first of all to make the fullest acknowledgement of his great debt to Dr. Sugden's work, without which this book could hardly have been written. He would also express his deep appreciation for sympathetic encouragement received from the Connexional Local Preachers' Secretary, the Reverend F. A. Farley, M.A., B.D., as also from the Methodist Publishing House, through the Reverend E. C. Barton. He would also take this opportunity of thanking his brother-in-law, the Reverend Alan R. Miller, a faithful upholder of our Church and 'our doctrines', for his help and advice in reading the manuscript.

COLSTERWORTH, LINCS
*16th July*, 1945.

# CONTENTS

PREFACE - - - - - - - - - - **vi**

FOR THE BEGINNER: HOW TO USE THESE NOTES - - - xv

WHY FORTY-FOUR SERMONS? - - - - - - - xix

NOTES ON WESLEY'S PREFACE TO THE STANDARD SERMONS - xxiii

## TITLES AND TEXTS OF SERMONS

SERMON

I SALVATION BY FAITH - - - - - - - 1
*By grace are ye saved through faith.*—Eph. ii. 8.

II THE ALMOST CHRISTIAN - - - - - 11
*Almost thou persuadest me to be a Christian.*—Acts xxvi. 28.

III AWAKE, THOU THAT SLEEPEST - - - - 17
*Awake, thou that sleepest, and arise from the dead, and Christ shall give thee light.*—Eph. v. 14.

IV SCRIPTURAL CHRISTIANITY - - - - - 24
*And they were all filled with the Holy Ghost.*—Acts iv. 31.

V JUSTIFICATION BY FAITH - - - - - - 37
*To him that worketh not, but believeth on Him that justifieth the ungodly, his faith is counted for righteousness.*—Rom. iv. 5.

VI THE RIGHTEOUSNESS OF FAITH - - - 55
*Moses describeth the righteousuess which is of the law, That the man which doeth those things shall live by them, &c.*—Rom. x. 5-8.

## CONTENTS

**SERMON**

**VII** THE WAY TO THE KINGDOM — 60
*The kingdom of God is at hand: repent ye, and believe the gospel.*—Mark i. 15.

**VIII** THE FIRST-FRUITS OF THE SPIRIT — 67
*There is therefore now no condemnation to them which are in Christ Jesus, who walk not after the flesh, but after the Spirit.*—Rom. viii. 1.

**IX** THE SPIRIT OF BONDAGE AND OF ADOPTION — 78
*Ye have not received the spirit of bondage again unto fear; but ye have received the Spirit of adoption, whereby we cry, Abba, Father.*—Rom. viii. 15.

**X** THE WITNESS OF THE SPIRIT — 86
*The Spirit itself beareth witness with our spirit, that we are the children of God.*—Rom. viii. 16.

**XI** THE WITNESS OF OUR OWN SPIRIT — 98
*This is our rejoicing, the testimony of our conscience, that in simplicity and godly sincerity, not with fleshly wisdom, but by the grace of God, we have had our conversation in the world.*—2 Cor. i. 12.

**XII** THE MEANS OF GRACE — 102
*Ye are gone away from Mine ordinances, and have not kept them.*—Mal. iii. 7.

**XIII** THE CIRCUMCISION OF THE HEART — 110
*Circumcision is that of the heart, in the spirit, and not in the letter.*—Rom. ii. 29.

**XIV** THE MARKS OF THE NEW BIRTH — 115
*So is every one that is born of the Spirit.*—John iii. 8.

**XV** THE GREAT PRIVILEGE OF THOSE THAT ARE BORN OF GOD — 123
*Whosoever is born of God doth not commit sin.*—1 John iii. 9.

## CONTENTS

| SERMON | | |
|---|---|---|
| XVI | SERMON ON THE MOUNT.—I. | 132 |
| | *And seeing the multitudes, He went up into a mountain: and when He was set, His disciples came unto Him, &c.*—Matt. v. 1-4. | |
| XVII | SERMON ON THE MOUNT.—II. | 135 |
| | *Blessed are the meek, &c.*—Matt. v. 5-7. | |
| XVIII | SERMON ON THE MOUNT.—III. | 140 |
| | *Blessed are the pure in heart, &c.*—Matt. v. 8-12. | |
| XIX | SERMON ON THE MOUNT.—IV. | 147 |
| | *Ye are the salt of the earth, &c.*—Matt. v. 13-16. | |
| XX | SERMON ON THE MOUNT.—V. | 151 |
| | *Think not that I am come to destroy the Law, or the Prophets: I am not come to destroy, &c.*—Matt. v. 17-20. | |
| XXI | SERMON ON THE MOUNT.—VI. | 158 |
| | *Take heed that ye do not your alms before men, to be seen of them, &c.*—Matt. vi. 1-15. | |
| XXII | SERMON ON THE MOUNT.—VII. | 162 |
| | *Moreover when ye fast, be not, as the hypocrites, of a sad countenance, &c.*—Matt. vi. 16-18. | |
| XXIII | SERMON ON THE MOUNT.—VIII. | 165 |
| | *Lay not up for yourselves treasures upon earth, where moth and rust doth corrupt, &c.*—Matt. vi. 19-23. | |
| XXIV | SERMON ON THE MOUNT.—IX. | 170 |
| | *No man can serve two masters: for either he will hate the one, and love the other, &c.*—Matt. vi. 24-34. | |
| XXV | SERMON ON THE MOUNT.—X. | 173 |
| | *Judge not, that ye be not judged, &c.*—Matt. vii. 1-12. | |
| XXVI | SERMON ON THE MOUNT.—XI. | 175 |
| | *Enter ye in at the strait gate, &c.*—Matt. vii. 13, 14. | |

## CONTENTS

| SERMON | | |
|---|---|---|
| XXVII | SERMON ON THE MOUNT.—XII. | 178 |
| | *Beware of false prophets, which come to you in sheep's clothing, &c.*—Matt. vii. 15-20. | |
| XXVIII | SERMON ON THE MOUNT.—XIII. | 182 |
| | *Not every one that saith unto Me, Lord, Lord, shall enter into the kingdom of heaven, &c.*—Matt. vii. 21-27. | |
| XXIX | THE ORIGINAL, NATURE, PROPERTY, AND USE OF THE LAW | 184 |
| | *Wherefore the law is holy, and the commandment holy, and just, and good.*—Rom. vii. 12. | |
| XXX | THE LAW ESTABLISHED THROUGH FAITH.—I. | 190 |
| | *Do we then make void the law through faith? God forbid: yea, we establish the law.*—Rom. iii. 31. | |
| XXXI | THE LAW ESTABLISHED THROUGH FAITH.—II. | 193 |
| | *Do we then make void the law through faith? God forbid: yea, we establish the law.*—Rom. iii. 31. | |
| XXXII | THE NATURE OF ENTHUSIASM | 195 |
| | *And Festus said with a loud voice, Paul, thou art beside thyself.*—Acts xxvi. 24. | |
| XXXIII | A CAUTION AGAINST BIGOTRY | 201 |
| | *And John answered Him, sayiug, Master, we saw one casting out devils in Thy name: and he followeth not us, &c.*—Mark ix. 38, 39. | |
| XXXIV | CATHOLIC SPIRIT | 209 |
| | *And when he was departed thence, he lighted on Jehonadab the son of Rechab coming to meet him: and he saluted him, &c.*—2 Kings x. 15. | |
| XXXV | CHRISTIAN PERFECTION | 215 |
| | *Not as though I had already attaiued, either were already perfect.*—Phill iii. 12. | |

## CONTENTS

| SERMON | | |
|---|---|---|
| XXXVI | WANDERING THOUGHTS | 226 |
| | *Bringing into captivity every thought to the obedience of Christ.*—2 Cor. x. 5. | |
| XXXVII | SATAN'S DEVICES | 229 |
| | *We are not ignorant of his devices.*—2 Cor. ii. 11. | |
| XXXVIII | ORIGINAL SIN | 232 |
| | *And God saw that the wickedness of man was great in the earth, and that every imagination of the thoughts of his heart was only evil continually.*—Gen. vi. 5. | |
| XXXIX | THE NEW BIRTH | 241 |
| | *Ye must be born again.*—John iii. 7. | |
| XL | THE WILDERNESS STATE | 246 |
| | *Ye now have sorrow: but I will see you again, and your heart shall rejoice, and your joy no man taketh from you.*—John xvi. 22. | |
| XLI | HEAVINESS THROUGH MANIFOLD TEMPTATIONS | 251 |
| | *Now for a season, if need be, ye are in heaviness through manifold temptations.*—1 Pet. i. 6. | |
| XLII | SELF-DENIAL | 255 |
| | *And He said to them all, If any man will come after Me, let him deny himself, and take up his cross daily, and follow Me.*—Luke ix. 23. | |
| XLIII | THE CURE OF EVIL-SPEAKING | 261 |
| | *If thy brother shall trespass against thee, go and tell him his fault between thee and him alone: if he shall hear thee, &c.*—Matt. xviii. 15-17. | |
| XLIV | THE USE OF MONEY | 264 |
| | *I say unto you, Make yourselves friends of the mammon of unrighteousness; that, when ye fail, they may receive you into everlasting habitations.*—Luke xvi. 9. | |

## INDEXES

I THEOLOGICAL SUBJECTS - - - - - - - 277

II HISTORICAL SUBJECTS - - - - - - - 284

III PRACTICAL AND ETHICAL SUBJECTS - - - - - 289

# FOR THE BEGINNER: HOW TO USE THESE NOTES

1. As you read Wesley's Sermons remember always that you are reading the work of one of the world's greatest men. You are reading to prepare yourself for the world's greatest and noblest task. Therefore, resolve that it is worth while to take some pains with these sermons. Those who give of their best to them will find here a study of fascinating interest. Those who hope to skip through them quickly will find very little. Expect to find something of value in every sermon; if not instruction in theology, then perhaps practical guidance on the way of life, a window into the heart and mind of Wesley, light upon the times and history of early Methodism, or a sample of noble eloquence or superb literary style.

2. In these notes Wesley's admirable system of headings, sub-headings, and numbered paragraphs is followed throughout. Look at the margin, and you can tell at a glance to which paragraph every note belongs.

3. First make sure whether your copy of Wesley's Sermons is a modern one with forty-four sermons, or an older edition with fifty-three. These notes use the modern numbering of the sermons, but in the footnote to each sermon there is a reference giving the appropriate number in the *'Fifty-three Sermons'*. The system of headings, sub-headings, and numbered paragraphs is the same in both cases.

4. If a note does *not* start with a word or sentence from Wesley, quoted in inverted commas, the note refers to the whole paragraph in general. It is best in this case to read the note first, and then the paragraph of the sermon.

5. If a note starts with a quotation from Wesley, the note is on that word or sentence in particular. In this case it is best first to read the paragraph of the sermon, then to turn back and read the note.

## FOR THE BEGINNER: HOW TO USE THESE NOTES

6. Always take the trouble to look up cross-references given in the notes.

7. If you wish to find out all that Wesley says on any given subject, or all that appears in these notes on any subject, refer to the index. There are so many matters treated of in these Sermons that this index presents the student with a complete outline of the more practical side of Christian theology, together with quite a lot of information about Wesley, the history of early Methodism, the practical problems of the modern preacher, etc.

8. Read Wesley's fine Preface to the Sermons, with these notes.

9. Summary list of the more important Sermons, and their main interest:

I. 'Salvation by Faith'—what faith is: what salvation is: salvation by faith.

II. 'The Almost Christian'—the religion of the heart (which theme occurs constantly in the *Sermons*).

IV. 'Scriptural Christianity'—the Methodist Revival and contemporary religion.

V. 'Justification by Faith'—Wesley's doctrinal background.

VIII. 'The First-Fruits of the Spirit'—advice to a convert: growth in grace.

IX. 'The Spirit of Bondage and of Adoption'—conversion.

X. 'The Witness of the Spirit'—Christian assurance.

XII. 'The Means of Grace'—the devotional life.

XV. 'The Great Privilege of those that are Born of God'—advice to a believer: growth in grace: meeting temptation.

XVIII. 'On the Sermon on the Mount: III'—the Christian way of life.

FOR THE BEGINNER: HOW TO USE THESE NOTES xvii

XIX. 'On the Sermon on the Mount: IV'—the active and useful Christian.

XX. 'On the Sermon on the Mount: V'—ethical religion.

XXIV. 'On the Sermon on the Mount: IX'—the Christian and the world.

XXVIII. 'On the Sermon on the Mount: XIII'—the religion of the heart.

XXX. 'The Law Established through Faith: I'—ethical religion.

XXXII. 'The nature of Enthusiasm'—defence of Methodism: place of common sense in religion.

XXXVII. 'Satan's Devices'

XL. 'The Wilderness State'

XLI. 'Heaviness through Manifold Temptations'—growth in grace: pressing on to perfection.

XLIV. 'The Use of Money'—the Social Gospel.

# WHY FORTY-FOUR SERMONS?

As soon as Methodism became possessed of land and property the Wesleys had to face the task of forming legal trusts to hold the same, and of securing legal recognition of the Methodist Connexion as a corporate body capable of holding property. The first step was the publication in 1763 of a pamphlet by John Wesley, known as the *Large Minutes*. This contained a form of trust-deed, designed as a model upon which the trust-deeds of Methodist property were to be drawn. A clause of this model deed provided that the preachers should preach 'no other doctrine than is contained in Mr. Wesley's Notes upon the New Testament, and four volumes of Sermons'. This provision was continued in all the succeeding editions of the *Large Minutes*. A further step was taken in 1784, when John Wesley enrolled in the High Court of Chancery a 'Deed of Declaration and Appointment'. In this he gave legal definition to the Methodist Conference, appointing 100 preachers (the 'Legal Hundred') to be the responsible governing body of the Connexion, as from the death of himself and his brother.

The Methodist Conference of 1832 adopted the 'Chapel Model Deed', to be used henceforth for all Methodist Chapels. This contained: (i) an account of the origin and constitution of Methodism; (ii) a recital of Wesley's Deed of Declaration; (iii) detailed provisions for the government of the property by the Trustees in accordance with the rules of Conference. In line with Wesley's own action Clause XX of the Model Deed laid it down that no person 'shall teach any Doctrine, or Practice, contrary to what is contained in certain Notes on the New Testament—of the said John Wesley, and in the First Four volumes of Sermons—written and published by him'. The purpose of these arrangements was: (i) to secure that Methodist Trusts should everywhere be drawn up on a uniform and approved plan, and that the Trustees be bound to administer them on behalf of the whole Methodist Church, in accordance with Methodist law; (ii) to secure legal power to exclude from ministerial office any person not recognized by Conference as a Minister; (iii) to secure legal power to exclude from Methodist pulpits any person holding opinions alien to the genius of Methodism; (iv) to secure that if in any local Church a discontented section wishes to sever itself from the Methodist Church as a whole, and from Conference, it shall not have the power to take possession of the trust property. To have these considerable legal powers in reserve is a valuable and necessary factor in maintaining the life of our Church as an ordered Connexion. When other branches of Methodism came into existence they adopted various model deeds of their own, for the same purpose of safeguarding connexional discipline. At Methodist Union provision was made in the Methodist Union Act, 1932, for a New Model Deed. In line with the long tradition of our Church, this repeats the clause regarding Wesley's Sermons and Notes. These circumstances are the basis of the rule of our Church, that all preachers shall read, and give general approval of, the Notes on the New Testament and Wesley's Sermons. It is hoped that this explanation will help the young preacher to feel that this reading which is set him is no mere formality, no dull piece of hide-bound tradition. It is an integral part of a discipline which admirably expresses a very vital spiritual principle, namely, that the Church is one cohesive body with a definite witness. Every member owes allegiance to one Lord and one Faith, and to every other member.

It has already been observed that older editions of Wesley's Sermons contain fifty-three sermons, which number is now reduced to forty-four. The reason for this is that the various editions of his sermons published by Wesley differ in contents, and confusion arose as to which edition was referred to in Clause XX of the Chapel Model Deed of 1832. In 1771 Wesley embarked upon the project of publishing all his prose works in a collected edition of thirty-two volumes. The first four of these contained sermons. They were reprints of the separate volumes of sermons published originally in 1746, 1748, 1750, and 1760 (containing in all forty-three sermons), together with ten additional sermons. This made fifty-three in all for the four

## WHY FORTY-FOUR SERMONS?

volumes. After Wesley's death, during the years 1829-31, a third edition of Wesley's '*Works*' was issued. In his preface the editor made himself responsible for the statement that the first four volumes of the series contained the sermons referred to in Methodist trust-deeds. This statement had already been made by the same editor in the preface to a two-volume edition of the same sermons published in 1825. Such was the impression gradually made that it became assumed throughout Methodism that the Standard Sermons numbered fifty-three. However, Wesley had issued another, and a final, edition of all his printed sermons in 1787-8, in eight volumes. In this, nine of the ten sermons added to the first four volumes in the 1771 edition were omitted, the one remaining being that on 'Wandering Thoughts'. Thus the first four volumes of the eight-volume edition comprise forty-four sermons. There is evidence that Wesley regarded the eight-volume edition as the authoritative edition of his sermons.

The long-standing assumption that the Standard Sermons numbered fifty-three was at length questioned by the Reverend Richard Green, in an article published in the *Methodist Recorder*, December 20, 1894. The matter was carefully discussed, and legal opinion on the points at issue finally sought. Counsel's decision was that the natural sense and proper intention of the phrase 'the first Four Volumes of Sermons' in Clause XX of the Chapel Model Deed of 1832 was a reference to the edition of 1787-8, and not to the sermons in the collected '*Works*' of 1771. A legal case to this effect was presented to Conference in 1914, and adopted (*Minutes of Conference*, 1914, pp. 614-26: reprinted also in Sugden, Vol. II, pp. 331-40). This had the effect of reducing our Standard Sermons in number from fifty-three to forty-four.

# NOTES ON WESLEY'S PREFACE TO THE STANDARD SERMONS

1. *'eight and nine years last past.'*

   This period goes back to the time of Wesley's great evangelical experience in 1738, for this Preface was written for the 1746 volume of Sermons. It is important to notice that most of the Sermons were written to be preached, and not specially for publication.

   > *'I am not conscious that there is any one point of doctrine, on which I am accustomed to speak in public, which is not here, incidentally, if not professedly, laid before every Christian reader.'*

   There are here no sermons on many great fundamental Christian truths, such as the Holy Trinity, the Divine Sonship and True Humanity of our Lord, the Person of the Holy Spirit, Revelation and Inspiration, &c. The reason for this is that the Sermons are not a standard of *doctrine* as such, but a standard of *practical and evangelical preaching*. Wesley certainly assumed as a matter of course that all his preachers accepted the main doctrines of orthodox Christianity. This was an indispensable foundation. However, he knew that orthodoxy did not necessarily make an evangelical preacher. He therefore set up these Sermons as a standard to secure a certain emphasis in the Methodist pulpit. So today, acceptance of these Standard Sermons presupposes orthodox Christian belief in our preachers. However, the *purpose* behind requiring them to be read and approved is not to secure a declaration of formal orthodoxy. They are a guide as to the sort of things the preacher ought to say in the pulpit. The great doctrines mentioned above are constantly assumed, and mentioned in passing, when preaching on other and more practical subjects. This is one of the most effective ways of preaching Christian theology.

2. *'curious readers'*: i.e., readers possessed of intellectual curiosity.

3. '*nice*': i.e. requiring precision, subtle.

'*Bodies of Divinity*': i.e., theological books.

'*To imagine, that a word which is familiar to ourselves is so to all the world.*'

Every preacher is advised to take this warning very much to heart. He should remember also that it applies to technical phraseology of every kind, not merely to theological terms.

4. '*I mean to speak . . . as if I had never read one author . . . excepting the inspired*': (i.e., the Bible).

By this Wesley means that he intends to preach plain Bible doctrine, and to avoid delving into those subjects which have been the frequent topics of theological and philosophical discussion. In particular, he is not going to draw a host of long words and difficult propositions from these writers. Wesley could not keep strictly to this. He had at times to meet and overturn certain common errors, which involved taking notice of what others had said and written about religion. Most emphatically Wesley does not intend to disparage wide reading. He was a great and various reader himself, as well as an ambitious publisher for his people. He dismissed as fanatics those who claimed that one ought to read only the Bible, and not books upon it. (See Sermon XXXII, 27.)

5. Here is a beautiful and revealing paragraph, splendid for its eloquence. Wesley indeed shows his inmost mind. He is both a saint of rare devotion and a careful scholar.

'*I want to know one thing—the way to heaven.*'

This is true, in the profound sense that Wesley's passion was for the salvation of the souls of men. He does himself less than justice, however, if the phrase be taken too literally. Wesley's religion was never 'other-worldly'. A token of this is that half the present sermons are on extremely practical matters of daily life, conduct, and piety. Many of the noblest in eloquence and most masterful in thought are of this class '*homo unius libri*': 'a man of one book'.

In his *Journal* for May 14, 1765, Wesley writes: 'In 1730 I began to be *homo unius libri*, to study (comparatively) no book but the Bible.' How wide an interpretation is to be given to 'comparatively' may be seen in the circumstance that he immediately goes on to testify to the great help he received at this very time from some of the great works of Christian devotion.

6. '*experimental religion*': i.e., the religion of experience.

'*to guard those who are just setting their faces toward heaven . . . from formality . . . and to warn those who know the religion of the heart . . . lest at any time they make void the law through faith.*'

Here is a guide to what one may expect to find in the *Standard Sermons*. On the one hand, there are evangelical and theological sermons. These set forth the great doctrines of the Gospel, as emphasized in the Evangelical Revival. On the other hand there are pastoral and practical sermons, which show how the Christian must hold to the Church and the means of grace, and must live an upright and useful life. The reader is warned not to neglect the latter class for the former. The practical and pastoral sermons are as numerous, as eloquent, as revealing of the mind and spirit of our great Founder, and as valuable in guidance to the preacher today, as are the sermons on 'our doctrines'. In every age the two great pitfalls in the path of the spiritual life are: (i) to forget that the Gospel is essentially the message of a change of heart miraculously worked by the power of God in Jesus Christ. This error leads men to reduce religion to a round of 'good deeds' and religious rites, which one must impose upon oneself in the strength of one's own resolution. Wesley repudiates this as 'formality'. (ii) To be so enwrapped in the joys of 'religious experience' as to forget that the necessary fruit of a change of heart is a complete change of life. This is to 'make void the law through faith'. It is not enough that the Christian should experience ecstasies of devotion and transports of joy. He must be upright in character, gracious of disposition, clean in life, steadfast in the service of God in the Church, and useful in citizenship. The great purpose of these sermons is to guide the preacher to a spiritual war on two fronts.

7. Wesley's assertion is in accord with the essential facts. The careful reader will, however, find that the passage of years produced more than one change of emphasis on minor points. Wesley was able to learn many things by long experience. What he would make plain is that he has not deserted the truth to pacify his critics.

8. Wesley's modesty in this paragraph is very touching, as is his humour in the following.

10. 'ἠΰτε καπνός':

'like smoke.' The reference is to the *Iliad*, XVIII, 110.

*Sermon One**

# Salvation by Faith

AT the head of this sermon we read that it was 'Preached at St. Mary's, Oxford, before the University, on June 11, 1738'. The sermon was thus first composed not to be printed, but to be preached. This raises a point of some importance in our understanding of Wesley's Sermons. The *Standard Sermons* are not a collection of dummy sermons. They are not dull theological discourses thinly disguised as spoken addresses. A few of them were indeed written specially for publication, but most of them are sermons that Wesley actually preached. Many of them were preached very frequently, to ordinary congregations, and even in the open air. Some have found it hard to believe this. For example, Dr. Dinsdale T. Young wrote in his book *Popular Preaching* (p. 139): 'Many have expressed wonder that such discourses should have awakened such all-but-unparalleled popular response. The plain and ready answer to such wonder is that it was not by those discourses that Wesley built up his popular pulpit.... The printed sermons were specially prepared as doctrinal standards for his preachers and people. Face to face with the multitude John Wesley preached in a very different style.' With all due respect it must be insisted that this common opinion is a misreading of the situation. It is certainly on record that Wesley enlivened his sermons with illustrations, even to the point that some conventionally-minded hearers objected to his manner as too anecdotal. There is little evidence of this in the present sermons. Wesley may well have had other sermons of a lighter sort, which he would naturally not choose for publication as a permanent and authoritative record of his message. We can also well imagine that as he preached the present sermons he would on occasion insert stories and examples that came to mind, so as to give application to his points. He would not feel it worth while to print these illus-

* No. 1 in *Fifty-three Sermons*

trations. At the same time, it is definitely unfair to dismiss the Standard Sermons as sermons only in form, or as mere skeletons of sermons. It is a baseless assumption that doctrinal preaching can never draw a crowd. This may not often happen today, but it has not always been so, and we have not a Wesley in the pulpit today. Furthermore, at least half the sermons are not essentially doctrinal at all, but deal most practically and plainly with questions of conduct and piety. The commanding personality and prophetic enthusiasm of the preacher should be considered, and likewise, the frequent strangeness of his message in those days. Violent controversy surrounded his person and his followers. All this would combine to fire these sermons with interest, and make them thrilling to the hearer. We invite the modern reader to come to them with confidence and sympathy, expecting to find here the stirring utterances of a great preacher.

'*Before the University.*'

The University Sermon was preached by those Masters of Arts who were in Anglican Orders, in turn, by appointment of the Vice-Chancellor. Wesley's turn came about once in three years. Five of the *Standard Sermons* were preached before the University, Nos. I, II, IV, and XIII by John, and III by Charles Wesley.

'*June* 18, 1738.'

This date is incorrect, and should be June 11. To judge from *Wesley's Journal* for June 8, the sermon was preached on the Sunday morning at the village of Stanton Harcourt, six miles away, and afterwards at Oxford. It is moving to remember that Wesley had found the experience of the heart strangely warmed only eighteen days before.

1. '*mere.*'

This word has since sunk in meaning. We would say: 'His pure grace.'

2. '*all unholy and sinful.*'

The strictness of this judgement is somewhat modified by Wesley's consideration of the case of the Centurion Cornelius (*Notes on the New Testament*, Acts x. 4). Here the prayers and alms of one who had not yet found faith in Christ are admitted as acceptable to God. They are not sins. However, the prayers and alms of one moved by a full faith are on a higher level. What Wesley is saying is simply:

> 'Not the labours of my hands
> Can fulfil Thy law's demands.'

'*righteousness at first impressed on his soul.*'

Wesley here makes the assumption, very common in Christian tradition, that the 'image and likeness of God' in the first man (Gen. i. 26) consisted in every perfection of intellect and morals. This is an assumption, and one which need not bind us today.


I. Notice the admirable system of headings and sub-headings. It may not always be best to read one's headings to the congregation, but to have systematic divisions clearly in mind is one of the first steps toward being easy to follow.

1. One aspect of faith is to acknowledge the truth about God. Non-Christians recognize part of this truth, and God expects them to live by it.

2. '*the faith of a devil . . . goes much farther than that of a Heathen.*'

    A satanic intelligence is free from human limitation, and has a perfect knowledge of the Gospel. This, moreover, is not saving faith, for there is no movement of the heart and will in loving obedience and trust.

3. The Apostles had a measure of devotion to Jesus in the days of His flesh, but as yet no grasp of the doctrine of the crucified and risen Lord.

4. *'a train of ideas in the head.'*

This is the other side to (3). There can be no faith without some ideas in the head, namely, that Jesus Christ is the Lord, and that in Him God has done all that is necessary for man to be forgiven, and delivered from the power of sin. However, these ideas are but the initial stage of faith. There must also be that movement of the affections and will. Wesley would be thinking as he spoke: 'And until eighteen days ago my Christian faith was too much a train of ideas in my head, too little a disposition of my heart.' Though many 'men of reason' of that day would be most uncomfortable at the large place allowed to 'mere feelings', modern psychology abundantly bears out the importance of this truth. Man is mainly moved to effective action by the emotions. Reason is also very necessary, but as the steering-wheel rather than the engine.

5. *'a trust in the merits of His life . . .'*

We would say today: 'A vivid sense that, on account of what was done *then*, for the whole *world*, God can and will do something for *me*, *now*.'


II. 1. *'a present salvation.'*

Wesley is objecting to those who would tone down the Gospel to the teaching that, if we trust in Christ, we may live in hope that in the end we will find ourselves saved.

4. *'a filial fear of offending.'*

The man who knows himself to be saved should not be cock-sure. He must remember his frailty. On the other hand, he need not spend his days in anxious fear, wondering whether he is a Christian indeed, or well-pleasing to God.

*'not from the possibility of falling.'*

The Calvinists, who made up the bulk of Evangelical Christians in that day, left no real place for human free will. The saved were saved solely because God had so ordained, not at all because they had chosen to accept His grace. God does not change His mind. Therefore, once a man knew himself to be chosen, he knew himself to be chosen for ever. He might have ups and downs, but it was impossible to imagine that he could ever be finally lost. This was the doctrine of Final Perseverance. The sense of assurance that it brought was one of the main reasons why Calvinism was so widely attractive. Wesley rejects this whole system, but can nevertheless preserve the sense of full assurance of salvation. It is an assurance based, not on the idea of God's unchanging purpose, but on a deep sense that what God is now doing in the heart is very real. This is the doctrine of Full Assurance through the Witness of the Spirit.

*'though perhaps not at all times, nor with the same fullness.'*

Wesley is certainly speaking from his new experience. He feels that one who has attained to genuine faith ought to be able to walk constantly in it. However, he is saddened to find that he does not live at this level, though he remains convinced of his salvation. Even those whose assurance rests on the Witness of the Spirit have their ups and downs. The moving and human account of the days May 24–June 1, 1738, in Wesley's *Journal* should be read. It is full of guidance for all who know that they are Christians, but who do not find the path easy.

5. *'saved from the power of sin.'*

Notice how the emphasis falls upon salvation from the power of sin, and not merely from the punishment for sin. Man is to flee from sin because it defiles him and grieves God, and not just because it will lead to Hell. Unhappily not all our preachers have maintained this high level.

6. Wesley is very sweeping here, and later modified these statements. With (1) we must agree. (2) is an over-simplification, and involves the assumption that all who have faith are adult in the faith. This point has been dealt with above (para. II, 4). Furthermore, in the *Minutes* of 1745 it is stated that, from the

moment of Justification, 'the believer gradually dies to sin, and grows in grace. Yet sin remains in him . . . till he is sanctified throughout.' Of (3) we learn that even the perfect Christian is not free from temptation, though he is from falling. (Sermon XXXV, I, 8.) The difficult question of 'sins of infirmity' (4) is further treated of in Sermon XXXV, I, 7.

7. *'taken in the largest sense.'*

Wesley more narrowly defines what he means by Justification in Sermon XV, 1–3.

'ἄδολον.'

Wesley doubtless quotes the Greek because the familiar rendering 'sincere' does not give the sense. The word means 'unadulterated'. There are many quotations in Latin and Greek in these sermons. Wesley practically always translates as he proceeds. Such original quotations were much more natural then, when it could be assumed that any well-educated man would know the classics. At the present day the ordinary preacher on any ordinary occasion should in general avoid bringing in odd phrases of Latin and Greek, particularly if he has only picked them up at second-hand from his reading.


III. 1. *'a faith which is . . . productive of all good works.'*

If faith is 'a train of ideas in the head' it can be imagined as separable from a good character. If it is a movement of the heart and will toward God and His truth it is bound to lead to a complete change of life.


2. *'comments that eat out all the spirit of the text.'*

Wesley here assumes that the Christian Gospel is the natural and necessary climax of the Jewish religion, with the consequence that those who do less than justice to the Gospel thereby do injustice also to the Law of Moses. This is essentially the argument used by St. Paul to meet those Jews who objected that his doctrine of Justification by Faith robbed the Law of its

# SALVATION BY FAITH

primacy as God's path to Himself. The Apostle agreed that the Law had indeed lost its ancient place, but claimed that this development was God's original plan, as forecast in the Law. The life of faith was but the true essence of Law now plainly revealed, free from all temporary concession to human unworthiness.

3. *'pride.'*

The objection Wesley here has in mind would run as follows: 'The man who trusts to earn merit in the sight of God by his own efforts in obedience to God's laws knows that he has not yet attained. He will be a humble man. He who has accepted free forgiveness knows that he has attained. Such a one is sure to be inflated with self-satisfaction and presumption.' This was one of the main arguments which induced many 'men of good sense' to shrink from Methodist preaching as fanatical. There is some ground for this fear. In the preaching of evangelical religion there is a temptation to pride and conceit, which will constantly come upon all who forget that they entered into the experience of forgiveness through penitence for their sins.

*'accidentally.'*

One meaning of 'accident' is, 'a property connected with a substance which is not essential to our very conception of that substance'. 'Accidentally' has a kindred meaning here. Wesley means that the temptation to pride may accompany the preaching of salvation by faith, but it is not an inevitable and necessary accompaniment. It is an abuse of the system, not a part of it.

*'of yourselves cometh neither your faith . . .'*

Yes: for every good thing is the gift of God, and man's salvation is His work alone. The Calvinist deduction from this does not follow, however, namely, that those who have no faith have it not solely because God has not given it. God offers His gift of faith to all who hear the Gospel, but forces it upon none. Some might say that human receptivity of the first stirrings of grace in the heart is a degree of faith. This degree of 'faith' cannot be described simply as God's gift to man, and as His work in him, without abolishing all human responsibility. However, this degree of 'faith' is much less than that saving faith whereby the believer knowingly devotes his heart in love to Christ, and embarks all his hope upon Him. Anyone who has shared this glorious experience will testify that it is nothing less than a miracle worked by God. Nevertheless, man remains free to reject those stirrings of grace. This is the truth of which Charles Wesley sings:

> No man can truly say
> That Jesus is the Lord,
> Unless Thou take the veil away,
> And breathe the living word.
>
> (M.H.B. 363.)

4. *'encourage men in sin.'*

It will, if in their blindness they suppose that the free mercy of God toward penitent sinners is a token that He condones sin: hence the cynical cry: 'God will forgive, that is His business.'

5. 6. *'this will drive men to despair.'* *'an uncomfortable doctrine.'*

This objection appears today in this form: 'If God will be satisfied by an honest life and a kindly disposition I may hope to be saved, for I can try to attain to this. If He demands a mysterious change of heart, which will lift me up to glorious spiritual communion with Him, I fear I am shut out. I have not that sort of temperament. Well do I know that nothing I can do will bring this to me.' Our answer, with Wesley, is: 'God *does* offer you this change of heart. Do not fear that He has created you a spiritual idiot, constitutionally incapable of recognizing your Father, and of responding to His love.'

7. *'not to be preached as the first doctrine . . . or to all':*

i.e., 'This doctrine of Justification by Faith may be true, but it is apt to be misunderstood. It is full of pitfalls for the ignorant or undiscriminating. You should keep this truth in reserve for those who can appreciate it. Such emphasis and such publicity is highly imprudent.' Such is still the way of the world with zealots.

'*they often except themselves from hearing.*'

This would thrust home! There were many such in the Oxford congregation.

8. '*Romish delusion.*' '*Popery.*'

There are some things in the Roman Church which we repudiate, and many regarding which we have doubts. We should, however, today certainly avoid hard phrases such as these.

'*the strong rock . . .*'

Quoted from the second part of the Anglican Homily, 'Of Salvation'.

'*this doctrine . . . first drove Popery out.*'

This is absolutely true. The Roman Church would emphatically claim that her teaching is that man is saved by the grace of God, through faith in Jesus Christ. Our misgiving, when stated aright, is that in the Roman system 'Faith' is too much expounded as acceptance of the authority of the Church, agreement with her Creeds, obedience to her discipline, and dutiful participation in her Sacraments. All too little is heard, at least by the multitude, of that faith which is the personal surrender of the soul to God, in a movement of heart and mind and moral will. Such preaching as this of Wesley rights the balance. It certainly strikes at the root of every error and abuse that may spring from this Roman lack of proportion. It is no accident that the great rallying-cry of the Lutheran Reformation was 'Justification by Faith'.

'*can you empty the great deep, drop by drop?*'

This is a telling rejoinder to those modern Humanists who cherish too sanguine a hope of the reformation of mankind by improved education and social organization, and who estimate too lightly the need for the conversion of the individual.

9. *'the adversary so rages.'*

Even as early as this Wesley was beginning to experience the opposition aroused by his new manner of preaching.

## Questions

1. Is it better today to preach a sermon avowedly on the subject of 'Justification by Faith', or to teach this doctrine by inference only, i.e., by taking more general subjects which presuppose this doctrine, and by making allusions to it?

2. What is the distinction between 'Faith' and 'The Faith'?

3. Did the writer of James ii. 19 mean the same thing by 'believing' as did St. Paul in Acts xvi. 31?

4. Is there any case for putting the soft pedal on 'only believe in Jesus' when preaching to the more insensitive and unintelligent type of congregation, and concentrating rather upon: 'keep off the drink'; 'don't get into debt'; 'come regularly to Church'; etc.?

5. Would the hearers find this a 'comfortable' sermon then? or now?

*Sermon Two**

# The Almost Christian

*Date. July 25, 1741.*

In his *Journal* for this date Wesley writes: 'It being my turn (which comes about once in three years), I preached at St. Mary's, before the University.... So numerous a congregation (from whatever motives they came) I have seldom seen at Oxford.' This is hardly surprising. Since the last sermon open-air preaching had been started, often accompanied by great excitement, the Societies had been formed, the Foundery had been opened for worship, and laymen had been allowed to preach. All this had created nation-wide controversy. Wesley had been excluded from many Parish Churches. It is to the lasting credit of the University, then entirely in the hands of the Church of England, that Wesley was allowed to take his turn. The responsible authorities of the Church might not agree, but they did not condemn unheard. Wesley had thought of preaching a vehement attack upon the lax life of the University (now printed as Sermon CXXXIV in Wesley's *Works*). He was fortunately dissuaded by Lady Huntingdon. The *Journal* for Sunday, June 28, 1741, shows that the present sermon had been preached already to a large London crowd in the open-air.

*Text.*

Wesley's warmest admirer must admit that this is an example of how not to treat a text. It is taken as though it read: 'Thou persuadest me to be an almost Christian.' The meaning of this phrase, the reply of King Agrippa to St. Paul's challenge, is very obscure. The King was probably trying to be evasive. He wishes neither to side with St. Paul nor to disown the Prophets. A probable sense is a sneering: 'You make short work of persuading me to play the Christian.'

* No. 2 in *Fifty-three Sermons*

I. (i) 1. 2. 3. *'Heathen.'*

According to the usage of the day this means simply: 'non-christian'. Wesley is thinking of the ancient Greeks and Romans, not of primitive tribes.

(ii) 4. *'a form of godliness.'*

We may perhaps say that 2 Tim. iii. 5, a favourite with Wesley, is the real text for this sermon.

*'the stranger that is within his gates.'*

Wesley assumes that the master of the house should seek to use his relationship with guests and servants to influence them to conform with his own religious usages. This is more in accord with the manners of that age than of this.

*'εὐτραπελία.'*

This word comes from Eph. v. 4, and is there translated 'jesting'.

*'a kind of virtue.'*

The proper meaning of the word is 'witty talk'. According to Aristotle, it is the happy mean between ribaldry and boorish stupidity. However, the word became degraded.

5. *'that plain rule':* i.e., the Golden Rule reversed.

In the next paragraph Wesley assumes that his 'almost Christian' also keeps the Rule positively.

7. *'not as the manner of some is.'*

There were widespread contemporary complaints that many Church services had more of the atmosphere of the social function and the fashion parade than of religious worship. This abuse is inevitable in any society which is dead to true religion, but which does not completely neglect a nominal Christianity. The avowed 'paganism' of the present day at least preserves us from this.

(iii) 9. '*Epicurean poet*': i.e., Horace.

This great Latin poet is hardly to be described as an Epicurean. He was of no definite school of philosophy, but sought in the teachings of them all such principles as would make life easier, better, and happier. The Epicureans were one of the most important schools of ancient Greek philosophy. The name is taken from the Athenian Epicurus (about 300 B.C.). He believed in the existence of gods, who, however, were entirely separated from the affairs of this world. Only thus could they exist in bliss. The world was made up of an endless series of chance combinations of the eternal atoms. A main aim of this school was to abolish the terrors of popular paganism by a sceptical attack, and to free man from the haunting fear of death by assuring him that there was no future life. The practical aim of life was the pursuit of happiness, though in a good sense of the word. Pleasures that produced painful effects were to be avoided, while such pains as contributed to lasting good were to be welcomed. It is easy to see how this system has given rise to the common degraded use of the term 'Epicurean', as of a person devoted to sensuous enjoyment.

'*this poor wretch*': A strangely perverse judgement.

'*oderunt peccare boni* . . .'

This is an incorrect quotation from Horace (Ep. I. xvi. 52). As they stand in the sermon the lines may be rendered:
> 'The good hate to sin through love of virtue;
> The evil hate to sin through dread of punishment.'

'*Non pasces in cruce corvos*':

i.e., 'You shall not feed the crows from the cross.' This phrase occurs a few lines before the previous quotation. They form the poet's answer to a slave who comes with the plea that he has not committed any offence. He has killed no man. It is pronounced a meet reward for this that he will escape crucifixion as a murderer. The moral of the whole argument is that one who refrains from crime merely from fear of punishment is not a good man.

11. '*Is it possible . . .?*'

This question may well be asked. For Wesley's answer, which reveals the essential intention of the sermon, see paragraph 13, with note (*infra*).

12. '*If I declare my own folly.*'

Wesley here moulds his language to that of St. Paul, in the moving plea of 2 Cor. xi. 1–xii. 13. There the Apostle undertakes to meet his detractors on their own ground, even though he well knows that his argument is in reality but foolish boasting.

13. '*I did go thus far for many years.*'

In Sermon I we surmised that Wesley was speaking from his own experience. As Sermon II proceeds it becomes clearer that the 'almost Christian' is Wesley's portrait of himself, as he was in the days before his heart was strangely warmed. Now, most appealingly, he takes off the mask. In this circumstance is the answer to the objection that has been raised by some to the argument of para. 11. Wesley is not there simply a victim of his own logic, carried into error by excess of zeal for the proposition that nothing in human life, however seemingly worthy, is good in the Christian sense unless it springs from the faith that works by love. He is not describing a purely hypothetical man who never could have existed, one who, contrary to the witness of Romans vii, has succeeded in keeping the law of God without the aid of the empowering grace of God. Wesley is here describing a real man, though a rare man. It is himself before the experience of Aldersgate Street. The type who is consumed by sincere zeal for the service of God, and who sustains this without the exhilaration of the full evangelical experience, will never be common. Such are those who, according to natural and inborn character, are the noblest of the race, the select and fortunate few. These are the genuine 'almost Christians'. The great point of this sermon is that God has something more to offer to man even than this. He will give to all His children not only an upright and sincere character, but also the unspeakable experience of conscious communion with Himself, of peace of mind and the witness of Full Assurance, and of the empowering Spirit in all the duties of the Christian life. All who lack this, however truly good, have missed the calling of God. It would be alike false and uncharitable to deny the title of 'Christian' to the 'almost Christian', yet an '*almost* Christian' he remains, for the best is still in store. To use a distinction found in Wesley's later writings, the 'almost Christian' has the faith of a servant of God, but not of a son. He did not question the salvation of such. For a commentary on this important point, see the *Journal* for January 29, 1738, with its later added footnotes, and Sermon CVI, 'On Faith', para. 11 (in Wesley's *Works*, Vol. VII).

II. (ii) 2. '*the enemies of God and their own souls.*'

Wesley had met many such during the past three years. To love these is perhaps a more testing calling than to love one's own enemies.

(iii) 4. The long quotation in this and the next paragraph is from the Anglican Homily, 'On the Salvation of Mankind', part III, somewhat abbreviated.

'*devilish*': i.e., the faith of a devil, as discussed in Sermon I.

5. '*our own Church*': i.e., the Church of England.

6. Notice how in these sermons Wesley admirably blends the appeal to the mind and to the heart. At this point he begins to pass from a closely argued address to a telling and passionate personal application. This is an excellent model to copy.

10. '*if any man die without this faith, &c.*'

We are not compelled to suppose from this that Wesley regarded his 'almost Christian' as eternally damned. Certainly this was not his later, considered teaching.

## Questions

1. Does the conception of the 'almost Christian' provide a satisfactory place in the Christian system for the devout Unitarian? or a member of the Ethical Society? or the nobler type of Moslem or Hindu?

2. Is 'the man in the street' an 'almost Christian'? Is he in the right when he resents statements by Christian preachers that he is not a Christian?

3. With all that is best in our national life in mind, would it be true to say that this country is an 'almost Christian' nation?

4. Is Methodism, as you know it, an 'almost Christian' Church?

*Sermon Three*\*

# Awake, thou that Sleepest

THE main interest in this fine sermon by Charles Wesley is the striking contrast between his work and that of his brother. The ground covered is much the same as in the two foregoing sermons, namely, that the Christian religion is no mere polite convention, nor even the most strict discipline of self-imposed morality, but a new life springing from a glorious change worked in the heart by God. Yet what a difference is here! There is almost nothing of argument with the hearer. In consequence, relatively few points arise of distinctively doctrinal interest. The theology is there, but it is assumed, not discussed. The direct appeal is not to the mind, but to the heart. What an appeal that must have been! The fervent passion of a mighty evangelist and a great lover of souls breathes in every line of this rhetorical sermon, together with the poet's fine sense of words. John Wesley was aware of his brother's different gifts, and once wrote to him: 'In connexion I beat you; but in strong pointed sentences you beat me.'

It is interesting to speculate why John Wesley should have included this among his Standard Sermons, seeing that it gives no additional information regarding Methodist doctrine, and also, as to the reason why only a single one was chosen. Perhaps it claims this place simply as a sample of fervent eloquence. It is recognized that the Sermons are neither a Creed nor a compendium of theology. They are a practical guide to the work of preaching. Wesley assumed as a basis that the Methodists accept the traditional body of Christian doctrine, particularly as taught in the Church of his upbringing. What he left to his followers was a guide to the parts of that system which ought most to be emphasized in the pulpit. The inclusion of this sermon is therefore perhaps more than a tribute to the gifts and

\* No. 3 in *Fifty-three Sermons*

toils of Charles Wesley. It is here to reflect the level of feeling and word-mastery that John Wesley fain would see among the Methodists. For this purpose he modestly prefers his brother to himself. He knows, however, that in giving information as to principles he comes into his own.

We can well believe the report that Charles Wesley was more powerful as a popular preacher than his brother. This sermon certainly makes less demand on the untutored mind (unless one is to ask the meaning of every Scripture citation!) together with a more sustained appeal to the heart. The *Methodist Magazine* for 1815, p. 457, gives a fascinating eye-witness account by Joseph Williams of Charles Wesley preaching at Bristol in September 1739. 'Standing on a table in a field, the preacher, with eyes and hands lifted up to heaven, prayed with uncommon fervour and fluency. He then preached about an hour in such a manner as I scarce ever heard any man preach. Though I have heard many a finer sermon according to the common taste or acceptation of sermons, I never heard any man discover such evident signs of a vehement desire, or labour so earnestly to convince his hearers. . . . With uncommon fervour he acquitted himself as an ambassador of Christ. . . . And although he used no notes, nor had anything in his hand but a Bible, yet he delivered his thoughts in a rich, copious variety of expression, and with so much propriety, that I could not observe anything incoherent or inanimate through the whole performance, which he concluded with singing, prayer, and the usual benediction.' (From Sugden, I. 69.)

An interesting side-light on the occasion of this University Sermon is given by Matthew Salmon, who wrote as follows in 1748: 'When I happened to be in Oxford in 1742, Mr. Wesley, the Methodist, of Christ Church, entertained his audience two hours, and, having insulted and abused all degrees, from the highest to the lowest, was in a manner hissed out of the pulpit by the lads.' The retort of Charles Wesley to this, in his *Journal* for April 15, 1750, was: 'And high time for them to do so, if the historian said true: but, unfortunately for him, I measured the time by my watch, and it was within the hour; I abused neither high nor low, as my sermon, in print, will prove;

AWAKE, THOU THAT SLEEPEST

neither was I hissed out of the pulpit, or treated with the least incivility, either by young or old.' (From Sugden, I, 70.)

The reader should notice the way in which every sentence of this sermon is either a quotation from the Bible, or an allusion, often veiled, to Scripture. This is reminiscent of Charles Wesley's hymns. Such an approach must have been most powerful in those days, when even the careless of religion gave a general assent to the proposition that the Bible was 'the Word of God'. It would be a useful exercise to look up as many of these references as may be found, and also to see how often the same references occur in well-known hymns.

I. 1. '*in which the sin of Adam, &c.*' See note, Sermon V, I (pp. 38 ff.).

2. '*figured out by baptism.*'

For the relation of Baptism to the New Birth, see note on Sermon XXXIX, IV, 2 (pp. 243 f.).

5. '*Laodicean.*' See Rev. iii. 14–22.

7. '*the sinews and flesh are come upon them, &c.*' See Ezek. xxxvii. 8.

By 'sinews and flesh' Wesley means the outward form of religion. Notice the quaint but effective way in which two quite different Biblical references to 'bones' are linked together to form a single picture. Wesley keeps on doing this.

11. 'ἔλεγχος' (conviction) 'Πνεύματος' (of the Spirit).

This phrase does not occur in the New Testament. The two words are brought together from different places. ἔλεγχος is the word rendered 'proving' ('evidence,' A.V.) in Heb. xi. 1, 'Now faith is the assurance of things hoped for, the proving of things not seen.'

II. 1. '*If thou wouldest escape them.*'

Wesley is probably thinking of Jonah, who accepted as

rightful the marks of divine wrath, and so was saved. (Jonah i. 12.)

3. *'It is to thee, who thinkest thyself unconcerned.'*

This is the eternal problem of the preacher.

*'on the brink of the pit, &c.'*

Charles Wesley comes nearer than his brother to threatening the sinner with hell fire.

5. *'Did not God create thee for Himself?'*

This echoes the celebrated word of St. Augustine (Conf. I, 1). 'Thou hast created us for Thyself, and our heart is restless till it finds rest in Thee.'

9. *'thou hast solemnly mocked God this very day'*:

i.e., by using the Collect at the beginning of the Holy Communion.

10. *'anointed with the Holy Ghost.'*

The reference is probably to Acts x. 38, though there it is our Lord, and not the Christian man, who is spoken of.

11. *'agonizing.'*

The point of this powerful rendering of Luke xiii. 24 is seen if it be remembered that the Greek for 'I strive' would read 'agonizo' if put into English letters. In his *Notes on the New Testament* for this passage, John Wesley translates, 'agonize, strive as in an agony'.


III. 6. *'Neither is it possible to have received Him: and not know it.'*

The rightness or otherwise of this was long discussed among the first Methodists. John Wesley's later mind is reflected in a letter to Melville Horne, quoted in Southey's *Life of Wesley*.

'When fifty years ago my brother Charles and I, in the simplicity of our hearts, told the good people of England that unless they *knew* their sins were forgiven, they were under the wrath and curse of God, I marvel, Melville, they did not stone us! The Methodists, I hope, know better now; we preach assurance as we always did, as a common privilege of the children of God; but we do not enforce it, under the pain of damnation, denounced on all who enjoy it not.'

8. Here speaks the 'reasonable' man, who objected to early Methodist preaching as fanatical.

9. '*Our own excellent Church*': i.e., the Church of England.

Sugden (I, 83) collects from the *Book of Common Prayer* the following references as illustrating this paragraph: Article xvii: 'The doctrine of Election is full of comfort to godly persons, and such as feel in themselves the working of the Spirit of Christ.' Ordering of Deacons: 'Do you trust that you are inwardly moved by the Holy Ghost to take upon you this Office and Ministration?' Visitation of Sick: 'The Almighty Lord . . . make thee know and feel that there is none other Name under heaven given to man, in whom, and through whom, thou mayest receive health and salvation.' Holy Communion: 'Cleanse the thoughts of our hearts by the inspiration of Thy Holy Spirit.' Ordering of Priests: 'Receive the Holy Ghost for the Office and Work of a Priest in the Church of God.' The difficulty is that the objector of para. 8 has a fair claim to share the *Book of Common Prayer* with Charles Wesley. The Prayer Book reflects the very comprehensive tradition of the Church of England, and was, indeed, deliberately designed as a happy mean between extremes. It is quite correct for Charles Wesley to claim that he can find there that enthusiastic evangelical religion which makes so much of the conscious personal experience of the believer. It is, however, equally true that the institutional and the 'common-sense' types of Christian, who respectively think of religion mainly in terms of the ordered life of the Church, and of the common decencies of human society, are likewise thoroughly at home in the Prayer Book.

10. *'enthusiasts.'*

This is an example of a word that has taken on a nobler usage in the passage of time. In the eighteenth century 'enthusiast' was almost always used in the sense of: 'one who holds extravagant and visionary religious opinions'; 'one who pretends to special divine illumination.' This was a stock term of abuse for the Methodists.

*'that falling away.'* See 2 Thess. ii. 3.

Wesley is not to be taken too seriously here. Some Christian preachers of many ages have pointed to the wickedness of their own times as a mark that the Second Coming of the Lord was at hand. Fortunately this strain was no real part of Methodist thought.

12. *'us of this place':* i.e., the University.

These were bold words for those days. The congregation must have been open-minded if it indeed treated the preacher with civility.

13. *'He lets us alone this year also, &c.'*

Britain was then engaged, with little success, in a war with Spain. Home government was at a low ebb. The fallacy that national misfortune is a mark of divine displeasure, and success of divine approval, is a very natural one in time of war. Wesley is not alone here.

15. *'our land become a field of blood.'*

Bonnie Prince Charlie was watching his opportunity to invade the country and secure his throne.

## Questions

1. Compare Sermon III with I and II. Which do you think would do most good to the first hearers? Which has the more lasting value?

2. In what ways does this sermon show a like authorship to Charles Wesley's hymns?

3. Is it justifiable to quote texts in senses other than the original, if a pleasing or forceful effect is obtained thereby?

4. Are you helped today by the sort of preacher who 'pours out texts'? If not, what has changed in the congregation? and in preachers?

*Sermon Four*\*

# Scriptural Christianity

*Date. August 24, 1744.*

This was St. Bartholomew's Day, and a Friday. In *A Short History of the Methodists* (1781), Wesley wrote of this occasion: 'And I am well pleased that it should be the very day on which in the last century, near two thousand burning and shining lights were put out at one stroke. Yet what a wide difference is there between their case and mine! They were turned out of house and home, and all that they had; whereas I am only hindered from preaching, without any other loss; and that in a kind of honourable manner.' It was on St. Bartholomew's Day, 1662, that 2,000 clergymen, including Wesley's grandfather, John Wesley, were expelled from their livings for refusing to take the oath prescribed in the Act of Uniformity. Wesley seems to have been determined to make a special occasion of the sermon, for he was supported by his brother, as well as by many Methodists. Charles Wesley's very human account is worthy of note. 'At ten I walked with my brother and Mr. Piers and Meriton to St. Mary's, where my brother bore his testimony before a crowded audience, much increased by the racers. (It was race-week.) Never have I seen a more attentive congregation. They did not let a word slip them. Some of the Heads stood up the whole time, and fixed their eyes on him. If they can endure sound doctrine like this, he will surely leave a blessing behind him. The Vice-Chancellor sent after him, and desired his notes: which he sealed up and sent immediately. We walked back in form, the little band of us four, for of the rest durst none join himself to us. I was a little diverted at the coyness of an old friend, Mr. Wells, who sat just before me, but took great care to turn his back upon me all the time, which did not hinder my seeing through him.' (*Journal*, Aug. 23, 1744.)

\* No. 4 in *Fifty-three Sermons*

Sugden (I, 89–90) further records two very interesting eye-witness accounts from non-Methodists. They are from Benjamin Kennicott, later eminent as a Hebrew scholar, and from William Blackstone, afterwards famous as a Judge, and as the author of the *Commentaries on the Laws of England*. Their impressions will be referred to later. We have already seen Charles Wesley, the preacher, as he appeared to a sympathetic outsider (Introduction to Sermon III). It is well to compare this with Kennicott's account of the preacher at the present service. 'When he mounted the pulpit, I fixed my eyes on him and his behaviour. He is neither tall nor fat; for the latter would ill become a Methodist. His black hair quite smooth, and parted very exactly, added to a peculiar composure in his countenance, showing him to be an uncommon man. His prayer was soft, short, and conformable to the rules of the University. His text, Acts iv. 31: "And they were all filled with the Holy Ghost." And now he began to exalt his voice. He spoke the text very slowly, and with an agreeable emphasis. . . . Under three heads he expressed himself like a very good scholar, but a rigid zealot; and then he came to what he called his plain, practical conclusion. Here was what he had been preparing for all along.'

2–5. There is no hard and fast distinction between ordinary and extraordinary gifts of the Spirit, though there is a rough and ready practical distinction between that work which has been general among all true believers, namely, love in the heart stirring up all Christian virtues, and such phenomena as visions, miraculous 'signs', and ecstatic speech ('speaking with tongues'). The latter have generally occurred at times of great spiritual excitement and tension. The attention of Wesley to this point is the first appearance of a theme which runs through much of this sermon. This is a parallel drawn between Methodism and the life of the early Church. Wesley does not say that he is making this parallel, but it is certainly there. He may have been unconscious of it himself. He may have pointed the parallel so often to his own people that when he set about presenting a picture of New Testament Christianity he instinctively arranged his material in the way he does. On the other hand, it is not improbable that the parallel is here by unavowed design. Wesley will describe the rise of the Christian religion in such a way that the hearer will be led to say to himself: 'How like all this is to the story of the Holy Club, and all that has come out of it!' Even if this effect was not planned we may well believe that many of the congregation had it presented to their minds. Thus the first part of the sermon may be regarded as a vindication of Methodism as 'Scriptural (i.e., in Wesley's parlance: "authentic") Christianity'.

Early Methodist preaching was often accompanied by a violent emotional response. Those convicted of sin would sometimes fall to the ground groaning or crying aloud, or would remain insensible for a time. Others were transported with joy. Such occurrences would cause misgiving today, even in quarters fundamentally sympathetic to evangelical religion. In those days these reports were the occasion of violent prejudice, particularly at a place like Oxford. The moral of Wesley's introduction surely is: remarkable phenomena occurred in the primitive Church. Why should we Methodists be condemned out of court for the same? These extraordinary gifts were but a small part of the life of the Apostolic Church. May not the same prove to be true of Methodism?

3. '*Whether . . . designed to remain.*'

Wesley gives his answer in Sermon LXXXIX, 2 (*Works*, Vol. VII). 'It does not appear that these extraordinary gifts of the Holy Ghost were common in the Church for more than two or three centuries. . . . The cause of this was not because there was no occasion for them because all the world was become Christian. The real cause was "the love of many" . . . was "waxed cold". . . . The Christians were turned heathens again, and had only a dead form left.'

'*the nearer approach of the "restitution of all things".*'

Wesley was not one of those to whom a vivid sense that the 'end of the world' is at hand was an important part of religion.

'*not one in a thousand.*' This is probably playing down the facts.

'*fidelity.*' See Gal. v. 22.

Wesley anticipates the Revised Version rendering of 'faithfulness', which is preferable to the Authorized Version word, 'faith'.

5. '*curious*': i.e., inspired by mere curiosity.


I. 1. '*beginning to exist in individuals.*'

It is correct to say that Christianity began to exist in individuals in the sense that there could obviously be no actual Church existing in this world apart from the existence of actual men having some measure of Christian faith. It is not, however, adequate as an ideal or theological principle of the Church to teach that men first become Christians, and afterwards associate themselves for mutual support. Christianity, being a life of love, is essentially social. It is impossible to imagine anyone coming to a real understanding of the Christian life, or practising it to any real effect, apart from some form of fellowship. In principle the Church comes first.

It seems clear that from the beginning our Lord looked upon the company of His disciples as the New Israel, i.e., the few and worthy, the 'Israelites indeed', picked out from the whole body of God's ancient Chosen People. The disciples were therefore inherently a community, for Israel was a community. In them Israel was given a new start, though the life of the two was continuous, and the New Israel was the legitimate heir of all God's promises to the Old. For example, there were twelve Apostles chosen, to answer to the traditional Twelve Tribes of Israel (cf. Matt. xix. 28.) Again, the distinctive Christian act of worship was to be a meal in continuation of the Passover, the memorial family meal of Israel. Furthermore, in actual fact the Christian experience first came to birth in a pre-existing fellowship. It is impossible to say whether the founding of the Church took place with the call of the first disciples, or the ordination of the Twelve, or the confession of St. Peter (though this was certainly seen by Jesus as a decisive event), or, as with Wesley here, at Pentecost. These were all so many stages toward full Christian experience in the life of the Christian community. These considerations are a sufficient answer to the questions: 'Did God intend the Church?' 'Did Jesus found the Church?' It is also St. Paul's justification for speaking of the Church as existing ideally in the realm of God long before it came into actual existence in this world.

'*instantly.*' Not invariably so, nor of necessity.

2. 'Ἔλεγχος.' See note on Sermon III, I, 11 (p. 19).

5. '*These had a peculiar place.*'

In Wesley's mind prayer for one's enemies would have special association with the fullness of evangelical experience. He would never forget that when his heart was strangely warmed the first impulse that came to him was to pray for his enemies. (*Journal*, May 24, 1738.)

8. '*the breaking of bread*': i.e., the Holy Communion.

9. Here is Wesley, of the Holy Club, Oxford. This and the preceding paragraph give a little picture of the typical activities of the first Methodists. Many would be the hearers who would remember them.


II. 2. '*bowels.*'

Primitive Hebrew psychology made the intestines the seat of compassion. The influence of Biblical language has unfortunately left much Christian writing marred by this inelegant expression.

'*brands out of the burning.*'

Wesley regularly applied this phrase to himself. The circumstance that in childhood Wesley had been narrowly rescued from the fire which destroyed Epworth Rectory gave him a special interest in it.

3. '*So the Christians of old did.*'

And, we are asked to remember, so do the Methodists today.

'*winked at.*' The Revised Version, 'overlooked', is better.

4. Wesley had spent the previous three days evangelizing the inns and alleys of Oxford.

5. '*His word ran and was glorified.*' '*The world in general were offended.*'

This, hints Wesley, is true also of later revivals of true religion.

'*his life is not like other men's . . . he maketh his boast, that God is his Father.*'

In this telling citation from the Apocrypha Wesley takes the very words out of the mouth of his detractors. The broad hint continues to good effect to the end of the paragraph.

'*movers of sedition.*'

One current slander was that the Wesleys were disloyal Jacobites.

7. So runs *Rules of the Society of the People called Methodists*, 1743: 'submitting to bear the reproach of Christ; to be as the filth and offscouring of the world, and looking that men should say all manner of evil of them falsely for the Lord's sake.'

9. '*Thus did Christianity spread.*' So now it spreads before you.

'*Here we tread a beaten path.*'

'And you,' in effect says Wesley, 'are those who tread it now.'

III. 1. '*a Christian world.*'

Despite his bitter experiences, Wesley did not despair of the ultimate redemption of the world. He was not one of those who conclude that the best God can do is to gather His elect out of the world, and let it go to the devil in its own way. It was his ambition for Methodism that it should 'spread Scriptural Holiness throughout the land'. He said: 'I look upon all the world as my parish.'

3. '*Here is no din of arms.*'

Wesley was the best of patriots. On occasion he even offered to raise volunteers for the defence of the realm. Yet he did not hesitate most ruthlessly to strip off the false glamour of war. There was no place for warfare in God's plan for the world. 'Here are forty thousand men gathered together on this plain. What are they going to do? See, there are thirty or forty thousand more at a little distance. And these are going to shoot them through the head or body, to stab them, or split their skulls, and send most of their souls into everlasting fire, as fast as they possibly can. Why so? What harm have they done to them? O none at all! They do not so much as know them. But a man, who is King of France, has a quarrel with another man, who is King of England. So these Frenchmen are to kill as many of these Englishmen as they can, to prove the King of France is in the right. Now, what an argument is this! What a method of proof! What an amazing way of deciding controversies!' Such recourse to arms is 'undeniable proof that the very foundations of all things, civil and religious, are utterly out of course in the Christian as well as the heathen world'. ('Original Sin,' (10): *Works*, Vol. IX.)

'*intestine*': i.e., 'internal'.

4. '*Neither saith any of them: that aught of the things which he possesseth is his own.*'

Wesley did not mean that a truly Christian world would adopt a communist basis for society. (See notes on Sermon

XLIV, pp. 264 ff.) The 'communism' of the primitive Church (see Acts iv. 32 f.: cf. ii. 44-5) to which reference is here made, was liberal alms-giving, prompted not by any political theory but by a simple impulse of good-will. This is all that Wesley intends.

6. Thus closes a noble vindication of Methodism as a revival of authentic New Testament Christianity, together with a stirring manifesto of its programme.


IV. '*a plain, practical application.*'

Here is a plain application indeed! 'Thou art the man!' suddenly thunders the prophet. It is impossible not to admire this utterance as a denunciation of social abuse. It is the voice of an Amos, a John the Baptist, a Savonarola. The effect, from the lips of a man of Wesley's commanding personality and fiery earnestness, must have been tremendous. For witness we have Kennicott. 'Then he came to what he called his plain, practical conclusion. Here was what he had been preparing for all along; and he fired his address with so much zeal and unbounded satire as quite spoiled what otherwise might have been turned to great advantage; for as I liked some, so I disliked other parts of his discourse extremely. . . . "Now," says he, "where is the Christianity to be found? Is this a Christian nation? Is this a Christian city?"—asserting the contrary to both. I liked some of his freedom, such as calling the generality of young gownsmen "a generation of triflers", and many other just invectives. But, considering how many shining lights are here that are the glory of the Christian cause, his sacred censure was much too flaming and strong, and his charity much too weak in not making large allowances. But so far from allowances, that, after having summed up the measure of our iniquities, he concluded with a lifted-up eye in this most solemn form: "It is time for Thee, Lord, to lay to Thine hand"—words full of such presumption and seeming imprecation, that they gave an universal shock.'

The modern reader may fail to appreciate the moral courage

required for an utterance such as this. Established institutions and men of privilege are on the defensive today. The public is accustomed to criticism of them, and they to justifying their continuance. It was otherwise in the eighteenth century. English sentiment was dominated by reaction to that prolonged civil and religious strife which had been, it was fondly hoped, brought to an end by the compromise of the 'Glorious Revolution' of 1688. All reasonable men felt that the aim of good government was to preserve order by maintaining the *status quo*. If a privilege had existed for a long time it was felt to be a rightful privilege. That an alleged abuse had gone unquestioned for many years was evidence that it was not an abuse at all. For a man to face his superiors gathered in august array, and publicly to call them to task, is never easy. At that time it was the role of a hero.

We cannot doubt Wesley's complete singleness of purpose. He had seriously considered making a flaming attack upon the failings of Oxford life in his sermon of 1741. (See notes to Sermon II.) His attack was therefore a careful and deliberate one. Kennicott is just in his observation: 'Here was what he had been preparing for all along.' Wesley certainly felt that his position in the University laid upon him a solemn duty to rebuke the evils he saw there. All honour is due to him that he did not shirk the task. There was every justification for his statements, for impartial witnesses agree that the life of the Universities was at a low ebb at this time. The abuses spoken of were actually there, though as usual in such cases, there were sheep among the goats. Wesley admittedly paints the dark side of the picture, and his standards for diligence and integrity were most exacting.

While we do not question Wesley's intentions, it is legitimate to express some doubt as to his judgement. Though still a Fellow of Lincoln College, the manner of his life and work made him in fact an outsider at Oxford. As such he could hardly hope to promote any practical measure of reform by an isolated outburst. Had his calling been to live and work at Oxford, his would have been the opportunity and obligation to work for reform. As it was, Wesley had a different, and not less worthy calling: to build up Methodism throughout the land. Untold good might have been done during the succeeding decades had he been in the position to secure that, every two or three years, the University should hear a reasoned and sympathetic exposition of Methodist life and teaching. It might well have ensured the continuance of a little group of 'Oxford Methodists', holding their original place in the High Church tradition of Oxford Anglicanism, yet understanding the new evangelical experience, and sympathizing with efforts to spread it. Had Anglicanism and Methodism thus been interpreted to one another there would have been profound and beneficial effects on the later development of both. However, the net result of the Sermon was that Wesley was afterwards excluded from the University pulpit. One could wish that for his 'practical application' the preacher had pointed the moral of his admirable sketch of 'Scriptural Christianity', had given a few examples of transformed lives within Methodism, and had appealed to his hearers to take an unprejudiced view of the Revival.

2. *'Non persuadebis, etiamsi persuaseris':* 'Thou shalt not persuade me, even though thou hast persuaded me':

i.e., 'However right your argument, I refuse to be moved by it'; or, 'A man convinced against his will is of the same opinion still.' If the Latin is a quotation, it is not apparent whence it comes.

3. *'our hearts.'* *'our lives.'*

Wesley graciously says 'our' and not merely 'your'.

7. *'Fellows, Students, Scholars.'*

These had an income provided by the endowments of their Colleges. The Fellows were responsible for the rule and tuition of the College.

*'even a proverbial uselessness.'*

The Fellows were appointed for life. In a generation such as that, which had largely lost its vision, the natural temptation of men enjoying a secure income was to become employed in trifles.

8. *'trusting that we were inwardly moved, &c.'*

This, and the following allusions, are to the Prayer Book Offices for the Ordering of Priests and of Deacons.

*'Who ... have been quickened by our word?'*

This is at all times a searching question for those engaged in the routine administration of a Church.

9. *'the youth of this place.'*

Kennicott admits, 'I liked some of his freedom'. The degeneracy of the rising generation may safely be deplored even in the eighteenth century!

*'gaming':* i.e., gambling.

*'What is perjury, if this is not?'*

A little more sense of humour would perhaps have saved Wesley here. The medieval Statutes of the unreformed Universities largely legislated for circumstances that had long ceased. They were partially unenforceable. Added to this, discipline was often slack. Furthermore, as Wesley admits in his own case, the Statutes were little read, being complicated and in Latin. An oath to obey cannot have a proper seriousness in conditions like this, and its enforcement is a thoroughly unhealthy custom. However, to describe this as habitual perjury betrays a lack of proportion. The real wrong was that the condition of the Statutes was a symptom of the unreformed state of the University. Kennicott answered Wesley's charge as follows: 'But this gave me no uneasiness; for in every oath the intention of the legislator is the only thing you swear to observe; and the legislators here mean that you shall observe all their laws, *or upon the violation of them submit to the punishment if required.*' This is a fair debating point, but evades the morals of the case, savouring rather of a legal quibble.

## SCRIPTURAL CHRISTIANITY   35

10. '*It is time for Thee, Lord, to lay to Thine hand!*'—'words full of such presumption and seeming imprecation, that they gave an universal shock.'

11. '*young, unknown, inconsiderable men.*'

Wesley here takes up a sneer natural to dons who still remembered the Wesleys as undergraduates. John was then forty-one, and Charles thirty-six.

'*Romish "aliens".*'

There had been a recent threat of French invasion to support the Jacobites.

In a letter Blackstone wrote: 'We were last Friday entertained at St. Mary's by a curious sermon from Wesley the Methodist. Among other equally modest particulars he informed us; first, That there was not one Christian among all the Heads of Houses; secondly, that pride, gluttony, avarice, luxury, sensuality, and drunkenness were the general characteristicks of all Fellows of Colleges, who were useless to a proverbial uselessness. Lastly, that the younger part of the University were a generation of triflers, all of them perjured, and not one of them of any religion at all. His notes were demanded by the Vice-Chancellor, but on mature deliberation it has been thought proper to punish him by a mortifying neglect.' This renders the sermon far less than justice.

Action was taken to prevent Wesley again taking his turn as University Preacher. His notes were required as precise evidence of what he said. His own comment is: 'I preached, I suppose the last time, at St. Mary's. Be it so. I am now clear of the blood of these men. I have fully delivered my own soul. The Beadle came to me afterwards and told me the Vice-Chancellor had sent him for my notes. I sent them without delay, not without admiring the wise providence of God. Perhaps few men of note would have given a sermon of mine the reading if I had put it into their hands: but by this means it came to be read, probably more than once, by every man of eminence in the University.' (*Journal*, Aug. 24, 1744.)

## Questions

1. Christians of all communions find their own systems in the New Testament. Is this due to 'wishful thinking'? or to the comprehensive nature of a book which contains the germ of all later systems? or to the circumstance that the New Testament gives no sufficient information?

2. In what departments of its life can present-day Methodism uphold a claim to be 'Scriptural Christianity'?—our Connexional and Ministerial system? our use of lay preachers and stewards? our evangelistic methods? our regular worship? our sacramental system? Would your answer be different under any of these heads in the case of the Wesleys?

3. What light does this sermon throw on the rights and wrongs of the separation of the Methodists from the Church of England?

4. Can an outsider usefully attempt to reform an institution? Are corrupt institutions *ever* reformed from within? What are the respective merits of denunciation and peaceful persuasion as weapons for the reformer?

*Sermon Five**

# Justification by Faith

Wesley preached a sermon on these lines, and from this text, on a number of occasions. The most notable of these was Tuesday, June 8, 1742, during the celebrated week when he preached daily in Epworth Churchyard, standing upon his father's tomb-stone. However, the sermon as we have it here savours more of the theological treatise than the open-air address. Unlike most, this is only a sermon in form. It is not unreasonable to suppose that Wesley re-wrote it with the aim of making as far as possible a complete and systematic exposition of his views on this particular matter. The sermon thus presents a strong contrast to the foregoing one, for there is missing the rich human and historical interest found there. Nevertheless, there is much of value here. The main interest for the present-day reader is to observe the way in which much of Wesley's detailed exegesis of the Bible is rejected by modern scholarship, and yet his essential message remains untouched. This should prove a reassurance to those who are diffident in accepting the results of modern Biblical study, lest the Gospel message suffer thereby. It is also a warning to such as would hasten to reject past evangelical tradition on account of 'science' and 'up-to-date views on the Bible'. We are also reminded that these Standard Sermons were left to us as a standard for preaching. They do not impose upon us canons of Biblical scholarship. We are fully entitled as loyal Methodists to disagree with Wesley on technical matters, when later research makes this necessary.

*Text. 'him that worketh not.'*

St. Paul here refers to the things commanded by the Mosaic Law. He means that the Christian trusts to be accepted by God

* No. 5 in *Fifty-three Sermons*

solely because Christ is his Saviour, and not at all because he has earned divine favour by his own efforts in obedience to the Law of Moses. It does *not* mean that the true Christian regards 'believing in Christ' as more important than an actual and practical change of life. Those who do not understand St. Paul as a whole can easily misunderstand this text in this way. It is therefore perhaps better to preach Justification by Faith from a different text today.

1. *'the wrath of God abideth on us.'*

To St. Paul 'the wrath of God' was a name for that self-acting process which produces progressive utter moral ruin for those who forget God. The process is sketched out in Rom. i. 18–32. God is responsible in the sense that He has made the world as it is, but 'the wrath' is not anything that God does, nor is it His attitude to mankind. In token of this, St. Paul often speaks of 'the wrath of God', but he takes care never to say: 'God is angry.' God's activity is to rescue man from this Nemesis he has brought upon himself. To Wesley, however, 'the wrath' *did* speak of 'an angry God': not of course in the pagan sense of One who flies into a rage because man has defied Him, but to the effect that an inflexibly righteous God cannot condone the smallest moral lapse.

I. 1–4. *'In the image of God was man made.' 'Such then was the state of man in Paradise.'*

In agreement with his times Wesley took the Genesis Creation-stories as literal history. We can do so no longer, because science has shown that the whole earth has gone through many complete changes, spread over ages almost inconceivably vast, and that all living creatures have, from the simplest of beginnings, evolved from type to type in response to those changes. At least so far as his physical frame and nervous constitution are concerned, man is a part of that which has evolved. Science has so far shown less light on how such

JUSTIFICATION BY FAITH 39

gifts as self-consciousness, moral free-will, and conscience may be imagined as developing. These are the factors that make man what he is. There is ample justification for regarding the origin of man as a distinct and marvellous episode in God's evolutionary creative plan. We need not hesitate to say that God specially created and specially endowed man. However, the Genesis story has to take its place among those other legends in explanation of 'how things came to be', which have commonly been developed among ancient races richly gifted with curiosity and imagination, though not with knowledge. Another factor is that it is now much better realized than in the days of Wesley that there were many other ancient Creation-legends. A comparison will show not only many striking similarities, but also, in particular, a striking difference. The primitive Hebrews were not ahead of the Babylonians, &c., in their science, but they marvellously excelled them in a sense of 'God in everything', in level of morality, and in psychological insight. Hence the Genesis legends are certainly to be described as inspired by God. These most beautiful stories rightly have a place in the Christian Scriptures. God has many methods of imparting spiritual truth other than historical narrative.

In Gen. i. 26 we read: 'And God said, Let us make man in our image, after our likeness.' It has been widely assumed in Christian tradition, as in Wesley here, that by this 'image and likeness' is intended every conceivable intellectual, moral, and spiritual perfection. This notion of Adam's Original Righteousness is something read into the Genesis account. A reader coming to the story with no pre-suppositions in mind would probably gain the impression that Adam and Eve were nearer in nature to children than to angels. They seem to have been imagined as similar to ourselves in powers of body, mind, and spirit, but lacking knowledge and experience of life. They were in consequence easily deceived. It is an interesting coincidence that science gives a not dissimilar picture of primitive man. In the evolution of the race the first beings to be accounted men in the full sense of the word were probably not very unlike modern men in body, and in inborn mental potentiality. Their minds would be, however, quite untutored, and their rudimentary moral sense as yet unawakened to the lessons of succeeding ages of social experience. However, it is no accident that generations of theologians have instinctively elaborated and emphasized this conception of Original Righteousness. Tradition has held that the whole race was condemned by God to eternal damnation on account of Adam's sin. There was no rhyme nor reason in a punishment of such inconceivable severity unless it was merited by a crime of inconceivable heinousness. Hence every effort was made to represent the sin of Adam as a test case of disobedience, a deliberate and utterly needless rebellion against God's known and wise law, done with complete knowledge of the frightful consequences, and with no excuse of overmastering temptation. The greater the estimate of the mental and spiritual endowment of Adam, the more awful the Fall. Here is certainly the motive behind the doctrine of man's Original Righteousness. The great commentary upon this theme is Milton's *Paradise Lost*. See also note to Sermon XXXIX, I, 2 (pp. 241 f.).

5. *'The moment he tasted that fruit, he died.'*

We are forced by the circumstance that, in the Genesis narrative, Adam and Eve continued to live after eating of the tree, to take God's warning of death as referring either to the soul alone, or else as having the sense of: 'the body (and soul) shall become *liable* to death.' The latter is more likely.

*'His body . . . became corruptible and mortal.'*

Wesley believed that physical death did not occur before the Fall. In Sermon LVI, ii, 1. (Wesley's *Works*, Vol. VI, p. 213) he says: 'God . . . made no corruption, no destruction, in the inanimate creation. He made not death in the animal creation; neither its harbingers—sin and pain.' At this time he also thought that, had man not sinned, he would have continued physically immortal. Physical death is, of course, original and necessary to man's physical being, as to all other living things. See note to Sermon XXXIX, I, 3 (pp. 242).

## JUSTIFICATION BY FAITH

### 6. *'as being contained in him.'*

The construction that Wesley placed upon the foregoing citation of Rom. v. 12 was: Adam, who sinned, was the ancestor of the whole race. All later men were, in a certain sense, in him when he sinned. In consequence they all sinned in his sin, and all die. We may be excused for regarding this as a far-fetched argument. It is, however, not quite what St. Paul intended, though the general effect is similar.

By way of illustration, consider the story of Achan (Joshua vj. 16–19, and vii). The punishment of the whole family for the sin of one member is to us a manifest injustice. The ancient Hebrews did not look at the matter in this way, however. They conceived of the tribe as a unit. The whole acted together. They were well aware that only one man had done the actual deed, but in doing it a part of the tribe had acted, and all were to some extent involved. Such is the conception of 'collective personality'. It is hard for us to take it seriously today, for it has been almost entirely obliterated as an element in actual life by the greatly enriched modern sense of personality, and by the consequent prevalence of the individualist outlook. The nearest modern parallel is the mind that reproaches the Jews of the present day for the death of Christ. This ugly custom is rightly condemned, for it is an unseemly survival of what was once universal. However, for St. Paul the conception of 'collective personality' was a living one. In his thought Adam was the 'Representative Head' of the human race. He was the one in whose action all men acted, not in the theoretical sense that an ancestor comprises all succeeding generations, but in the real sense that he was the head of a tribe that was a unity. St. Paul, being a Hebrew, did not employ abstract nouns as we do, but 'Adam' is his equivalent for our 'humanity'. It is quite likely that he thought of Adam as an actual man who really lived, though we cannot be certain. He certainly had enough mental subtlety to distinguish between a real and a typical Adam. Which ever be the case, no difference is made to his argument, for the *interest* of St. Paul is not in Adam as an individual man, but in Adam as standing for the race.

7. *'another common Head of mankind, &c.'*

This is the corresponding side to St. Paul's thought as applied to Christ. It is correctly reflected by Wesley. The Apostle's explanation of the saving work of Christ was somewhat as follows: the human race was in bondage to sin, to death, to the curse of the Law, and to the evil spirits. In becoming Man the Son of God placed Himself in the proper sphere of influence of all these malign forces. By sin He was tempted. At the hand of death He went to the grave. The curse of the Mosaic Law was fastened upon the Crucified One. (Gal. iii. 13.) The Satanic powers did Him to death. (1 Cor. ii. 8.) The resurrection was the pledge of complete and final victory in every part of this manifold contest. One asks: 'How does this victory, wrought out once and for all *then*, affect *me, now?*' St. Paul answers: 'Christ, a real Man, was your Representative Head. He played the part of a second, and a victorious Adam. If you make yourself one community with Him and with His, by going to Him in penitent faith and making trust in Him your sole hope in life, by taking upon yourself His Name and allegiance, and by joining His People the Church, all He did belongs to you.' With some confidence we may claim that such is the heart of St. Paul's explanation of the Atonement, while most other parts of the New Testament move on similar lines.

*'that one oblation of Himself, once offered.' 'a full, perfect, and sufficient sacrifice.'*

These are from the Prayer of Consecration in the Order for Holy Communion.

8. *'God hath now "reconciled the world to Himself".'*

This is sound Pauline doctrine. (See particularly, 2 Cor. v. 19.)

9. *'God is so far reconciled to all the world.'*

St. Paul nowhere speaks in this way, as though God, as well as man, had to come to another mind.

To conclude upon this section, we may say that, whatever

be the result of speculation regarding the historical origin of sin, the 'general ground of the whole doctrine of justification' remains firm. Every man of any spiritual insight, the world over, and in every age, will agree that he is a sinful man, in need of divine forgiveness and aid. However to be explained, the universality of sin is a dreadful and manifest fact of experience. The explanation of the fact is of secondary importance.

II. 1. *'it is not the being made actually just and righteous.'*

By justification the Roman Church means not only forgiveness, but also that change of character and activity which results in the forgiven, i.e., she includes in justification that which Wesley describes as sanctification. This difference in terminology largely explains the Roman objection to the Protestant thesis: 'Justification by Faith alone, and not by works.'

*'some rare instances.'*

Perhaps Rom. iv. 25; Rom. viii. 30; 1 Cor. vi. 11.

2. *'conceit':* i.e., 'thing conceived', 'notion'.

*'clearing us from accusation, particularly that of Satan.'*

It does not appear precisely what Wesley had in mind. He may be referring to the theory that, man having sold himself to the devil, God bought out Satan's 'just rights' over man at the price of His Son (whom Satan found himself powerless to hold).

4. *'Least of all does justification imply that God is deceived, &c.'*

This is a most important point, for many have been guilty of careless expressions which can be misinterpreted in just this deplorable manner. It is a serious error to speak of justification as if there were an element of pretence associated with it. See below.

5. *'The plain scriptural notion of justification is pardon, the forgiveness of sins.'*

This is an admirable exposition. The teaching of Jesus was that a righteous and loving Father freely forgives penitent man. St. Paul was himself a man, and moved among men, who by deeply ingrained habit of mind thought of man's relation to God in terms of *law*. God was always conceived of as the Judge, and man as the defendant. The question always was: 'What is the verdict?' In trying to make the Gospel plain to such hearers, St. Paul was impelled to express the idea of free forgiveness in law-court language. The only way of doing this was by using the startling paradox that God *acquits the guilty*, or, to use the familiar form of words, that He *justifies the ungodly*. The word in St. Paul's Bible which in our English version is rendered 'to justify' meant 'to acquit'. How startling the paradox would seem then is seen when we remember that, in the Scriptures of that day, the stock phrase for the unjust judge who corrupted justice was that he 'acquitted the guilty'. Whatever we may think of the Apostle's attempt to translate the message of Jesus into this other idiom, it is impossible to improve on Wesley's simple definition as a description of St. Paul's intention.

With this in mind, the modern preacher is well advised, when explaining justification, to avoid such phrases as: God imputes righteousness to him that believes, or: He does not impute, or reckon, sin. This language certainly has the authority of Scripture, but, unfortunately, to the average modern mind 'imputing' smacks of a matter of form or a legal fiction. The idea is almost irresistibly conveyed by this word that God chooses to account the penitent sinner as other than he actually is. For the sake of what he *will* be, God 'writes the sinner up' as though he were *now* a good man. Justification is made into a mere technical change of legal status, which is not the real intention of St. Paul, or of the Bible as a whole. The misconception condemned in paragraph 4 is then close to hand. It is both much plainer to the average modern congregation, and closer to the spirit of St. Paul, to keep to the simple usage: justification=forgiveness.

If justification is forgiveness it is emphatically not a mere matter of form. Rather is it the initial stage of a *real* change of life. The grace of God is both His attitude of loving-kindness towards man, and His prevailing power at work in the heart of man. 'Justifying Grace' answers to both these aspects. Once God's gracious attitude of forgiveness is realized a continuing gracious divine work begins in the heart. The great obstacle to starting a new and better life is disbelief in the possibility of good, despair of oneself, shame at past failures, and the load of a guilty conscience. However, if God still believes in me and calls me, if He does not despair of me, if He loves me and pardons me, *then* I *can* start again, in His strength. It may be theologically convenient to separate justification from sanctification, just as it is administratively convenient to introduce a legal distinction between infants and adults. Actually, however, there is no hard-and-fast line. Justification has the same relation to sanctification as a baby has to a man.

*'for the sake of the propitiation.'*

The word in the Greek Old Testament (as used by St. Paul), rendered 'to propitiate', means: 'to perform an act whereby guilt or defilement is removed'. (It is in *pagan* Greek writers that it generally means 'to placate'. Unfortunately for the common understanding of St. Paul, it is just this sense of 'appeasement' which instinctively presents itself to the mind of 'the man in the street' when he hears the word 'propitiation'.) In primitive times, when the Hebrews thought of religion largely in terms of mysterious 'taboos', propitiation referred mainly to ceremonial acts of 'spiritual disinfection'. Under the influence of the Prophets Jewish religion became increasingly ethical. It was more and more felt that defilement in the sight of God was not merely a matter of taboo. Rather did it consist in man's moral failings. Here was a defilement which only God could wipe away, by His forgiveness of the penitent sinner. In proportion as later parts of the Old Testament represent this development, so does the verb 'to make propitiation' take on a new usage. It comes to be used, with God as subject, in the sense of 'to forgive'. Thus, when St. Paul speaks of the death of Christ as 'making propitiation for sin', his intention is that the Cross is the means whereby man can come to the forgiveness of sin, and the barrier of guilt between man and God be done away. He does not say that Christ's death *placates* God.

'*He "showeth forth His righteousness" (or mercy).*'

In Biblical language the Righteousness of God is the action God takes to vindicate the distressed cause of right, and to rescue His People. It is salvation. (See Isaiah li. 5, 6.) It is the expression of God's mercy. Certainly it is not the *opposite* of His mercy, as some have held. God's Righteousness is not the attribute of severe and inflexible justice. The complete moral uprightness of the character of God is shown, not so much in an insistence upon due punishment for every sin, even to the last jot and tittle of the law, but in the circumstance that it is the *righteous* man whom He chooses to uphold.

'*Not the hearers of the law, but the doers of the law, shall be justified.*' (Rom. ii. 13.)

We cannot uphold Wesley's exposition here. St. Paul is arguing that every man, Jew and Gentile alike, is judged by the moral standard he knows. The mere possession of the Law of Moses as part of the national heritage gives the Jew no position of advantage in God's sight. It simply provides a higher standard by which he is to be judged. To profit by his national religion the Jew has to *obey* the Law, not just *hear* it.

### III. 2. '*those who . . . contend that a man must be sanctified . . . before he can be justified*':

i.e., those who by justification mean a completed change of life and character, and not only the simple forgiveness of the penitent sinner (St. Paul's general usage).

'*under the notion of a sinner*': i.e., considered as a sinner.

5. For the quotations in this paragraph see the Anglican *Articles* XII and XIII. The argument of this and the succeeding paragraph suffers somewhat from a certain excess of zeal to prove

that the 'good works' of such as are not converted Christians are not really good. (See also note to Sermon I, 2; p. 3.) The Christian preacher is on sounder ground if he sticks to the simple proposition that no man, no matter how truly upright he be, can come to the fullness of that good to which God calls him, apart from the experience of salvation.

IV. 1. ' *"that He might be just, and"* (consistently with His justice) *"the justifier of him which believeth in Jesus".*' (Rom. iii. 26.)

The words in brackets represent a case where Wesley, in company with multitudes of others, has read into St. Paul something which is probably not there. If it be assumed that the Righteousness of God is the attribute of inflexible justice, and that God shows Himself to 'be just' by insisting on punishment to the utmost for every sin, then there is an antithesis in this verse. There is a strong contrast between God as He is righteous and just, and God as He justifies (forgives) him that has faith. Two opposite activities of God are placed over against one another. As Isaac Watts sings:

> But when we see Thy strange design
>    To save rebellious worms,
> Where vengeance and compassion join
>    In their divinest forms;
> Here the whole Deity is known,
>    Nor dares a creature guess
> Which of the glories brightest shone,
>    The justice or the grace.

However, if the Biblical Righteousness of God be regarded as the action which a right-loving and merciful God takes to succour His righteous ones (see note on II, 5, pp. 44 ff.), this sharp antithesis quite disappears. The Righteousness is not 'vengeance', and the Justification, by contrast, 'compassion'. They are but two names for one and the same redeeming activity of God. Righteousness mainly refers to God's care for His cause and People, justification mainly to His care for the individual. With some confidence we may say that in this verse (or elsewhere), St. Paul does not speak of righteousness and forgiveness as though they represented opposing claims, claims which had to be squared with one another by the death of Christ. There is hence no need to insert 'consistently with' to bring out the full meaning of Rom. iii. 36, or to write of 'The justice *or* the grace'.

*'What law do we establish by faith?'*

It is unlikely that in Rom. iii. 31 St. Paul had in mind a clear distinction between the ritual ordinances of the Law of Moses, which are to pass away, and the moral law, which is to be established in Christ. He probably simply meant that the inward intention and true essence of the Jewish religion was right living before God and man, and that faith in Christ was the only way in which man could attain to this.

2. '$\text{ἔλεγχος}$.' See note to Sermon III, I, 11 (p. 19).

3. *'the words of our own Church.'*

Here are abbreviated quotations from the Anglican Second Homily on the Passion, and the First Part of the Homily on the Sacrament. It is noteworthy how, after some years of Methodist revival, and after many differences with individual Anglicans, Wesley so openly bases himself upon the authority of 'our Church', the Church of England. There is here forcibly brought to our attention a feature that will be encountered many times in the reading of these sermons. This most Methodist of books is also in a sense an Anglican book. Whenever Wesley speaks of 'our Church' he always has the Church of England in mind, never a separate Methodist Church. He constantly makes appeal to the doctrinal standards of the Church of England, and quotes the *Book of Common Prayer*, the Homilies, &c., with affectionate approval. Through long familiarity he instinctively cites the Psalms after the Prayer-Book version. In loyalty to the Prayer Book he affirms his belief in Baptismal Regeneration. (Sermon XIV, 1; XXXIX, IV, 2.) He asserts that the rule of the Church by Bishops is Scriptural and right (Sermon XXXIV, II, 2). These utterances cannot be dismissed as ill-considered. They stand in sermons which bear the marks of revision in the light of long experience. The fact is that Wesley filled a dual position. He was a life-long member of the Church of England, both devoted and strict, and also the Methodist of Methodists. To the reader who knows only Methodism as she is today, and not as she was at the beginning, a few of the notes upon these Sermons may read like attempts to assimilate our Church to the Established Church. Assurance is given that this is not the intention. The 'Anglicanism' is already there in the Sermons, and it is impossible to make candid comment upon them without taking account of this factor.

Regarding the bearing of this upon present-day Methodist Church life two things are to be said. On the one hand, Methodism is not bound to John Wesley. She is a Free Church, and can order her beliefs and customs in any way that seems right to her, subject to those general loyalties which are binding upon all Christians. In not a few things she has actually departed from Wesley, and in some cases, at least, with undoubted rightness. On the other hand, when advice is to be sought upon present issues Methodism will surely recognize that no other human voice from within herself carries quite the same weight of authority as does that of Wesley. In virtue of this the Methodist Church looks toward the Church of England to a somewhat greater extent than do her sister Free Churches. We certainly recognize that the other British Free Churches are our nearest spiritual neighbours within the vast community of the Universal Church. We cherish our present close and happy fellowship with them. At the same time, we cannot forget that in time past these great Churches have definitely and in principle repudiated the Episcopal government and the Liturgy of the Church of England. By contrast, following Wesley, we have in fact departed from Episcopacy, and to a less extent from the Prayer Book also, but to do this has never been a part of the avowed principles or essential genius of our Church. While that which corresponds to the ways and views of Wesley may not be binding upon all Methodists, it can hardly be repudiated as false to Methodism.

This intermediate position between our sister Free Churches

and Church of England has an important practical bearing in these days when the unity of Christendom is so widely seen by Christians of vision to be a vital issue. The Methodist may be confronted with the Episcopal Orders and discipline, the doctrinal formularies, and the Liturgy of the Church of England. He may have to make up his mind what arrangement he would be willing to make regarding these things for the sake of fuller Christian unity. The only question he is then bound to ask, in loyalty to the past tradition and present experience of his Church, is the severely practical one: 'What organization of the Church will today most make for the advancement of the Gospel?' This would have been Wesley's sole question, for Wesley both loved these elements of Anglicanism, and was prepared to sacrifice them when the necessity of the work of God seemed to demand it. The issue of Bishop or no Bishop, of Liturgy or no Liturgy, is not one of vital principle in our Church. The Methodist is freer in this matter than the Independent, or even the Presbyterian. These have the issue complicated for them by the further painful question: 'Is it the Lord's will that I should now compromise the Church polity to which my forefathers witnessed, and for which they suffered?' Thus Methodism possibly has it in her to become the bridge between the other Free Churches and the Church of England, in much the same way as the Anglo-Catholic may become a link between the Greek Orthodox Church and the main body of Anglicans.

5. '*"He made Christ to be sin for us,"* (2 Cor. v. 21) *that is, treated Him as a sinner.*'

This interpretation is too harsh. St. Paul was deeply moved by the circumstance that the form of execution suffered by Jesus was one involving a curse of excommunication, according to the Law of Moses. (Gal. iii. 13.) To the Jew, to whom the Law was the supreme revelation of God, the statement that the Messiah had been crucified was an inconceivable and blasphemous paradox. This was the 'offence of the Cross', of which the Apostle so often speaks. To St. Paul, however, the Messiahship of the Crucified had been vindicated by the Resurrection. He resolved the paradox in the other way. That the curse of the Law had been attached to God's Messiah was evidence of the bankruptcy of the Mosaic Law as a religious system. So 'Christ is the end of the law'. (Rom. x. 4.) That Christ, by dying an accursed death, should bring to an end the dispensation of Law, and open the Gospel of Grace, was God's plan. This is what St. Paul means by saying that God made His Son to be sin. He would most probably have said that it was man, and not God, that treated Christ as a sinner. That Christ was crucified was not a mark that He was accursed for a time in the sight of God. It was rather the opposite. We have no conclusive evidence that St. Paul could have spoken of God 'punishing Him for our sins'.

7. '*It does not become poor . . . worms . . . to ask of God the reasons of His conduct, &c.*'

There is much truth in this, for the proper approach of man to God is always that of awed submission. At the same time, it is God who has given us both the power and the urge to ask such questions, and we cannot believe that it is wrong to inquire reverently.

'*This is the very point . . . in the ninth chapter of this Epistle.*'
    (Romans.)

Calvin had regarded Romans ix as teaching the doctrine of Election, i.e., that those who have faith have it solely because God has so chosen, and those who have it not lack faith solely because God wills to leave them to the damnation deserved by all alike. Divine grace was limited: 'Even as it is written, Jacob I loved, but Esau I hated' (i.e., rejected) (Rom. ix. 13). Arminius led those Protestants who rejected the doctrine of Election in favour of the conception of God's grace extending to all, with man free to accept or reject it. Wesley, who was always firm in declaring himself an Arminian, here adopts the argument used by Arminius to explain away the difficulties which were apparently presented to his doctrine by Romans ix. Actually,

Calvin and Arminius are alike in error by speaking of 'Jacob' and 'Esau' too much as if they were individual men, and the whole chapter as if it were dealing with the problem why one man is saved and another not. 'Jacob' and 'Esau' are 'Representative Heads' of different nations. St. Paul is really trying to show that in God's plan for the world one nation is called to play one role, perhaps more honourable, and another a different and perhaps less honourable role, yet that in the end everything will work out for the glory of God and the blessing of all men. This is quite another problem, which has nothing to do with 'justifying faith'.

8. *'to hide pride from man.'*

This is a profound reason. As Wesley goes on to show, a humble preparedness to make oneself utterly dependent upon God is a main requisite for coming to Him. There is, however, surely a more profound reason why justification is by faith. 'Saving faith' is nothing less than the humble, trustful, and affectionate outgoing of man, in heart and mind and will and every activity of life, to his Father God. (See notes on Sermon I, I, pp. 3 f.) Such faith is the self-evident condition for man to be united to God as His penitent, forgiven, reconciled, obedient, and happy child.

*'Pride had already destroyed the very angels of God.'*

cf. 2 Peter ii. 4 and Jude 6.

To conclude: the reader may well ask whether the real value of this sermon has not been taken away by the wide divergence of much modern exegesis of St. Paul from that of Wesley. Assurance may be given that this is not so. In that day the universally accepted system of Pauline exposition centred around the so-called Penal Substitution theory of the Atonement. This theory was that God laid upon Christ, as He hung upon the Cross, the actual curse and penalty due for the sins of all men. So, and only so, could the claims of justice be satisfied, and the Father enabled to forgive without violating His own moral law. Thus Charles Wesley wrote of:

## JUSTIFICATION BY FAITH 53

> ... the Father's vengeful ire
> Which my Redeemer bore:
> Into His bones the fire He sent
> Till all the flaming darts were spent,
> And Justice ask'd no more.

Though we must not suppose that all sound writers are agreed upon every point, or even upon the main principle, it yet remains that among reverent and progressive evangelical scholars there is a strong tendency to find that this Penal Substitution theory is no part of St. Paul's theology. One of the best of the many books that may be recommended as giving further information on this matter is Dr. C. H. Dodd's *Romans* in the *Moffatt Commentary*. This result is the central point among many points where the traditional exegesis of St. Paul is being revised. Most of the divergences mentioned in the foregoing notes are to be explained as cases of this revision.

We have therefore moved quite a long way from this sermon in our understanding of St. Paul, and this in a matter of real importance, namely, the explanation of the death of the Lord. It is most important to keep clearly in mind that these changes, however significant, only affect the details, and not the substance of the Christian Gospel. The *essential* things for a man to realize, if he is to be saved are: (i) that in Jesus Christ God has done all that is necessary for him to be forgiven if penitent, and accepted as the well-pleasing child of God: that God has pledged His goodwill toward man, His belief in man, His love for man; (ii) that in Jesus Christ God has decisively conquered the power of sin, and of everything that can hold the spirit of man in chains: that God has pledged His sufficient power to redeem and restore. The various ancient theories of the Atonement, including that of Penal Substitution, helped men of bygone days to grasp these two essentials. In every case, however, it was the *fact* of the Atonement that saved, rather than the *theory* propounded to explain the fact. We may rightly adopt new theories of the Atonement (one such has been briefly summarized in the note on I. 7, p. 42), if they seem to be demanded by Biblical scholarship, or by our sense of spiritual fitness. Yet we do not thereby in the least call in question the great fact of the saving work of Christ. Many will differ from some of the opinions expressed in this sermon, but no one need depart in the slightest from the Gospel here proclaimed with such profundity and systematic thoroughness.

## Questions

1. 'This man went down to his house justified rather than the other.' Does our Lord's Parable of the Pharisee and the Publican (Luke xviii. 9–14), teach 'Justification by Faith'?

2. Is it necessary for a man to have some sort of reasoned explanation of the saving work of Christ for him to be saved?

3. Is a deep sense of the guilt and power of sin an indispensable preliminary to justification?

4. Would God's plan of salvation have miscarried had the Jews as a whole accepted Jesus as their Lord, teacher, and hero, so that He had not been crucified?

5. Have changed views concerning the Fall and Original Sin helped to produce that dulled sense of personal, as distinct from social, sin, which is such an impediment to evangelical preaching today?

6. Was the 'old-fashioned theory of the Atonement', with its directness and simplicity, a better weapon for the evangelist than 'modern notions', however admirable in principle?

*Sermon Six**

# The Righteousness of Faith

THIS sermon covers much the same ground as No. V. It is, however, a true sermon, though a definitely doctrinal sermon. It is not a theological treatise in sermon form. In consequence, this sermon much excels the foregoing one in personal application, though it is inferior in systematic completeness and clarity of thought. Here is an example of how 'Justification by Faith' may be *preached*.

*Text.* Rom. x. 5–8.

St. Paul's quotation is from Deut. xxx. 11–14. The original meaning is that the Law of Moses is not too hard for man to keep. It is not utterly remote from man, but in his heart already. St. Paul picks this passage out as an example of the religion of faith contained in the Law. There is real insight in the choice, for Deuteronomy represents the Law as influenced by the Prophets. Deuteronomy is less concerned with ceremonial than the older Leviticus, and more with ethical and humane conduct. Here is Jewish religion on its more inward and spiritual side. However, basing himself on the theory that the Old Testament contains Christian doctrine in veiled form, St. Paul goes on to read into the text a fanciful 'prophecy of Christ'. He interprets Deut. xxx. 11–14 to mean that Christ is not an inaccessible heavenly Figure (like the Messiah of Jewish expectation), nor yet a dead prophet. He is a present and living Lord. Charles Wesley takes up this passage as the theme for a most beautiful hymn (*M.H.B.* No. 530).

1. '*the covenant of works, made with Adam while in paradise.*'

The idea that Adam was set to maintain himself in favour with God by his own efforts in perfect obedience has been explained fully in Sermon V, I, 2–4. Seventeenth-century

* No. 6 in *Fifty-three Sermons*

Protestant theologians formed the habit of describing this stage of religion as the Covenant of Works. Wesley here misrepresents St. Paul's meaning. The Apostle had no notion of this supposed Covenant of Works. Rather did he teach that God's Saints lived by faith in the days before the Law of Moses was given. St. Paul contrasts with the religion of faith not the Covenant of Works, but the Mosaic Law, *in so far as this was an external and ceremonial system.*

I. 1. *'This law, or covenant . . . given by God to man in paradise.'*

Wesley's initial confusion of the text runs on throughout the sermon. When he speaks of 'the righteousness of the law' he has the Covenant of Works in mind. However, 'The man which doeth these things shall live by them' properly refers to the Law of Moses. Observe that this, and the next four paragraphs, are based upon the assumption that Adam was so gifted in spiritual insight as perfectly to understand, and so endowed with spiritual grace as perfectly to perform, the whole will of God.

7. *'This was in part revealed to Adam.'*

An ancient belief, much popularized by Luther, was that Gen. iii. 15 was a first mysterious forecast of Christ's victory over the devil. Actually it is a part of the theme: 'how things came to be'. The legend seeks to explain the common aversion felt for snakes.

*'that in thy Seed.'*

Here is another traditional example of a 'prophecy of Christ' read into an Old Testament narrative. The original sense is: 'Thy descendants shall become a blessing to all nations.'

8. *'the propitiation which He hath made.'*

See note on Sermon V, II, 5 (pp. 44 ff.).

*'imputes'*: i.e., 'reckons', 'accounts'.

9. *'wrath.'* See note on Sermon V, 1 (p. 38).

13. *'Him who hath paid the price for us.'*

Despite the observations regarding St. Paul's theology of the Atonement, made in discussing Sermon V, we certainly need not hesitate to use this phrase. Whatever theory we entertain in explanation of the death of Christ, His saving work was costly to Him. It was exceeding costly in self-sacrifice, in spiritual and physical agony. Christ paid a great price on our behalf. We only go astray when we ask: 'To whom was the price paid; to Satan, or to the Father?'

II. 4. *'one single breach . . . utterly destroys our whole claim to life.'*

This is a severe statement indeed, though it flows logically from the theory of the Covenant of Works. Looked at from one aspect it is true. Even the smallest moral lapse will not be condoned by God, and may be the beginning of grievous faults. Nevertheless, the conclusion lies dangerously close to hand that, in judging men eternally, God is not too careful to mark whether an offender has fallen into many and heinous sins, or into but few and slight. This would impugn the justice of God.

5. For a discussion of this extreme view of the total depravity of man, see notes to Sermon XXXVIII (pp. 232 ff.).

8. *'mere grace':* i.e., 'pure grace'.

III. We come now to a powerful and practical application. As II. is aimed at the unawakened and careless, so this is adapted to the earnest man who has a sincere desire to please God, yet who is a stranger to the evangelical experience. There are probably more of the latter than of the former in the average congregation of today. We can learn much from Wesley here. He well knows every 'cave of refuge'. No evasion escapes challenging notice.

**2.** '*wash away thy sins.*' Acts xxii. 16.

The original reference is to Baptism.

**3.** '*It may be, thou wilt not weep much, till thou lovest much.*'

Some remain strangers to the evangelical experience because they cannot bring themselves to see that the moment has come for the venture of faith, through undue mental preoccupation with a great and thrilling emotional disturbance they suppose they should have. Faith is a condition of mind and will, as well as of feeling. We cannot say which part of the gift of faith should be more prominent first. God deals in different ways with men of various temperaments.

The quotation is the last two lines of the hymn, 'Behold the Saviour of mankind' (*M.H.B.* No. 193), by Wesley's father, Samuel Wesley, senior.

**4.** '*I grant . . . it were meet and right, &c.*':

i.e., 'You must live this moment as if it were your last, and the act of closing with Christ in faith the only thing you will ever have time to do. Yet you must also expect to find that your faith will work itself out in obedience, if opportunity is given you.'

**5.** '*if there be anything good in sincerity: why dost thou expect it before thou hast faith?*'

As a counter-balance to this statement see Sermon IX, IV, 1. Wesley there rightly finds room for sincerity in non-believers. However, it is certain that the experience of faith will increase the spirit of sincerity, as of every other Christian temper. The truest sincerity comes after faith.

## THE RIGHTEOUSNESS OF FAITH

### QUESTION

Imagine as listening to section II the average decent man, who intends to be an honest and humane citizen, yet who makes no profession of being a devout Christian; or alternatively, the adherent who comes to service at times, yet without being a deep partaker in the spiritual life of the Church. He would say to himself: 'I admit that my character is not perfect. I do not walk as close to God as the great saints, or have the same zeal for prayer and the service of God. Were I entirely different, I would be a much better man. All this I concede. However, it is preposterous to suggest that my ordinary and common failings are grievous sins, which will set my life on the course for utter moral shipwreck, and for which God will severely hold me accountable on the Day of Judgement. Wesley is stretching a point!' How would you re-cast section II in an attempt to awaken folk like this?

*Sermon Seven*\*

# The Way to the Kingdom

THIS sermon, or at any rate the first part of it, seems to have been the first of the series of 'tombstone sermons'. On Sunday, June 6, 1742, Wesley was at Epworth, and unsuccessfully offered his services to the curate. The sequel is described in the *Journal* for this and the following days. 'After sermon John Taylor stood in the churchyard, and gave notice, as the people were coming out, "Mr. Wesley, not being permitted to preach in the church, designs to preach here at six o'clock." Accordingly at six I came, and found such a congregation as I believe Epworth never saw before. I stood near the east end of the church, upon my father's tombstone, and cried, "The kingdom of heaven is not meat and drink; but righteousness, and peace, and joy in the Holy Ghost".' Wesley preached daily in the churchyard for eight days, his texts being: Monday, Eph. ii. 8 (Sermon I); Tuesday, Rom. iv. 5 (Sermon V); Wednesday, Luke xviii. 10; Thursday, Rom. viii. 15 (Sermon IX); Friday, Ezek. xxxvii. 1; Saturday, Rom. x. 5 (Sermon VI); and on Sunday, Matt. v. 1 (Sermon XVI). In a letter to Mr. John Smith, dated March 25, 1747, Wesley remarked: 'I am well assured I did far more good by preaching three days on my father's tomb than I did by preaching three years in his pulpit.'

I. **1.** *'true religion, here termed by our Lord "the kingdom of God".'*

This is hardly a satisfactory definition of the Kingdom of God. It would be widely agreed today that the phrase is to be understood as: 'the Kingly Rule of God', or, 'the sovereignty of God'. The Kingdom of God is not the territory or the society governed by God, nor, to use the celebrated phrase of Ritschl, is it 'the organization of humanity through action inspired by love'. The Kingdom is not the ideal state of human

\* No. 7 in *Fifty-three Sermons*

society. It is not the Church, as in much Christian tradition. The Biblical 'Kingdom of God' is in the first place the omnipotent power of God, who from eternity is supreme over nations and men. It is that divine attribute by virtue of which it is right and necessary that man should acknowledge God as his Lord and his King. However, this power does not operate in a void. The King has subjects. In the second place, then, the Kingdom of God is the sphere in which the kingly rule is exercised. Dr. Flew would therefore render the term 'the Domain of God', because the word 'domain' 'preserves the sense of the sphere in which a Lord exercises his dominion rather than the actual people who live in the domain'. (*Jesus and His Church*, p. 34.) The announcement, 'the Kingdom of God is at hand', which was the very essence of the message preached by Jesus, thus implied: 'the long-awaited power of God, which shall purify and subdue the nation, and redeem the People of God, is even now at work in the world. It is immediately available to you. Daily I loose men from sin, teach them of God, and bring healing and blessing. This mighty work of God going on before your very eyes is nothing less than the first stage of a new and great manifestation of the Kingly Rule of God. Because I am here the Kingdom is here.' (See Luke vii. 18–23; x. 9; xi. 20; xvii. 21, R.V. marg.) Thus the Kingdom of God is hardly to be defined as 'true religion'. It is more nearly the power which makes true religion possible.

3. '*the Apostle declares.*'

One of the most memorable things in the life-work of St. Paul was that he led the resistance to those conservative elements in the primitive Church, described in para. 2, who would have made of Christianity a reformed and re-invigorated Judaism. (This wing of the Church finds expression within the New Testament in the Epistle of James, and, more moderately, in the Gospel according to St. Matthew.) St. Paul, and such followers as St. Luke, contended vigorously that the Christian faith was a new religion, though continuous with the old. It was entirely free and spiritual, the principle of external Law being done away. In consequence, it was most wrong to try to induce Gentile converts to adopt Jewish national and religious customs, so as to keep Christianity within the bounds of Judaism.

4. '*the vulgar*,' i.e., the general crowd.

This word has become debased in usage, in the same way as 'common'.

'*and it were superstition to object.*'

The superstition of an unreasoning objection to all religious ceremonial as such, even if 'ever so expressive of inward things', has not been unknown in Methodism.

'*or that religion cannot subsist without them.*'

It is doubtful whether this is sound psychology, save perhaps in the case of those rare men whose religious experience is purely contemplative and intellectual. The royal road to a deepening of the impression in the heart is expression. We cannot express apart from words and acts. Religious ceremonial may be utterly simple in form or very elaborate, and yet equally expressive of inward things in either case, depending on the temperament of different types of worshippers. No dispute shows a greater ignorance of human nature than controversy whether simple or complicated ritual is in universal and essential principle the more helpful to true religion. It is not a matter of universal principle, but of various circumstance. So far as Wesley is concerned, we know that he was most sensitive regarding the propriety, dignity, purity, and expressiveness of forms of religious worship. In this paragraph he is, however, anxious to place such considerations in their proper perspective.

5. '*one may act from the love of God, and the other from the love of praise.*'

This statement is true in principle, provided that 'love of praise' be extended to include *all* kinds of second-rate motives. Nevertheless, it is an over-simplification. In actual fact, most people do most of their 'good deeds' from a mixture of motives, good and less good.

6. '*as orthodox as the devil.*' See Sermon I, I, 2.

7. '*the first and great branch of Christian righteousness.*'

If the love of God is to be this there is demanded, not only a sincere motion of love, but also an adequate realization of the ethical character of God. Wesley does not mention this side here, though he was not unmindful of it. Failure to understand the nature of God as strictly pure and just is the great root of all such religious devotion as may exist apart from right living. This is the besetting weakness of pagan religion. It may also be found within the Church. As Dr. Sugden effectively observes: 'It is the general experience of missionaries to the less civilized races, like the Fijians or the Australian aborigines, that their converts very quickly attain to a remarkable degree of religious emotion, without any commensurate development of the ethical sense. A negro may give a most rapturous address in a love-feast, with tears of sincere joy running down his face, and then go away and rob a hen-roost without any sense of incongruity. One of the most unscrupulous business men I ever knew could pray like a seraph and preach like a prophet; and I do not think he was a hypocrite either.' (Sugden, I, 151-2.)

8. The second commandment of the Lord follows of necessity, if man knows the God he loves. Wesley proceeds to a powerful exposition of ethical religion.

'*prevents.*'

To prevent properly means, 'to go before', 'to anticipate'. (See note to Sermon XII, II, 1, p. 105).

10. '*happiness as well as holiness.*'

The man whose heart is warm with the love of God will find this elevated course of life a joy, and not a grim duty. Yet we must not assume that the Christian can be invariably of good cheer, as though he were insensitive to the distressing experiences of life. He will have sorrows, but will not repine over them, nor allow them permanently to disturb his faith in God.

11. 'καταλλαγήν.'

As so often, Wesley here anticipates the improved reading of the Revised Version (Rom. v. 11). For this word the old version reads 'atonement', which in 1611 would not be incorrect, for then 'to atone' (i.e., 'to at-one', 'to put at one'), had not lost its original general meaning of 'to reconcile'. The new version reads 'reconciliation', which is demanded by the modern special sense of 'to atone'.

'*the testimony of the Spirit.*'

See Sermon X, and notes thereon (pp. 86 ff.).

12. The former lines quoted are the second half of verse six of No. 164 in the Wesleys' *Hymns on the Lord's Supper*. The second quotation is the conclusion of a paraphrase of the 'Song of the Three Holy Children', or Benedicite, by the Rev. Mark Le-Pla, vicar of Finchingfield, Essex. The first line should run: 'Thee, therefore, Lord, safe shielded by Thy pow'r.' The Benedicite is an apocryphal insertion into the Book of Daniel, taking the form of a hymn sung by Shadrach, Meshach, and Abed-nego, as they walked in the Burning Fiery Furnace. It is printed in the *Methodist Hymn-book* as Chant 3.


II. The former part of this sermon has been in fact based on Rom. xiv. 17. Wesley now at length turns to the text with which he heads the sermon.

1. '*And, first, "repent"; that is, know yourselves.*'

This is hardly a full definition of repentance, though self-knowledge in the light of God leads to it. Properly speaking, repentance is a steadfast turning of the whole man, in mind, will, affection, and act, from evil to God.

*'original righteousness.'*

See Sermon V, I, 1-4, with notes (pp. 38 ff.), and VI, I, 1-4.

4. *'ἔνοχός ἐστι . . . &c.'* (Matt. v. 22.)

Wesley's attempted emendation is incorrect. ἔνοχος means 'liable to', not 'under sentence of'.

*'quick':* i.e., 'alive'.

9. *'He pardoneth and absolveth, &c.'*

These words are from the Absolution in the Order for Morning Prayer.

10. *'as some have fondly conceived.'*

Wesley is probably thinking of the error of John Glas and Robert Sandeman, who taught that faith was a merely intellectual assent to the truth of the Gospel, and that 'the bare death of Jesus Christ, without a thought or deed on the part of man, is sufficient to present the chief of sinners spotless before God'. Much harm was done for a time to London Methodism, when Thomas Maxfield and George Bell fell into this heresy, and even went so far as to deny that good works are necessary for sanctification. Bell said: 'God has done with all preachings and sacraments.'

*'I, even I, am now reconciled to God.'*

See note to Sermon X, I, 7 (pp. 91 f.).

13. *'mere enthusiasm':* i.e., 'mere fanaticism'.

## SERMON VII

### Questions

1. 
> I will not cease from mental fight,
>   Nor shall my sword sleep in my hand,
> Till we have built Jerusalem
>   In England's green and pleasant land.

Is this the Gospel of the Kingdom? What would Wesley have said? Is it a part of the Christian message? Would Wesley have agreed with your answer?

2. The disillusioned or apathetic man says: 'There always have been wars and rumours of wars, and rich and poor. There always will be, because you can't change human nature.' What message has this sermon for such?

3. 'The not increasing thy debt would not discharge it.' (II, 5.) Do you seriously think that God reckons like this? Would Wesley have been on sounder ground had he confined himself to: 'thou art not able to perform it; no, not in any one point, &c.'? (II, 6.) What would St. Paul have said?

*Sermon Eight**

# The First-fruits of the Spirit

THIS sermon is most interesting, important, and instructive. In seven sermons Wesley has laid down the main principles of the Gospel of grace. He now essays the task, never easy, of applying the theoretical to the practical and the ideal to the actual. He has, furthermore, shown how to call man to conversion, and has pointed out beforehand something of what the believer is to expect of the new life. Now the field-preacher and evangelist gives way to the pastor, and we see Wesley as he faces his converts in the Society-Meeting. This sermon, indeed, does not seem often to have been preached. It is more likely largely based on the exposition of the Epistle to the Romans which Wesley was accustomed to give to his Societies. Out of his memory of the days and weeks succeeding his own experience of the heart strangely warmed he will give his people some practical advice for the daily life of faith. This advice is most practical for the preacher of today, who faces a well-intentioned company of believers, and of those who *think* themselves believers, more often than he does the unawakened and ungodly throng.

We can observe Wesley struggling, and to good effect, with two personal characteristics which did not make easier for him this work of practical application. It is the instinct of the logician to say that everything which is not definitely 'A' is definitely 'not-A'. Wesley was possessed of a severely logical mind. Logic was his subject at Oxford. Now he faces a world whose affairs rarely permit of these definite distinctions. Furthermore, it is the enthusiastic impulse of the prophet to dismiss as worthless all that is not perfect. Wesley was such a prophet. Now he has to move among men who are not all either black or white. We must therefore make a few

* No. 8 in *Fifty-three Sermon*

allowances in this sermon, yet we may feel true gratitude and admiration for it.

1. '*St. Paul evidently means, those who truly believe in Him.*'

This is only true if care be taken to give the fullest possible content to the word 'believe'. Faith must be conceived as a complete out-going of every part of man, heart, mind, will, and action, in loving trust to God. By 'being in Christ' St. Paul meant a spiritual union going beyond simple forgiveness, or justification. See note to VIII, I, 1 (*infra*).

2. '*conversation*': i.e., 'behaviour'. See the Revised Version.

3. '*untaught of God*': 'of God' is an addition to the sense of the text.


I. 1. '*These . . . are properly said to be in Him, &c.* (to end of paragraph).

'Being in Christ' is one of the dominant conceptions of St. Paul, and one of the richest. In the Church, and in the heart of the believer, dwells the spiritual Presence of God, unseen, powerful, manifest. This Presence can be thought of in terms of Old Testament prophetic experience as 'the Spirit of the Lord'. Described in terms of distinctively Christian experience the Presence is the Spirit of Christ. He is the Risen Christ, unseen in the midst in plenitude of power. The two terms are hardly distinguishable in the thought of the Apostle. (See Rom. viii. 9.) Not only does the Christian possess Christ in his heart, but his life is wrapped up in the life of a community, the Church, which possesses Christ as its moving principle and basis of unity. The believer is a member incorporate in that Body of which Christ is the Head. The Presence is indeed the very atmosphere in which he lives and moves and has his being. Thus the Christian is 'in Christ'. To be 'in the Spirit' is a parallel conception, though lacking the same strong sense of communion with and unity around a *Personal* Head. By parity of reasoning, St. Paul speaks of the unbelieving as 'in the flesh'. They belong to that sphere where rules rebellion against God.

## THE FIRST-FRUITS OF THE SPIRIT

2. *'The flesh, in the usual language of St. Paul, signifies corrupt nature.'*

Exactly so, though those who have been inclined to equate holiness with the denial of natural bodily instincts, or with the avoidance of pleasure, have often shown little realization of St. Paul's meaning. The careful reader of the list of vices in Gal. v. 16-21 (see Sermon VIII, I, 3), will observe that they are by no means all sins arising from excess or abuse of bodily desires. Some of them are purely spiritual, or mental. This illustrates the most important fact that St. Paul does not write as though the body of flesh and blood were in itself that which separates man from God. He did not think of the body as the 'prison-house of the soul'. 'The flesh' in St. Paul is human nature, alike body and mind and spirit, *as it is found in rebellion to God.*

*' "lust" (or desire).'*

The second word is the better translation. The original Greek word indicates all the desires of the body and mind, and not necessarily in a bad sense. Since the translation of the Bible the word 'lust' has come to be narrowed down from the general sense of 'desire' to denote evil desire, particularly sexual.

*'ἵνα μὴ ... &c.'*

Wesley assumes, in accordance with the usage of classical Greek, that this construction necessarily expresses purpose. This gives the rendering: '*in order that* ye may not do the things which ye would'. (The words 'in order' really need to be placed before the first translation of the Greek clause, if Wesley's contrast of renderings is to be made obvious.) Actually this rule of classical Greek does not invariably apply in the New Testament. The translation rejected by Wesley is correct. Thus Moffat reads: 'the two are at issue, so that you are not free to do as you please'. The sense is much the same as that of Rom. vii. 19.

3. *'have crucified the flesh.'*

To those who understand St. Paul as a whole this is a most expressive metaphor. In the case of Christ, execution was the preliminary to glorious life. The Apostle holds that the same is true of the believer in his attainment to life. The Christian is united to, and identified with, his Lord in the experiences of death and resurrection. Baptism is the beginning of the Christian life. As the admission ceremony into the Church it is the outward sign of repentance and turning to Christ. Indeed, it is commonly the means of grace which is the occasion of conversion. It is in the light of this that we may appreciate such a passage as Rom. vi. 1-14. 'To be put to death with Christ' can most fittingly denote 'to renounce sin', because the renunciation of sin is the preliminary to 'coming to life with Christ'. However, St. Paul's metaphor labours under a great disadvantage in the pulpit today. The meaning is not self-apparent to most modern hearers, for they are not sufficiently familiar with the system of thought of which it is a part. Hence it is commonly used as a piece of conventional phraseology, without adequate understanding of its significance. The preacher is therefore wise to be most cautious in the use of such phrases as, 'crucified with Christ', 'crucified to sin, to the flesh, to the world'. They are formulae which themselves require explanation, rather than those which explain.

> *'Although they feel the root of bitterness in themselves, yet they are endued with power from on high to trample it continually underfoot, so . . . that every fresh assault . . . only gives them fresh occasion of praise.'*

Here we are introduced to the profound and very practical theme of this sermon. In principle the justified believer is no longer in the flesh, but in the Spirit. He is in Christ. He has passed over the border-line. Yet he cannot at once begin to live as though he had never been a sinful man. He cannot ignore the past, for a shadow of it still lives with him. Sin has suffered a decisive defeat, and cannot recover its position so long as faith remains. Nevertheless, the guerrilla-warfare that sin can carry on, though hopeless in the final issue, is very troublesome. The change of masters, though ideally complete, is not immediately complete in actual fact. The convert should not imagine that God condemns him, or calls in question his status as a true believer, because he is found in this condition for a while. He need not destroy his peace of mind, nor doubt the reality and sufficiency of his faith, because he does not find himself in that ideally perfect condition where the after-effects of sin and human frailty trouble him no more. Yet man is not entitled to compromise with sin of this account, and to settle down to a second-rate quality of life. His heart rightly tells him that he *ought* to be perfect. He can never *quite* forgive himself for his weakness. There is a type of man whose Christian experience suffers through an excessive fear of the searching judgement of God. He is a rare type today, for it is all too true that the modern man is not worrying about his sins. However, such have it in them to become the noblest and most devoted servants of God. This sermon is full of comfort for these. For the general run of Christians perhaps the main value is that the sermon also serves as a caution against too severe judgement of one's neighbours.

Wesley now most effectively describes the initial stage of the campaign for mopping-up the hosts of wickedness. The convert is sorely tempted by doubt and sin. The struggle is hard. There are moments when it seems to him little more than indecisive. Yet the power of God always suffices for victory. Every victory confirms faith. The result of every struggle is the learning of some useful lesson. It is significant that Wesley's words are reminiscent of his account of the night after the Aldersgate Street meeting where his heart was strangely warmed. 'After my return home, I was much buffeted with temptations; but cried out, and they fled away. They returned again and again. I as often lifted up my eyes, and He "sent me help from His holy place". And herein I found the difference between this and my former state chiefly consisted. I was striving, yea, fighting with all my might under the law, as well as under grace. But then I was sometimes, if not often, conquered; now, I was always conqueror.' (*Journal*, May 24, 1738 (16).)

From this point Wesley proceeds to trace out the strait and narrow path between the opposite errors of careless compromise with sin, and the impatient and timid spirit of the one

## SERMON VIII

who will give himself no peace. Thus he mediates between the ideal and the real.

5. *'conversation'*: i.e., conduct.


II. 1. *'the sins that are past.'*

In Rom. iii. 25 this phrase applies to the ages before Christ, not to the individual before justification.

3. Wesley gives a fuller treatment of this problem in Sermons XL and XLI. He there distinguishes between *darkness*, which is always caused by sin, ignorance, or temptation; and *heaviness*, which may be due to illness, calamity, or bereavement. Darkness implies that faith is lost or decayed. Heaviness is consistent with faith in God. The general sense of this paragraph would then seem to be: If one finds love waning, moral will weakening, the mind gladly entertaining doubts regarding the goodness and power of God, then sin is nigh. However, the purely emotional element is a less stable factor. It is less under control. The sensation of joy in God may be invaded by natural sorrow, yet the believer need not accuse himself of weakness in the faith.

Modern psychology has thrown much light on the phenomenon of conversion. Normally, a person who is working up to a conversion is conscious of some measure of inward conflict. Two ways of life are contending for the whole man, heart, mind, and will. Conversion is the decisive act of will which throws the whole personality over from one side to the other. Thus the conflict is resolved. The by-product of this psychological change is a wave of joy, and a sudden bound of nervous energy which carries the convert zealously along the new path. There may later be a reaction to this. Thus 'joy in God' is not of the *essence* of a true Christian conversion, though it is a norma accompaniment. It may not always come equally, or immediately, and there may later be a reaction into 'heaviness'. The conversion nevertheless remains.

It is most significant that Wesley clearly recognized this as

THE FIRST-FRUITS OF THE SPIRIT 73

a matter of actual experience, though not of psychological theory. Immediately after he has written: 'I felt my heart strangely warmed . . . and an assurance was given me, that He had taken away *my* sins, even *mine*.' Wesley continues: 'But it was not long before the enemy suggested, "This cannot be faith; for where is thy joy?" Then was I taught, that peace and victory over sin are essential to faith in the Captain of our salvation: But that, as to the transports of joy that usually attend the beginning of it, especially in those who have mourned deeply, God sometimes giveth, sometimes withholdeth them, according to the counsels of his own will.' (*Journal*, May 24, 1738 (15).) The *Journal* then goes on to show that Wesley had a long period of darkness after his evangelical experience. Furthermore, in the *Minutes*, of June 25, 1744, we find: 'It is certain, a believer need never again come into condemnation. It seems he need not come into a state of doubt, or fear, or darkness; and that, ordinarily at least, he will not, unless by ignorance or unfaithfulness. Yet it is true that the first joy does seldom last long; that it is commonly followed by doubts and fears; and that God frequently permits great heaviness before any large manifestation of Himself.'

4. '*he cannot sin, because he is born of God.*'

This becomes reasonable if it be remembered that these repeated assaults of dying sin within are not strictly *guilt-bringing* sins. A further complication is the unhappy circumstance that believers so commonly show needless and sinful, though impermanent, lapses into genuine and blameworthy unbelief.

'*the law does not lie against a righteous man.*'

Wesley's emended rendering of 1 Tim. i. 9 is incorrect. The phrase is to be translated: 'Law is not enacted for a righteous man.'

5-13. The channel between Scylla and Charybdis narrows as the voyage proceeds. It is easy to reason concerning the uncertain emotional state of a believer. A harder problem is to be faced in that the after-effects of past sin remain also in the spheres of moral will, knowledge of good, and freedom of action. In principle, the individual has conscious control in these matters, with consequent moral responsibility. Actually this control is at times compromised by circumstances, which at the best can only be surmounted gradually as the result of prolonged discipline. Thus the Christian is painfully aware that his actions are not always perfect in the sight of God. He need not, however, feel borne down by a load of guilt on this account, provided he is constant in watching and prayer. Martin Luther's dictum, 'Sin bravely', was a crude and paradoxical statement of this proposition, and one that has naturally been widely misrepresented to his discredit.

5-6. This knowledge of '*inward sin*' is a sensibility of the fact that one is a frail being, in utmost need of divine support. Even when he gives himself to his best deeds the Christian can never be sure that his motives are *only* the highest and the best. He trusts that these are his real and sufficient motives, but he has insufficient knowledge of himself to be *certain* that other and inferior motives are entirely excluded. Furthermore, no matter how earnestly he gives himself to prayer, or the public worship of God, he cannot fix his mind upon it as he would. The Christian is bitterly humiliated that his conscience should be so clouded, his spirit so unresponsive. He knows that he would not be like this had he in past time walked as closely to God as he ought. Yet he is not filled with painful guilt, for he knows that he is now doing the only thing that man can do if he is to be lifted to a higher plane. No man with any degree of spiritual insight would dare to claim to live above this sense of humiliation.

8. '*sins of infirmity.*'

As Wesley observes, this is an ambiguous expression. If a lapse is entirely due to infirmity it is not a sin. There is no guilt, for there is no responsibility.

9. This rule is sound, but hard to administer in practice. Take the example that Wesley gives. Suppose the sickness be a severe headache, coming on in the first part of the service. There may be some cases when one might rightly say: 'I cannot profit by remaining to the Holy Communion today, for I am in no frame of mind to take in what I am doing.' Yet how easily and commonly is such an argument a mere excuse for forsaking the worship of God.

10. '*Like as the hart, &c.*'

    These are reminiscences of the Prayer Book Psalter.

11. '*sins of surprise.*'

    The path between this precipice and that here narrows almost to a razor-edge. Nevertheless, the soul has at times to walk this way, and the pastor must be guide. At the best, however, it is difficult to escape doubtful judgements.

    '*as there is more or less concurrence of his will.*'

    The principle is undoubtedly sound, but the practice hard. None can tell for certain even in his own case whether there has been a concurrence of the will. Still less can he speak for his neighbour. No man need feel condemned on finding, too late, that he has been entrapped into a fault, even a serious fault, through being suddenly confronted by some entirely unforeseen circumstance, there being no opportunity of judging the right of the matter. There are also more frequent but less serious occasions of falling, particularly into sins of temper, where surprise frees from blame. However, the Christian ought always to feel deep humiliation at such a fall, for he cannot forget that had he previously been living nearer to God the surprise would have been less overwhelming. (See para. 12.) In proportion as a man is pure within, the unpremeditated impulse of the heart is likely to be good. (Matt. xii. 36.) Therefore the surprised one must feel penitent for his fault, and seek to learn from it. There is certainly no occasion for condoning 'trivial faults' in the doctrine of 'sins of surprise'.

III. 4. For the lines by Charles Wesley, see *Methodist Hymn-book*, No. 465, v. 4

5. '*The rule which some give.*'

Some evangelical enthusiasts had gone so far as to say that wilful sins should not disturb peace and joy in God. Wesley is rightly dubious of this proposition, as reflecting an insufficiently serious view of sin. However, even the knowledge that one has committed a wilful sin should not be allowed to shake faith and filial trust in God, and so to drive one from Him.

## Questions

1. Is this a comfortable or an uncomfortable sermon?

2. Has a believer who fully reaps the 'first-fruits of the Spirit' attained to Christian perfection (i.e., perfect love)?

3. A man hits his thumb with the hammer, and cries: 'Damn the —— thing!' Is this a blameless sin of surprise? Consider the cases of: (i) a lad from a disorderly slum home, who has just been brought into the Mission; (ii) the Superintendent of the Mission.

4. So that he may keep his job, a civil servant in a Fascist country swears allegiance to the tyrant, puts on the badge, parades on occasion, but takes as little active part in public affairs as possible, because he is inwardly revolted at the system. Is there 'no condemnation' to this man for something 'which it is not in his power to help'? What then of an assistant in a store, who is instructed by the manager that some small lie is to be told about the goods?

5. Is a Christian who finds that his country is at war faced with evils 'which it is not in his power to help'?

6. A man has an inborn craving for drink, for he had drunken parents. So as to keep straight he resolves to be a total abstainer, but later decides to be 'moderate'. He is found the worse for drink. Is this sin due to an 'infirmity'?

7. Would you say that to lay undue emphasis upon a state of happiness as a mark of the work of God in the heart, and too little upon the stern resolve of the will and the fixed opinion of the mind, is likely to be the besetting error of an evangelist whose own conversion was an occasion of great joy to him? How does the average 'revival chorus' square with the conversion experience of Wesley, regarding the joy of the believer?

## Sermon Nine*

# The Spirit of Bondage and of Adoption

THIS sermon is the other side of the picture to Sermon VIII. The difficulties that may beset the convert are traced out there. Here are described the greater and more calamitous difficulties that beset the unbeliever, together with the joy, peace, and power that are born of faith. Thus we have here an introduction to one of the most important and typically Methodist of all the Sermons, that on 'the Witness of the Spirit'.

*Text. Rom. viii. 15. 'adoption.'*

Adoption was a much more widely recognized custom in the old Roman world than with us. Men of high position who lacked an heir would often legally adopt some young man, generally a relative, with a view to his succession to office. Thus in St. Paul's time 'adoption' was a striking phrase whereby to describe the glorious status of a Christian.

*'Abba.'*

The word means 'Father'. It is Aramaic, a language akin to Hebrew, and the tongue commonly spoken in Palestine in the time of our Lord. When a member of the original Church in Jerusalem, filled with the sense that God was his Father, expressed his feelings in a raptured cry, the word used would be 'Abba!' This set a custom that was carried on into the Greek-speaking Gentile Churches, such as that of Rome. It is with this custom in mind that St. Paul writes the word for 'father' twice, once in Aramaic, once in Greek. To give the proper effect in English the Aramaic word has to be left untranslated, to represent a single foreign word remaining in the Greek text of Romans. Another interesting example of an Aramaic phrase lingering in the Greek-speaking Church occurs in 1 Cor. xvi. 22.

* No. 9 in *Fifty-three Sermons*

# THE SPIRIT OF BONDAGE AND OF ADOPTION

'Maran atha' means 'Our Lord cometh!' Another rendering is 'Marana tha', i.e., 'Our Lord, O come!'

1. '*have drank.*'

Here is an example of a change in English since Wesley's day.

2. '*some of them may be styled His servants.*'

Wesley has in mind Christians who have not yet attained to the full evangelical experience.

4. '*ye " received the spirit of fear".*'

It is surely not needful to assume, as here, that the Christian must, as a matter of course, pass through the initial stage of the fear of God before he finds the love of God. However, Wesley is certainly right in saying that even the lower state of religion, that of hard and self-imposed duty, is a work of God in the heart.

5. By those who are 'under the law' St. Paul normally meant pious Jews, who were trying to put themselves right with God by their own efforts in obedience to the Law of Moses. However, any person who is attempting to attain to a noble character by applying himself in his own strength to moral precepts is in an analogous spiritual condition. The arguments of the Apostle fit his case equally well. It is quite legitimate, therefore, for Wesley to adapt St. Paul's phrase 'under the law' to describe the 'almost Christian', who is trying to justify himself by good works.

I. 1. '*a state of sleep.*'

A more common description in the New Testament is 'a state of death', e.g., Eph. ii. 5, and St. John's Gospel and First Epistle.

*'ignorance of whatever he is most concerned to know.*

How exact and how terrible a description of the tragic plight of multitudes.

**2.** *'secure.'*

The original meaning of this word was 'free from anxiety'.

*'Epicurean.'* See note to Sermon II, I, (iii), 9 (p. 13).

*'swallowing up all . . . His . . . essential hatred of sin.'*

Modern theology has rightly tried to place 'the Heavenly Father', of whom Jesus taught, firmly in the centre of the picture, even though this has to some extent involved displacing into the background the Old Testament Lord, terrible in righteousness. Some, however, in undiscriminating zeal, have failed at times to do justice to God's 'essential hatred of sin'. Any teaching is in grievous error which encourages men to think lightly of sin, and idly to say: 'God is merciful.'

*'he fancies that the obligation hereto is ceased, &c.'*

There is no inconsistency between the saying of our Lord, that He had not come to destroy the Law, but to fulfil it, and St. Paul's all-important general thesis that Christ is 'the end of Law'. (Matt. v. 17-20; Rom. x. 4, &c.) Jesus loved and valued all that was best and most spiritual in the religion of His people. He certainly regarded His teaching as the natural outcome and necessary completion of this, the *true* Judaism. Thus He came to fulfil the Law and the Prophets. St. Paul, in his turn, firmly grasped this truth. [7] However, in actual fact the bulk of the Jewish people unhappily failed to rise to this 'true Judaism'. Zeal to maintain intact their ancient place of religious privilege, as well as to preserve the outward institutions of their faith, led all too many of them to reject the Christian way. In particular, St. Paul, the champion of spiritual freedom for the Gentile Christians, was singled out for violent attack. When he wrote of 'the Law' he did so under the shadow of strong controversy. He thought not so much of the 'true Judaism' that ought to be, but of the Judaism that actually was, and that all too often

THE SPIRIT OF BONDAGE AND ADOPTION          81

rejected the Gospel of free grace. Thus to Jesus 'the Law' was the religion of Deuteronomy, Isaiah, and the Psalms. To St. Paul it was the religion of the self-justifying Pharisee in the Temple. Has the obligation to God's law ceased? If we have in mind the broad sense of Jesus, the answer is 'No.' The Christian religion is the worship of a righteous God, who requires in His worshippers inward purity of heart and outward uprightness of behaviour. This part of our tradition comes down as a precious heritage from Judaism. If we have in mind the specific theological sense found in St. Paul's writings, the answer is 'Yes'. Man is not called, and is unable, to set himself right with God by his own deeds or religious observances, however good they be.

3. *'no fear but he will make it good!'*

Here is some gentle sarcasm from one who well knew what was in man.

4. *'the absolute necessity of such freedom, in order to constitute man a moral agent.'*

It is an elementary proposition of philosophy that if man is morally responsible for his actions, those actions must be of his own free choice, and not forced upon him by some external necessity. Those who deny that man has a free moral spirit, e.g., the dialectical materialist thinkers of Communism, are logically compelled also to deny that man is morally responsible. An action may be stigmatized as harmful to society, but it is idle to regard it as guilty. All Christian thought assumes that man is morally responsible, and is therefore driven to the conclusion that man is in some real sense free. Wesley does not really wish to deny this. In the previous sermon he has shown himself fully aware that an action is not sinful unless it is voluntary (VIII, II, 8-13). He explains his views on free-will in his treatise 'Predestination Calmly Considered' (1752) para. 45. (*Works*, Vol. X.) After quoting from the Westminster Confession (a celebrated statement of Calvinist theology), to the effect that 'God hath endued the will of man with that natural liberty that is neither forced, nor, by an absolute necessity of nature, determined to do good or evil'; Wesley says: 'I do not carry free-will so far; I mean, not in moral things; natural free-will in the present state of mankind, I do not understand; I only assert that there is a measure of free-will supernaturally restored to every man, together with that supernatural light which "enlightens every man that cometh into the world".' The meaning of this judgement is that, suppose a sinful man be imagined as entirely left to himself by God, he would have no power to do right, and therefore no free-will. However, the grace of God rests on all men to some extent, even though they do not know it. One of the works of this grace is that all men have a measure of free-will. Wesley states the theory of free-will in an unusual way, but agrees in the fact. In the present paragraph, however, he has fixed his attention upon another, and more practical problem. Granted that all men have a limited measure of genuine free-will, sufficient to render them morally accountable for their actions, it yet remains that a sinful man has not the power to repent of his sins and to turn to God *as and when he will*. This is a dreadful fact of experience. Man can only truly repent when empowered by the grace of God.

6. '*at liberty . . . from the prejudice of education*':

i.e., that he has not been brought up as a bigot.

7. '*does not Solomon say, &c.*'

There follows the worldly man's comforting misquotation of Prov. xxiv. 16: 'A just man falleth seven times, and riseth up again.' The reference in Proverbs is not to falling into sin, but into misfortune.

6–7. These paragraphs contain an admirable portrait of the agreeable and well-meaning person who has not faced the serious issues of life. We know many such today. Would that we could 'stab their spirits broad awake' as Wesley could!

## THE SPIRIT OF BONDAGE AND OF ADOPTION 83

II. 1. *'By some awful providence, or by His word applied':*

i.e., by some calamity, or other occurrence, which may give a man 'furiously to think'; or else by the effective presentation of the Gospel. These are undoubtedly the main factors in awakening the careless.

2. *'obnoxious to':* i.e., 'liable to'.

3. '*τετραχηλισμένον.*'

Wesley gives one of several interpretations of this difficult word in the Greek of Heb. iv. 12.

6. *'a lively sense of the wrath of God.'* See note to Sermon V, 1 (pp. 38 ff.).

*'the devil, the executioner of the wrath ... of God.'*

There is very little in the Bible to uphold this most dubious proposition.

*'Yea, sometimes it may even border upon distraction, &c.',* to end.

Wesley's *Journal* is full of accounts of persons so carried out of themselves by conviction of sin as to fall to the earth groaning, &c.

7. *'Such is the freedom of his will; free only to evil.'*

This is not to be understood as a formal denial of the principle of human free-will. See note to para. 4 (p. 81).

9. *'I was alive without the law once.'* (Rom. vii. 9.)

Here St. Paul actually refers to his childhood, before he was of age to assume the obligations of the Mosaic Law. He idealizes those early days as happy, carefree, and innocent. He then continues his auto-biography in this moving chapter to show how, when the commandment came home to him, sin sprang to life. Stern prohibition excited inward rebellion. So in succeeding verses he traces that process by which he grew up at once devoted to the Law and sickened by its bankruptcy.

'*or rather*, that I . . . *that man I am now personating.*'

This is not the sense of Rom. vii. 25, which is more accurately represented by the usual: 'So then I myself with my mind serve the law of God.'

'"*but with my flesh*," *with my body.*'

This definition is not sufficiently accurate. See note to Sermon VIII, I, 2 (p. 69).

10. We need not fear that no one can have a full experience of salvation who does not feel conviction of sin with such an intensity of agony as is here described.


III. 8. '*The Heathen, baptized or unbaptized.*'

Wesley would certainly have described a godless man who had been baptized in infancy as an apostate Christian, not as a non-Christian. (See Sermon XIV, and notes (pp. 115 ff.); and Sermon XXXIX, IV, and notes (pp. 243 f.).) All he means here is that a purely nominal Christian is not, merely on account of his baptism, actually any the better for it, as compared with a non-Christian.

IV. 2. '*these several states of soul are often mingled together.*'

This is a most valuable paragraph, which admirably serves to bring the sermon down to solid earth. First there is stated the theory, with crystal clarity. Then account is taken of the actual confusions of human affairs.

3-4. The sufficient commentary on this is Sermon II, 'The Almost Christian'.

## QUESTIONS

1. Is there not a sense in which the Christian living under grace continues to fear God?

2. Someone defending the Theosophists, Christian Scientists, &c., says: 'I think that you orthodox folk are very unfair to them. They are most sincere people.' What would Wesley have said in reply?

> O that I could repent!
> With all my idols part,
> And to thy gracious eye present
> A humble, contrite heart;
> A heart with grief opprest
> For having grieved my God,
> A troubled heart that cannot rest,
> Till sprinkled with thy blood.
>
> Jesus, on me bestow
> The penitent desire;
> With true sincerity of woe
> My aching breast inspire;
> With softening pity look,
> And melt my hardness down,
> Strike with thy love's resistless stroke,
> And break this heart of stone!
>
> (Wesley's Hymns, No. 102.)

Are these lines, by Charles Wesley, rightly omitted from our present hymn-book?

4. Consider the Methodist people you know. What proportion would you judge live mainly in the legal, and what mainly in the evangelical, state? What is to be done about it?

*Sermon Ten**

# The Witness of the Spirit

### Discourse I

THIS is one of the most important of the Standard Sermons. Other Evangelical movements have borne like testimony to Salvation by Grace, Justification by Faith, &c. No substantial movement has equalled Methodism in giving a witness, at once emphatic and sanely balanced, to the doctrine of the Witness of the Spirit, and to the sense of Christian Assurance based upon it. In a most particular sense, therefore, this is one of 'our doctrines'. The subject of this sermon merits the most careful attention. .

Multitudes of believers outside Methodism have, of course, rejoiced in a faith which was a triumphant certainty to them, and not merely a wistful hope. They have been aware of God speaking immediately to the heart, granting abounding peace and joy and zeal. Many of these have lived as detached individuals within the great institutional Churches of Christian tradition. They have, in general, loyally accepted the dogmatic and sacramental systems of their own day, though loyalty to these has sometimes been but a small part of their own personal religion. Conversely, the majority of their fellow-Churchmen have commonly known little of their experience, and it has found little recognition in official expositions of the Christian faith. Most notable among such individuals are the Mystics of the Roman Church. (See also note, Sermon XLII, 4, pp. 255 f.). On the other hand, in Methodism the religion of warm personal conviction has been openly preached as the accepted doctrine of a substantial religious communion. Again, there are others who have drunk deeply of the religion of personal communion and individual inspiration, but at the price of drifting out of the

* No. 10 in *Fifty-three Sermons*

THE WITNESS OF THE SPIRIT 87

main stream of Christian tradition. These have been individualists pure and simple. Rejecting the wholesome discipline of a Christian society, they have been in constant danger of falling into all manner of eccentric and extreme opinions. These they have defended as the special illumination of the Holy Spirit, to the consequent discredit of the whole notion of personal religion. In contrast, Methodism was guided by a leader possessed of strong practical common sense, and one who was devoted to the solid institutions of the Church of England. This was an untold blessing, for the Methodists remained firmly attached to sane and orthodox theology, while the discipline of a closely-knit social life encouraged enthusiastic converts rapidly to live down individual extravagances.

An example of this process is most apposite to the present subject. As is well known, Wesley first heard from the Moravians the idea that a believer should have a full assurance of his salvation, witnessed by the Spirit of God. (But see note, Sermon XIII, I, 9, p. 111 f.) Thus, of the days immediately after his return from America he writes: 'When Peter Böhler (the Moravian), whom God prepared for me as soon as I came to London, affirmed of true faith in Christ . . . that it had those two fruits inseparably attending it, "Dominion over sin, and constant Peace from a sense of forgiveness", I was quite amazed and looked upon it as a new Gospel.' (*Journal*, May 24, 1738 (11).) On the other hand, however, Wesley gradually came to see that many of those who had so wonderfully brought him to a new experience of God were unbalanced extremists in other directions. Religion was to many Moravians too purely a matter of inward experience. They did not attach sufficient value to the discipline of the ordered life of the Church, with her divinely ordained means of grace. Wesley was repelled by the Moravian doctrine of 'stillness', i.e., that one should simply wait for the gift of faith, without using the means of grace, because for the searcher after God to be diligent at Communion, prayer, Bible-reading, &c., was a sign that he was trusting in his own works of righteousness, and not in God alone. (See notes to Sermon XII, pp. 102 f.) Hence came the separation of Methodism from the Moravian Church, and the hard words that Wesley frequently had for 'mysticism'. Our Church is thus in the happy position of giving the fullest official recognition to the religion of warm, inward, personal experience, yet of avoiding the individual eccentricities of fanatics. She gives neither too little, as do the great institutional Churches, nor too much, as do the cranks of every age. In consequence, this sermon explores the teaching of Wesley on an all-important subject.

We have already noticed the Calvinist doctrine of Assurance, based upon the knowledge that one was eternally of the number of God's Elect. (See note to Sermon I, II, 4, p. 4 f.) Wesley, who denied the doctrine of election, preferred to found himself upon the great utterance of St. Paul which is the text for the present sermon. Our founder teaches that the change of emotion, will, mind, and activity, worked by the grace of God is so striking and indisputable that it is impossible for him who experiences the change to doubt its reality. Christian salvation is so glorious as to be its own evidence. That this should be so is the result of a special and marvellous work of the indwelling Spirit of God. That this work is mysterious does not detract from its certainty, any more than is the case with the mystery of natural life. Some may ask whether this teaching of Wesley does not in effect open the door to rank individualism, for the fanatic is of all men the most forward with the claim that he is *certain*, 'deep down in the heart'. The answer is that this doctrine is open to this objection, unless those who rejoice in it whole-heartedly embrace the life of the Christian fellowship. If the believer is well content to learn of the experience of as many others as he may, as well as of his own, the truths he lacks will be made up to him. His extravagances will be corrected. If the believer is humble enough to see himself as others see him, he will not be in doubt whether he has arrived at a real and obvious change for the better in every part of life, or is merely the victim of some obscure psychological derangement. This great sermon can only be appreciated if we have in mind the strong Churchmanship of Wesley, and his emphasis upon the value and duty of Christian fellowship.

The first and very natural instinct of Wesley after his full

## THE WITNESS OF THE SPIRIT

evangelical experience was to assert that true faith was lacking to anyone who could not claim the Witness of the Spirit to Full Assurance. He gradually revised the strict judgement, to make allowance for the variety of Christian experience. The stages of his thought are collected by Sugden (I, 200-1). 'As early as January 25, 1740, Wesley says, "I never yet knew one soul thus saved without what you call the faith of assurance; I mean a sure confidence that by the merits of Christ he was reconciled to the favour of God." In the *Minutes* of 1744, in answer to Q. 8, "Does any one believe, who has not the witness in himself, or any longer than he sees, loves, obeys God?" he says, "We apprehend not." In the *Minutes* of 1745 he dares not positively say that there are not exempt cases, and allows that there may be infinite degrees in seeing God. In 1746 he admits that it is hard to judge of individual cases, as we do not know all the circumstances; but he affirms that all sincere persons who are striving for this assurance will surely find it before they die....

In 1747, a month after the Conference, he writes to Charles: 'By justifying faith, I mean that faith which whosoever hath not is under the wrath and curse of God. By a sense of pardon I mean a distinct, explicit assurance that my sins are forgiven. I allow (i) that there is such an explicit assurance; (ii) that it is the common privilege of real Christians; (iii) that it is the proper Christian faith which purifies the heart and overcomes the world.... If justifying faith necessarily implies such an explicit assurance of pardon, then every one who has it not, and every one so long as he has it not, is under the wrath and curse of God. But this is a supposition contrary to Scripture and experience (Isa. i. 10 and Acts x. 34).' Finally, in a much later letter, Wesley writes: 'When fifty years ago my brother Charles and I, in the simplicity of our hearts, told the good people of England that unless they *knew* their sins were forgiven, they were under the wrath and curse of God, I marvel they did not stone us! The Methodists, I hope, know better now: we preach assurance as we always did, as a common privilege of the children of God; but we do not enforce it, under the pain of damnation.'

1–3. Notice how ably Wesley fills in the background of his subject. He will treat of a most precious doctrine, which is yet one easily and commonly abused, and which is therefore in needless disrepute. The method, typical of Wesley's common sense, is to strike the happy mean between opposing extremes.

I. 1. *'The same Spirit, &c.'*

Wesley is certainly wrong in his attempt to improve upon the usual rendering. There is no evidence that any copies actually read τὸ αὐτὸ Πνεῦμα, which would yield 'the same Spirit'. The text is certainly Αὐτὸ τὸ Πνεῦμα, which must be translated 'the Spirit itself'. Nor can we uphold the rendering of συμμαρτυρεῖ as 'He witnesses *at the same time*'. 'But I contend not.' Wesley himself is aware that he is on insecure ground.

2–3. By the witness of *our own* spirit, bringing assurance of salvation, is meant the simple proposition: 'I am aware that my life has in actual fact been transformed by Christ. Therefore, whatever my state of feeling, I must be a genuine Christian.' Hence follows the significance of the last line of the familiar verse:

> 'His Spirit to us He gave,
> And dwells in us we know;
> The witness in ourselves we have,
> And all its fruits we show.'

(M.H.B. 377, v. 7.)

2. *'reason . . . which religion was designed not to extinguish, but to perfect.'*

Some of the Moravian 'mystics', in unbalanced emphasis upon religion as solely a matter of mysterious inward illumination, had renounced all use of the reason as a means to the knowledge of God.

4. Some who made much of inward illumination affected to despise as quite beneath them the use of an argument like this.

## 5. '*How does it appear to ourselves: not to others?*'

We cannot be very happy about the limitation introduced here. It is indeed obvious that 'the witness of our own spirit' must be the witness of *ourselves* to ourselves, and not of *others* to ourselves. Nevertheless, no one is entitled to be *too* sure of the witness of his own conscience unless he finds it to be supported by the judgement of unprejudiced friends. This is particularly true of the graces of the Christian character. I may be sure, apart from the testimony of others, that I '*remember the Sabbath-day to keep it holy*', for this concerns visible action. I cannot so easily be sure that I am '*kindly affectioned to all mankind, and full of gentleness and long-suffering*'.

## 7. '*But perhaps one might say; &c.*' to end of paragraph.

These profound words should be noted as one of the most important passages to be found anywhere in Wesley. One asks: '*How* does God speak direct to my heart, to give me an unspeakable conviction of the most glorious truth that I am indeed His forgiven, restored, and well-pleasing child?' The answer is: 'It is impossible to say, yet the fact remains that this is just what God does!' Thus the most that Wesley can attempt is to *describe*, not to *explain*. One inquires again: 'I accept that the Witness of the Spirit is a fact, though a mysterious fact; but what is the experience like? How would you describe it?' For answer Wesley instinctively flies back to the night at Aldersgate Street, as the present paragraph shows. 'Hath loved *me*' —'for *me*'—'*my* sins blotted out'—'*I*, even *I*.' These are almost the very words he had written in his *Journal* all those years before. 'I felt my heart strangely warmed. I felt I did trust in Christ, Christ alone for salvation; and an assurance was given me, that he had taken away *my* sins, even *mine*, and saved *me* from the law of sin and death.' (*Journal*, May 24, 1738 (14).) 'The Witness of the Spirit' is for Wesley really a theological name for 'the heart strangely warmed'. It is that degree of personal realization which raises to a white heat the proposition: 'Christ died for all, I suppose, therefore, He died for me.' The cool and calculating 'I suppose' slips out. The 'me' goes into italics of joyous surprise. Thus 'the Witness of the Spirit' does not denote another theological proposition. It denotes the proper emotional tension demanded of him who views the amazing theological propositions involved in the Gospel of Christ crucified. By way of illustration, the filament of an electric lamp remains the same substance when the current is switched on, but the temperature is raised, and the light shines. So when God gives the Witness He does not reveal a new truth. He raises the temperature of truths already known, so that the believer radiates joy, peace, and convincing speech. To teach that the Spirit of God witnesses a Full Assurance of Salvation is a precise and emphatic way of saying that God's gift of faith is not only a train of ideas in the head and an inclination of the will. It is also a powerful impulse of the heart. Hence Wesley was right in teaching that the Christian ought to *expect*, but not to *demand*, this seal of his faith. The main motive power of human personality is emotional. It is when a man's imagination is kindled and his affections stirred by the truth that he begins effectually to act upon it. It is surely God's will that His servants should possess the mainspring of effectual action. Nevertheless, there is something inherently involuntary and unstable about the emotional state of man. A man is not so accountable for his affections as he is for his ideas and wishes. Thus we do not condemn as an unbeliever the Christian who lacks the Witness of the Spirit, though we do stir him up to pray for it, reminding him that without it he lacks a chief privilege of the child of God, and the one thing which is above all else needful if the child is to be a useful servant.

8. *'this testimony of the Spirit of God must needs . . . be antecedent to the testimony of our own spirit.'*

Wesley contradicts this a little later (II, 5), on the ground that the one who is born of God must surely have the witness of his own spirit, i.e., be aware that his life and character is in fact changed. The confusion arises through using these various terms as though they were names for successive stages in a process. When one seeks to describe the Christian experience it

THE WITNESS OF THE SPIRIT 93

is convenient to speak in terms of Faith, Justification, the New Birth, Adoption, Sanctification, and Assurance. These are placed in a certain order *in thought*. We should not on this account fall into the error of supposing that they are to be placed in this order *in fact*. Actually they are but names for *different aspects of one and the same process*. By way of example, when the rainbow is described we name the colours in a certain order, but we always see them all together. It is impossible to see one colour at a time, because each is alike an inherent part of the whole scheme. So, man does not first see the love of God, and then afterwards realize that he loves God. The two loves grow up in the heart together, God's love being the cause, man's the effect. So also, a man does not come first to the sober conviction: 'My life is changed for the better; I must have been born again'; and afterwards to the rapturous conviction: 'He loved *me*, and gave Himself up for *me*!' (or vice versa). The two convictions are rather diverse evidences of a single work of God, the change of the whole man, in heart, and mind, and will.

It may surprise some that Wesley should show looseness of thought in dealing with a subject so peculiarly his own. This is a mark that his genius was one of practical application rather than of constructive thought. He was not one who wrought out new treasures so much as one who saw the true value of gems already lying hidden in the systems of others, and who realized they could be fitted together to make a perfect whole. For example, Wesley did not discover the experience or formulate the doctrine of the Witness of the Spirit. He received them from the Moravians. The service he rendered was to rescue both experience and doctrine from much that was doubtful, to place them in a worthy setting, and to put them before the world in a manner both sober and emphatic. Wesley had a powerful and logical mind. Where he received from his religious background a piece of systematic doctrine, e.g., 'Justification by Faith', he could expound that system with admirable clarity and cogency. He received no such systematic doctrine in the case of the experience of Full Assurance. He failed to construct one on his own account.

11. *'the soul as intimately and evidently perceives when it loves . . . God, as when it loves . . . anything on earth.'*

It is important to insist on this truth in times when the reality of religious experience is often attacked in the name of 'science'. So long as believers have the widest possible fellowship with one another, so that the fancies and illusions of individuals may be corrected in the sober light of the experience of others, it may rightly be insisted that the facts of religious experience are as solid and real as any other facts of human life.

12. *'Such knowledge is too wonderful and excellent for me.'*

This is the healthy and realistic attitude of man to the things of God. However, modern psychological investigation has shed much valuable light on how the process of conversion, &c., takes place. This does not in any way take away from the unspeakable wonder of the grace and love of God. It simply shows something of the manner in which God works.

II. Many a man has been firmly convinced that he is under the immediate inspiration of God, when all the while he is the victim of some delusion conjured up from his desires, his pride, or from the disorder of his subconscious mind. No man is harder to correct of his error than this. Here, also, is an error more likely to afflict him who is by nature a zealot for religion. On the other hand, the man of intellectual integrity is of all men the first to go in fear of anything in the least savouring of this error. It is upon one of the most precious parts of the Christian faith that the discredit falls, if such delusion is abroad. All these circumstances conspire to make the following discussion of the greatest possible practical importance to the Christian preacher.

4. *'Scripture describes repentance . . . as constantly going before this witness of pardon.'*

It would perhaps be truer to say that the man who enjoys the genuine witness of the Spirit will always be found a penitent

THE WITNESS OF THE SPIRIT 95

man at the present moment. The question in what order the penitence comes should not be pressed too far. Some measure of penitence is the natural gateway to forgiveness, but the fullest realization of penitence is often the fruit of the Christian experience.

'*He pardoneth and absolveth, &c.*'

The quotations are (i) from the Words of Absolution in the Order for Morning Prayer; (ii) from the Words of Absolution in the Order for Holy Communion; (iii) from the General Confession in the Order for Holy Communion.

5. '*which must precede the witness.*' See note to I. 8 (p. 92 f.).

6. Here is the fanatic, drawn to life.

7. Here likewise is the antinomian, the one who, oblivious of the ethical nature of God and the strictness of His demands, is absorbed in a religious experience which is solely a wave of feelings to be enjoyed, and not also a radical change of will and action. Here is certainly the deadliest temptation of those who have had a vivid evangelical experience.

4-8. The essence of these paragraphs is: none can be regarded as enjoying the genuine Witness of the Spirit unless he shows a changed character and life, i.e., the Witness of the Spirit must be confirmed by the witness of one's own spirit.

9. '*and this difference also is immediately and directly perceived.*'

Certainly this is so '*if our spiritual senses are rightly disposed*'. Much hangs upon that 'if', for the matter is not self-evident The 'experience' of the deluded is just as real to him as is the experience of the Saint. Here is another thing to be tested by the evidence of a changed life, i.e., by the witness of one's own spirit (cf. paragraphs 12, 13). The authentic Christian experience is not simply that which 'seems real'. It is that which results in a better life. To this criterion we would add another The authentic experience is also that which prompts a man to lay firm hold of the historical facts of the life of Jesus, and to that explanation of them which has stood the test of experience with multitudes of believers in every age and in many lands, i.e., which leads the mind to orthodox theology, particularly as regards its more practical and less speculative elements.

10. The latter consideration is the answer to the difficulty raised here. The Christian has at times to attempt to answer the question placed in the mouth of Agrippa. Suppose that St. Paul had attempted an answer, his statement would probably have been somewhat as follows: 'I knew the vision to be of Jesus because of what I knew about Him beforehand as a matter of fact. I accepted what He said as the voice of God because to see Him alive proved the truth of the claim that He was risen from the dead. I had long realized that the resurrection, if a fact, would vindicate His claim to be the Messiah of God.' This would be the argument back to the historical facts about Christ, and to the practical religious significance of those facts.

11. *'he who hath that witness in himself cannot explain it to one who hath it not.'*

A Christian can explain the various propositions of the faith to an unbeliever. What he cannot get across is that proper spiritual temperature, that emotional tension, which should be excited by the facts.

## THE WITNESS OF THE SPIRIT

### QUESTIONS

1. Wesley writes: 'I asked a little gentleman at St. Just what objection there was to Edward Greenfield. He said, "Why, the man is well enough in other things; but his impudence the gentlemen cannot bear. Why, sir, he says that he knows his sins are forgiven!"' What answer would you give to the 'gentleman'?

2. In *Saint Joan* Bernard Shaw writes of the interview of Joan of Arc with Captain Robert de Baudricourt:

JOAN. I hear voices telling me what to do. They come from God.

ROBERT. They come from your imagination.

JOAN. Of course. That is how the messages of God come to us.

What is there to be said for St. Joan, and what for Captain Robert?

3. We hear it said: 'Religion is caught, not taught.' How far is this true?

4. Wesley taught that *all* Christians ought to *expect* the gift of the witness of the Spirit, yet without questioning the salvation of believers who do not attain to it. Is this standard suitable only for a time of 'revival', or should it be applied to the whole Church in all ages?

*Sermon Eleven**

# The Witness of our own Spirit

3. *'wrote.'*

An example of change of usage in our language; note also 'chose' in 5.

*'every man of an honest heart will soon understand the thing.'*

Wesley is much too optimistic. The nature of conscience has been one of the great topics of philosophical dispute down the ages, hence the 'large and numerous volumes'. It is impossible to dismiss the matter as casually as this.

4. Originally 'conscience' and 'consciousness' were alike in meaning, but usage has made them quite distinct.

5. *'Some late writers':*

i.e., Lord Shaftesbury, writing in 1699, and Francis Hutcheson, writing in 1728 and 1755.

*'a faculty or power, implanted by God . . . of perceiving what is right or wrong.'*

We must bear in mind that many opinions regarding conscience can be defended. It is probably more satisfactory to say that conscience is an impulse which tells us that we must do the good we know, and must not do what we know is wrong, rather than a faculty of perceiving what the right actually is. Something of this sort does seem to be inherent in human nature. However, in view of the endless variety of standards of right and wrong, and the difficulty in getting men to agree, it is perhaps more in accordance with the facts of human life to maintain that knowledge of what is actually right and wrong depends on environment, education, experience, and reason,

* No. 12 in *Fifty-three Sermons*

rather than on an immediate 'voice within'. The Christian views this impulse 'to do the right' as implanted by God. To those who deny the existence of God it merely reflects the instinctive desire to be on right terms with the rest of the herd, and the power of custom.

6. *'whereby their conscience is to be directed.'*

If conscience needs external information to direct it, it can hardly itself be 'a faculty . . . of perceiving what is right or wrong'.

*'the law written in their hearts.'*

St. Paul had the insight to observe that even the heathen, who were not instructed by the Hebrew Scriptures, had some sort of moral standards; and to teach that these standards also were derived from God, and that God would judge the heathen in the light of them.

*'the writings of the Old and New Testament.'*

This appears to ignore the wide divergence of moral standard between the teaching of our Lord and the more primitive portions of the Old Testament, e.g., the Book of Judges.

*'or by undeniable inference.'*

The difficulty is to get various Christians to agree what is the undeniable inference of a given passage, and also the circumstance that some will cling mainly to one text, some to another. The controversy about Christian Pacifism illustrates this point.

*'Whatever the Scripture neither forbids nor enjoins, &c.'*

This does not make sufficient allowance for judgements in circumstances which never arose in the experience of Bible writers, e.g., the ethics of birth-control, total abstinence, &c. Alongside the Bible we must surely place the present-day guidance of the Holy Spirit, mediated through the consensus of opinion of faithful souls who hold fellowship with one another in the Church.

## SERMON XI

8. *'we perceive, as in a glass, all that is within ourselves.'*

   The sense of 2 Cor. iii. 18 is not that the purity of Christ is the mirror in which we see our own deformity, though this is a profound truth. St. Paul actually says that our transformed lives are the mirror which reflects Christ.

11. *'in simplicity and godly sincerity.'*

    Some ancient versions of 2 Cor. i. 12 give this reading, though the most authoritative manuscripts have 'holiness'. The two words are such as to be easily confused in the Greek manuscript.

12. *'simplicity regards the intention itself, sincerity the execution of it.'*

    Actually the two words mean much the same.

13. *'to prevent our mistaking . . . it with the sincerity of the Heathens.'*

    St. Paul had no thought of such a distinction in the present text.

14. *'we can hardly conceive any who was more highly favoured, &c.'* to end.

    All this is fully justified. St. Paul was one of the world's great geniuses. There was a fine Greek University at Tarsus, which could not but affect Paul's environment, even though it is doubtful whether a young Pharisee would be allowed by his parents to attend. Gamaliel was one of the most celebrated of the great Jewish Rabbis, and one of the most open-minded. The best of the Pharisees were the cream of the Jewish nation.

15. That grace has this two-fold meaning is a consideration important for the understanding of Christian theology.

17. *'an adult Christian rejoiceth.'*

    The word 'adult' was added by Wesley in the edition of 1771. He also gave his reason in a note at the end: 'It may easily be observed that the preceding discourse describes the experience of those who are *strong* in faith; but hereby those that are *weak* in faith may be discouraged; to prevent which, the following discourse may be of use': i.e., the sermon on Sin in Believers. Wesley was well qualified to describe the abounding joy of God's heroes, who suffer and labour for their Lord.

18. **19.** These paragraphs admirably describe a vital element of true Christian experience.

19. This spurious and fatal 'liberty' is today much spoken of among some who affect to be 'emancipated' and 'progressive'.

The quotation is verse 10 of the hymn by Charles Wesley, 'Watch in all things'. A selection of other verses, set to a noble tune, appears as No. 478 in the present hymn-book, to form a fine hymn which deserves to be more used.

We are forced to admit that this sermon is not up to Wesley's usually fine standard, apart from the last few paragraphs. It is marred by dubious exegesis of the Bible, and by a tendency to pass by difficulties.

*Sermon Twelve**

# The Means of Grace

THIS fine sermon, packed with cogent argument and many a telling thrust, represents Wesley at his best. Here he shows himself passionate and earnest, yet broad-minded and moderate, and most practical in application. In the early days of Methodism the topic of this sermon was a matter of burning practical concern. Mention has already been made in the introduction to Sermon X to the noble witness of the Moravians to the fact that it is the privilege of the Christian to experience a conscious change of heart. Immediate communion with God should fill his heart with unspeakable joy and peace, and assure him of his salvation. We have also noticed that the Moravians were often quite unbalanced in their emphasis upon this vital truth. Frequently they fell into the error of making religion too purely inward and individual. The main issue between the Moravians and the Methodists was joined on the doctrine of 'stillness', i.e., that one who was seeking, but who had not yet attained, full salvation, should not use the means of grace and worship, for this would be to trust not God only, but one's own 'good works'. The disciple should rather be 'still', and, doing nothing, simply wait upon God. This teaching is clearly the abuse through gross excess of 'Justification by Faith'.

In the Preface to the second part of his *Journal*, para. 8 (*Works*, I, p. 81), Wesley wrote as follows of the Moravians: 'But about September, 1739, . . . certain men crept in . . . greatly troubling and subverting their (i.e., the Methodists) souls; telling them, they were in a delusion; . . . and had no true faith at all. "For", said they, "none has any justifying faith, who has ever any doubt or fear, which you know you have; or who has not a clean heart, which you know you have not: Nor will you ever have it, till you leave off using the means of grace (so called); till you leave off running to church and

* No. 16 in *Fifty-three Sermons*

## THE MEANS OF GRACE

sacrament, and praying, and singing, and reading either the Bible, or any other book; for you cannot use these things without trusting in them. Therefore, till you leave them off, you can never have true faith; you can never till then trust in the blood of Christ."' In the first days of Methodism Wesley had to fight hard against this error of 'stillness', for a number fell to it, and even Charles Wesley was affected for a short time. The result of the dispute was that on July 20, 1740, the Methodists left the Fetter Lane (Moravian) Society, and on July 23 met instead at the Foundery, which became the first meeting-place for Methodism as a separate movement. Thus the subject of this sermon was the occasion for one of the most momentous steps in the life of our Church.

The error of 'stillness' is rarely met with today in this open and extreme form. It appears in a modified form in the disinclination of some to take part in acts of worship unless they 'feel like it'. So one will say: 'I do not pray regularly every day: I think it better to wait until I feel a strong desire to do so, otherwise my prayer is only a matter of form.' Another will say: 'I went to the Holy Communion once or twice, but I never felt that Real Presence of Christ of which some have spoken; so I stopped going.' And another: 'I do not fancy going to Chapel since my husband died. I fear that I should imagine the coffin standing there, and it would bring it all back to me.' Again: 'Since I came to live out here I have never felt at home in Church. The building feels strange, and the folk are not so warm. It was different at home. I do not feel that it is worth while to come.' All such statements reflect an insufficient sense of *obligation* in the Christian life. There is insufficient realization that, whatever the state of his inward feelings, the earnest Christian should patiently and expectantly persevere in those acts of worship which have been ordained by God as the way in which He is to be found. Religion such as this is too much dependent on the emotions. It is too little a solemn resolve of the will, and a fixed principle accepted by the mind. It is too purely individual. There is not enough sense that to be a Christian involves allegiance to the Church, with consequent acceptance of a regular and health-giving discipline. This is the spirit of 'stillness'.

l. 1. *'This question could never have been proposed in the apostolical church.'*

This is certainly the case. The New Testament gives no answer to the oft-debated point: 'What of Christians who are outside the Church?' because the question had then never been asked. It was assumed as a matter of course that all believers joined together in the means of grace.

2. *'Others seemed to imagine, &c.,'* to end.

Wesley puts his finger unerringly upon the commonest and most dangerous abuse of the means of grace. The sheer formalist abuse, mentioned in the first part of the paragraph, has not been unknown in the Church. It is, however, a manifest error, from which the soul will probably turn. On the other hand, to hope that diligence in those works of piety so definitely ordained of God will serve in some way to counterbalance faults of moral character is a more subtle and clinging error. It has been the besetting fault of multitudes zealous for the Church and means of grace.

3. *'to draw a general conclusion, &c.'*

Here is the natural but dreadful consequence of the abuse. It is among reformers, and zealots for spiritual religion, that there is most likely to be found the error of an excessive reaction against externalism in religion. There is here a standing warning for evangelical Christians.

4. *'till certain men arose, &c.'*

Wesley has in mind the so-called Mystics of the Church, already referred to in the introduction to Sermon X. In general these have taught that the highest form of religion is the immediate union of the soul with God, in soaring contemplation and ecstatic rapture, quite apart from outward forms of prayer and worship. Wesley had real appreciation for such of these Mystics as lived within the solid institutions of the ancient Church, and the Roman Church of later times. He saw that

THE MEANS OF GRACE 105

their witness in some degree counter-balanced the frequent externalism of their times. Writing in 1773 he says: 'There are excellent things in most of the Mystic writers. As almost all of them lived in the Romish Church, they were lights whom the gracious providence of God raised up to shine in a dark place. But they did not give a clear, a steady, or a uniform light.' Wesley had much less patience with Mystics nearer his own time, such as some German Protestants, many Moravians, and, in England, William Law, and the Quakers. This was doubtless due to his unhappy differences with the Moravians.

6. Wesley speaks from experience here. He remembers what it had cost him to separate from the Moravians, to whom he owed so much. He knows what attraction many of his enthusiastic converts had felt for 'stillness'.

Notice how full this whole section is of typical English moderation, and of eighteenth-century common sense.


II. 1. *'preventing.'*

'To prevent' properly means 'to go before'. 'Preventing grace' (the more usual expression is 'prevenient grace') is that grace of God which acts before a man has any real thought of turning to the truths of the Christian faith, and which brings him to those first stirrings of heart. Wesley taught that all men, however apparently ignorant and abandoned, are under the influence of prevenient grace.

*'our own Church . . . teaches us.'*

The Anglican Catechism runs: A sacrament is 'an outward and visible sign of an inward and spiritual grace given unto us, ordained by Christ himself, as a means whereby we receive the same, and a pledge to assure us thereof'.

*'The chief of these means are prayer, &c.'*

Wesley here definitely speaks as an Anglican, defending against Moravian 'stillness' the well-tried and well-loved piety of his Church. He says nothing here of those means of grace which were becoming so typical of Methodism, hymn-singing and the fellowship-meeting. He also seems to assume that his hearers have been baptized.

3. '*the whole power is of Him.*' '*He is able to give the same grace, though there were no means.*'

Whoever firmly grasps these truths will never suppose that he is saved *by* the priest who administers the means of grace, or by his *own diligence* in attending upon them. We should remember that Wesley here speaks for the whole Church, in principle even for such institutionalized Churches as the Roman. However, the principle has often in practice been obscured in the eyes of the multitude by undiscriminating emphasis upon the paramount necessity of loyalty to the ecclesiastical machine.

4. '*By the expression some have used.*'

'Christ is the only means of grace' was a Moravian maxim, true or false according to the sense in which it is taken.

III. 3. '*we may receive of God . . . by importunately asking.*'

It is improbable that in this parable our Lord intended to teach that we should try to move God to act by persistence in asking. Rather is the parable a humorous story to enforce the simple moral: 'Those who ask, get; have faith to ask.' Jesus taught that God is quite unlike an earthly judge, who may on occasion have to be constrained before he will avenge the right. 'I say unto you, that *He* will avenge them *speedily*' (Luke xviii. 1-8).

6. '*gross, blasphemous absurdity.*'

There is no justification for the use of such strong language over a difference in Biblical interpretation. Wesley's excuse is that he is desperately anxious to secure that no man shall use the word 'faith' in anything less than its profoundest sense. In the Epistle of James 'faith' certainly bears something less than 'the full Christian meaning', and Wesley's point is essentially sound.

## THE MEANS OF GRACE

7. *'shamelessly false.'*

'Ερευνᾶτε τὰς γραφάς can equally well mean 'Ye search the Scriptures', or the imperative: 'Search the Scriptures'. Only the context can decide, and no text has been more commonly misused than this, through neglect of the context. In John v. 39–40 our Lord points out that His Jewish hearers are being disappointed in their hope of finding eternal life in those Old Testament Scriptures that they so diligently search. Life is to be found only in Himself, not in the Jewish Scriptures, though these have a value in that they witness to Him. Thus the sense is almost the opposite to that for which Wesley so vigorously contends. (See Revised Version reading.)

8. *'All Scripture is given by inspiration of God.'*

Here is another sentence capable of two translations. Thus the Revised Version reads: 'Every Scripture inspired of God is also profitable, &c.' This is something less than a statement that the whole of the Old Testament is actually divinely-inspired Scripture. However, St. Paul certainly believed that the entire Hebrew Scriptures were actually inspired of God, so the preferable rendering of the text makes no *effective* difference to Wesley's argument. Wesley, of course, shared with all believers of his day the view that the infallibility of every part of the Bible was a fundamental assumption of the Christian faith.

11. Wesley rejected the view that only the soundly converted should come to the Holy Communion. He would remember that his own mother had come to the full evangelical experience at the Lord's Table, and that this was the case with many others. So in the *Journal* for June 27, 1740, he writes: 'But experience shows the gross falsehood of that assertion that the Lord's Supper is not a converting ordinance. Ye are the witnesses. For many now present know, the very beginning of your conversion to God . . . was wrought at the Lord's Supper.' Wesley goes on to state that only one thing is necessary for a man rightly to come to the Holy Communion, that is, a sense that he needs forgiveness and the assistance of God's grace. Wesley

was not, of course, discussing the rightness of the rule of the Church of England, that only those who have been confirmed may communicate. We may well believe that at this stage of his life he would have upheld the rule, and told the penitent seeker that it was his duty to be confirmed. However, the modern Methodist usage of a Communion open to all who sincerely desire to take it is in accord with the spirit of Wesley's rule.

IV. This section clearly reflects many an hour of debate with the Moravians.

1. '*The first and chief of these, &c.*'

This was the great Moravian plea. This perverse error is clearly an undiscriminating reaction to those who *have* trusted rites and ceremonies for salvation.

4. 5. 6. Here Wesley gives some sound and sensible exposition of the Bible.

V. 4. '*But, because God bids, therefore I do.*'

This is the essence of the whole matter, and this paragraph gives the best possible counsel to the Christian. Those who keep this advice in mind will neither contaminate Christianity with formalism or with superstition, nor will they neglect the Church, with her worship and Sacraments.

'*take care . . . how you congratulate yourself.*'

Here is a wise and necessary word. Few that find themselves zealous for the Church and her ordinances escape being assailed by this temptation.

## Questions

1. Our rule for the use of the means of grace is: 'Because God bids, therefore I do; because He directs me to wait in this way, therefore here I wait.' But does God's commandment *ever* breathe the spirit of:

> 'Their's not to reason why,
> Their's but to do *or* die.'

May we not perceive a reason why God commands us so to wait?

2. If we are to wait upon God by using the means of grace, is it possible to be saved, in any adequate sense of the word, apart from the Church?

3. A troubled soul comes to a minister for advice. One says: 'Repent, trust the grace of God, and open your heart to the good Lord!' Another says: 'Start coming to the Holy Communion, and join my Fellowship.' Which advice is likely to be more helpful? Or is there anything else you would say?

4. The Leaders' Meeting says: 'We have the evangelist coming for his special services. How can we ensure success? We must have plenty of prayer-meetings, for if we do we can be certain of revival.' Do you agree with them?

*Sermon Thirteen**

# The Circumcision of the Heart

A MOST interesting thing about this sermon is its early date. It is the first of Wesley's University Sermons. At the time he was simply the young and earnest Fellow of Lincoln College, and leader of the Holy Club. His voyage to America, with all he learned there by sad experience, his fruitful contact with the Moravians, and the gift of 'the heart strangely warmed' on his return to England in 1738, were then all experiences well in the future. Yet after long experience of the Methodist revival Wesley could pass this sermon to the world as part of the standard for Methodist preaching, with only a single, though significant, addition (the latter half of I. 7). In the *Journal* for September 1, 1778, we read: 'I know not that I can write a better sermon on the Circumcision of the Heart than I did five and forty years ago. Perhaps, indeed, I may have read five or six hundred books more than I had then, . . . but I am not sensible that this had made any essential addition to my knowledge in divinity.' In excess of zeal to magnify the glorious novelty of the evangelical revival many Methodists have drawn too sharp a distinction between Wesley before Aldersgate Street, and Wesley after. They have been treated as if they were two different men, the former almost not a Christian. Here we have evidence of the falsehood of this position.

*Text.*

The physical act of circumcision is very widespread as a tribal custom, invested with magical or religious significance. To the Hebrews circumcision was, and is, one of the most precious marks of the Covenant with Jehovah. Thus 'circumcision' could naturally be given an extended and metaphorical meaning, to denote 'religion'. So the prophets, and later, St.

* No. 17 in *Fifty-three Sermons*

Paul, in preaching spiritual and ethical religion, as opposed to mere ceremonial, pleaded for 'the circumcision of the heart'.

1. *'An excellent man.'* We do not know who this is.

*'which difference.'*

Or, as we would now say, in a less graceful word: 'which differentiate.'

I. 2. *'circumcision of heart implies humility.'*

This putting of humility as first among Christian graces, an order which may seem strange to some, is clearly a mark of the great influence that William Law, author of the celebrated *Serious Call to a Devout and Holy Life*, had upon Wesley in his young days. Wesley later decisively broke with Law, on account of his 'mysticism'.

*'conceits':* i.e., 'conceptions'.

7. The second half of this paragraph ('but likewise the revelation of Christ in our hearts, &c.'), was added by Wesley in the edition of 1748. It is significant that the one thing he felt he had to add was a clearer definition of saving faith.

9. We notice, perhaps with some surprise, that Wesley taught the doctrine of the Witness of the Spirit *before* he came to the experience of the heart strangely warmed. (See also II. 5.) We must, however, leave room, after the experience of Aldersgate Street, for a stronger apprehension of what the doctrine involved, else Wesley could hardly have written of Peter Böhler's teaching regarding 'Dominion over sin, and constant Peace from a sense of forgiveness': 'I was quite amazed, and looked upon it as a new Gospel.' (*Journal*, May 24, 1738 (11).) We can well imagine that the present statement was largely a matter of theory to Wesley, demanded by fidelity to the teaching of 'Romans'. Later it came with new understanding and emphasis, being a matter of vital experience also. So in the

present paragraph the 'clear and cheerful confidence', 'that good assurance', seems to be interpreted mainly as a confident *hope*, rather than a present attainment. We may well imagine that had Wesley penned this later he would have found it more natural to say that the Christian knows that he enjoys life, not merely that he is assured that he is 'in the path which leadeth to life'.

12. *'Nor yet does it forbid us (as some have strangely imagined) to take pleasure in anything but God.'*

This in answer to an attack on the Oxford Methodists which had appeared shortly before in *Fog's Journal*: 'They avoid, as much as possible, every object that may affect them with any pleasant or grateful sensations, &c.'

*'He has inseparably annexed pleasure to the use of those creatures':*
i.e., God has ordained that food is necessary to life, and that eating brings pleasure.

II. 1. *'whereby he is very far gone from original righteousness.'*
This is quoted from the Anglican Article IX, On Original Sin.

2. *'that blind leader of the blind . . . natural reason.'*

Wesley is here moved by reaction, natural in one possessed by his zeal for God, against the cool and rationalistic moralism that in his day often passed for Christianity. We need not assume that Wesley would have denied that reason is also a God-given faculty, whereby man may know the truth about God.

3. In line with the above, this paragraph betrays a certain unnecessary degree of impatience with philosophical investigations which, though not of the essence of religion, are of real value, and quite legitimate.

*'Either these accounts of the grounds of Christian duty coincide with the scriptural, or not; &c.'*

There is a very real danger in 'a cloud of terms, whereby the easiest truths are explained into obscurity', but surely, if reason is a gift of God, sound reasoning ought to agree with and support God's revelation of Himself through the prophets. The Bible is our supreme source of religious knowledge, but it does not thereby render all other sources superfluous.

5. On the Witness of the Spirit, see note to l. 9, pp. 111 ff.

*'So greatly have they erred, &c.'*

This has been a common position of philosophers. The immediate reference is to Cudworth and the Cambridge Platonists, who taught that man ought to aim at the realization of absolute good for its own sake, without any regard for its consequences. The Christian is certainly right in looking to the goal of his strivings, but the philosophers are profoundly right too.

7. Wesley is abundantly justified in what he says here. However, the statement does savour slightly of Wesley before, rather than after, his evangelical experience.

8. *'as a late author strongly expresses it.'*

The reference is to William Law's *Christian Perfection*. Wesley does not mean that Law was dead, but that the book had been recently published.

9. *'Though I speak with the tongues of men and of angels, and have not love.'*

Wesley here anticipates the much more adequate rendering of the Revised Version for 1 Cor. xiii.

10. *'those children of God':* i.e., the Mystic writers.

## SERMON XIII

### QUESTION

In his *Journal* for February 1, 1738, Wesley records his reflections on landing in England, upon his return from Georgia. 'It is now two years and almost four months since I left my native country, in order to teach the Georgian Indians the nature of Christianity: But what have I learned myself in the meantime? Why (what I the least of all suspected) that I who went to America to convert others, was never myself converted to God.' (A later added footnote here runs: 'I am not sure of this.') . . . 'This, then, have I learned in the ends of the earth . . . I am "a child of wrath" (Another later footnote here reads: 'I believe not'), an heir of hell.' *Works*, I, 75-6. What light does this confession throw upon Wesley's thought and experience immediately before his evangelical experience? What light do these footnotes shed upon the result of his mature reflection? Why did Wesley print for his followers *both* the original *Journal*, and the later footnotes?

*Sermon Fourteen**

# The Marks of the New Birth

THIS is another fine sermon on the religion of the heart, and covers ground which will by now be familiar to the reader of Wesley. The main interest particular to this sermon is that Wesley mentions, in passing, the relation of Baptism to the New Birth. In the opening paragraph we read: 'These privileges (the being born of God, and of the Spirit; the being a child of God) . . . are ordinarily annexed to baptism,' i.e., the promised and proper result of Baptism is the divine gift of Regeneration ('the New Birth'). (See also section IV, 5, and note on p. 122.) Some will find surprising the occurrence of this statement in the Standard Sermons, because most Methodists today regard Baptismal Regeneration as a dubious, or even erroneous doctrine, as well as one associated with the theology of those Churches commonly described as 'Catholic'. It is clear that Wesley was prompted to this statement by loyalty to the doctrinal standards of the Church of England, the Church of his upbringing. Thus in Sermon XXXIX, IV, 2. we read: 'It is certain our Church supposes that all who are baptized in their infancy are at the same time born again; and it is allowed that the whole Office for the Baptism of Infants proceeds upon this supposition.' As Sugden observes: 'The Anglican Article (XXVII), Of Baptism, is not explicit. It states that baptism is not only a sign of profession, but also a sign of regeneration or new birth; and that thereby "the promises of the forgiveness of sin and of our adoption to be the sons of God by the Holy Ghost are visibly signed and sealed"; but it does not definitely say that the baptized infant is regenerated. The Office for Baptism is, however, much more definite; prayer is offered, "Give Thy Holy Spirit to this infant, that he may be born again, and be made an heir of everlasting salvation"; and after the administration of

* No. 18 in *Fifty-three Sermons*

the sacrament, the priest shall say, "Seeing that this child is regenerate and grafted into the body of Christ's Church, let us give thanks to Almighty God"; and again, "We yield Thee most hearty thanks, most merciful Father, that it hath pleased Thee to regenerate this infant with Thy Holy Spirit".' (I, 280–1.)

We should first seek to understand the thought underlying the formula, 'Baptismal Regeneration', for the phrase is misleading, and widely misunderstood. Essentially and originally Holy Baptism is the admission ceremony into the Christian Church. The Holy Spirit dwells in the Church, and to be 'in the Spirit' is descriptive of the atmosphere in which live those who are genuine members of the Church. Thus, to bring anyone into the Church, and actually to incorporate him into the fellowship of believers, places him in the sphere of influence appointed by God for the saving work of the Spirit. The reader of Acts will find that in the formative days of the Church this principle was often set forth in visible and striking manner. Those (adults) who, to signify their faith in Christ and allegiance to His Church, were baptized, often then showed such manifest 'gifts of the Spirit' as 'speaking with tongues'. (Acts ii. 38; xix. 5–6: but compare x. 47.) In the case of the Baptism of an unconscious infant this change is real, though potential, i.e., the infant is truly placed upon the road of the Christian life, though the actual journey has yet to start. By way of illustration: imagine two babies born, one in a godly home, the other, next door, in a drunken and blasphemous home. There is a very real difference of spiritual status between the two, for one is joined to a society which will give him every chance to become an actual Christian as he grows up, while the other is joined to a society which will almost certainly do much to blight him. Yet the difference is potential. The babies are actually still the same, for there has not yet been time for the diverse environments to exercise their effect. Thus the general intention of those who teach Baptismal Regeneration is to affirm that the Spirit-filled environment of the Church has a prevailing beneficial effect upon those who enjoy it, with the consequence that to be incorporated into the Church by

## THE MARKS OF THE NEW BIRTH

Baptism is to be placed on the high road to salvation. Thus the divinely-intended, the ordinary, and the expected, effect of Baptism is the initiation of the Christian life, though this ideal does not always come about in fact. So Wesley writes: 'These privileges . . . are *ordinarily* annexed to baptism.'

If he has an adequate conception of the place of the Church in the Christian life, the evangelical Christian also will probably accept these basic ideas, though he will probably object to expressing them in the formula, 'Baptismal Regeneration', and still more to the use of such phrases as: 'baptism implants a seed of salvation.' The objection to this language, typical of 'Catholic' Christianity, is that it tends to fix the uninstructed or unthinking mind upon the virtue of the *rite* of Baptism, rather than upon the *actual fact* of incorporation into the Church. The Methodist will certainly wish to make it plain that a child who is in fact brought up in a Christian home, and in the fellowship of the Church, will receive the full blessing that comes of union with the people of God, even though the normal and proper admission ceremony to the community has not been performed. Furthermore, we would wish to state, following Wesley, that one who has been duly baptized can reduce the holy rite to a mere form if, as years go by, he shows no sign of Christian grace in his life. The language of 'Baptismal Regeneration' is such as to conceal these truths from those who have but slender knowledge of theology, and to give simple people occasion for supposing that there is some mysterious value in it apart from that actual Christian life in the Church of which it is intended to be the beginning. It is needlessly uncharitable to accuse the Roman or Anglo-Catholic of contaminating the Christian faith with magic, though we may rightly expostulate with him in a friendly way because, through loyalty to certain venerable formulae, he uses language not understood by the people.

In Sermon XXXIX, 'The New Birth', Wesley very significantly records how he met the practical problem of these misunderstandings. The moving passage runs: 'But perhaps the sinner himself, to whom in real charity we say, "You must be born again", has been taught to say, "I defy your new doctrine:

I need not be born again; I was born again when I was baptized. What! would you have me deny my baptism?" I answer, first, ... Was you devoted to God at eight days old, and have you been all these years devoting yourself to the devil? Was you, even before you had the use of reason, consecrated to God the Father, the Son, and the Holy Ghost? And have you, ever since you had the use of it, been flying in the face of God, and consecrating yourself to Satan? ... O be ashamed! blush! hide yourself in the earth! Never boast more of what ought to fill you with confusion, to make you ashamed before God and man!' I answer, secondly, you have already denied your baptism; and that in the most effectual manner. You have denied it a thousand and a thousand times; and you do so still, day by day. For in your baptism you renounced the devil and all his works. Whenever, therefore, you give place to him again, ... then you deny your baptism.' (Section IV, 4.) Doubtless this was the reason why in later years, and after reflection, Wesley abridged the Prayer-Book Office for Baptism in the *Sunday Service of the Methodists* (1784 and 1786). The three passages quoted above, as teaching Baptismal Regeneration in the Prayer Book, were omitted by him, so that the word 'regenerated' only appears in the citation of John iii. 5 in the introductory exhortation. However, the objection of Wesley would seem to have been to the *phrase*, rather than to the *principle*, or he would hardly in this same year (1784) have given legal sanction to these sermons, still containing the passages in question, as the doctrinal standard for Methodism.

Later Methodism has been at still greater pains to exclude every suggestion that an infant is born again simply by the act of Baptism. When the *Book of Offices* was revised in 1882 the reference to John iii. 5 was left out, and the prayers 'grant that the old Adam in this Child may be so buried, that the new man may be raised up in him, &c.' were transferred to the end of the service, to avoid the supposition that they were meant to be answered there and then in the act of Baptism. The Methodist Church has certainly been right in using every effort to avoid any occasion for the supposition that there is in Baptism some kind of magical change, i.e., that some blessing is conveyed to the baptized for life, and quite apart from his actual manner of living. The difficulty is that this is a *negative* policy. Those whose interest is that Baptism shall not be allowed to mean *too much* are in danger of not letting it mean enough. In consequence, many of our people have become content to see Holy Baptism as merely *declaratory*, i.e., that it is nothing more than a solemn occasion for declaring that all children, and this child in particular, do actually belong to God, and that He loves them; together with a promise by the parents and the Church that the child is to be brought up as a Christian. The practical outcome of this is that children are too often baptized 'to please the parents', or 'to give him a name', without any real guarantee that the promise to treat the child as part of the Church is taken seriously. This is much less than the New Testament doctrine, or the standard left us by Wesley. (Baptism is, of course, declaratory of certain truths.) With these considerations in mind one should read carefully our present beautiful Office for Baptism.

I. 3. Compare this paragraph with the Anglican Homily, 'On Salvation', whence are drawn a number of quotations.

5. '*God plainly saith, "He doth not commit sin"; and thou addest, habitually! &c.*'

Wesley protests a little too much here. The author of 1 John states in a most uncompromising fashion the proposition that the believer is freed from sin. This is the ideal, and certainly must be preached. Wesley rightly repudiates those who would water down 1 John iii. 9 in the way indicated, with the inference that occasional lapses in difficult moments 'do not matter very much'. However, account has to be taken of the circumstance that even the best Christians are not ideal Christians. Their faith is not constant and perfect; so that they do at times succumb to temptation, though sin does not prevail over them to their ruin. Wesley deals with this problem in the next sermon, and in effect modifies his present very outspoken statement. If we interpret Wesley's intention aright we may say that there is demanded of the true Christian a standard much higher than the mere avoidance of habitual sin, yet at the same time, the name of Christian is not to be denied to all but the theoretically perfect.

'μεθοδεία πλάνης.'

These are the words rendered 'wiles of error' in our translation of Eph. iv. 14. κυβεία ἀνθρώπων is represented by 'the sleight of men'.

7. *'whatsoever is, is best.'*

This is a reminiscence of the line in Pope's *Essay on Man*.
'One truth is clear, "Whatever is, is right".'

II. 1. *'because there is also a dead hope.'*

What Wesley says is true, but he errs in finding it in this text. The contrast here is not between a well-founded and a presumptuous hope, but between a living and a languid hope.

πληροφορίᾳ πίστεως—the words translated 'in fullness of faith' (R.V. marg., 'full assurance of faith'), in Hebrews x. 22.

πληροφορίαν ἐλπίδος—the words translated 'the fulness of hope' (R.V. marg., 'full assurance of hope'), in Hebrews vi. 11.

4. *'Ye, as many as are the sons of God, . . . We, the apostles, &c.'*

Wesley again makes a distinction where none is. If St. Paul had wished to make this distinction he could have used the appropriate pronouns for emphasis, but they are not here. It is, however, a sound point that all believers should look for the full experience of the Apostles.

III. 1. *'their reconciled and loving Father.'*
See note to Sermon V, I, 8, 9 (pp. 42 f.).

4. *'But some may possibly ask, &c.'*

This would be the objection of those who considered that the Methodist emphasis upon the religion of the heart savoured of fanaticism, and who maintained that they preferred a 'common-sense *practical* religion', i.e., a self-imposed set of conventional 'good deeds'.


IV. 1. *'so that ye are constrained to love all men.'*

An example of one such is surely Wesley himself.

2. *'The question is not, what you was made in baptism, &c.'*

Wesley here uncovers those who would take refuge in loose talk about Baptismal Regeneration. See introduction to this sermon, and Sermon XXXIX, IV, 4.

*'You was.'*

In Wesley's day this was the regular form for the second person singular, in place of the old 'thou wast'. Thus the paragraph has a direct personal application of great power.

3. *'your circumcised predecessors':*

i.e., the baptized sinner is in the same position as those denounced by our Lord, those who, though undoubtedly marked as Hebrews by the rite of circumcision, were not God's people in actual life.

4. *'To say . . . that there is no new birth but in baptism, is to seal you all under damnation':*

i.e., if it be indeed true that there is no hope for the New Birth in any who have sinned away their Baptism, what hope is there for the great multitude of Wesley's hearers?

*'And perhaps some may think this just and right, &c.'*

This refers to the ecclesiastical zealot, who interprets earnestness in religion in terms of rigour in enforcing the ordinances of the Church.

'*Amalekites.*' See 1 Sam. xv. 18.

'*You will say, "But we are washed"; &c.*'

The man who has kept every rule of the Church is confident that in pronouncing the just damnation of the openly careless he is himself safe in the favour of God. Wesley strips off his self-righteousness. God's standard is not outward, but inward.

5. '*Who denies that ye were then made children of God, &c.*'

This is Wesley's position regarding Baptism in a nutshell. He will not deny the highest significance to the Sacrament, but he will not allow the careless to *presume* upon its virtues. Whatever be our views regarding Wesley's precise opinions, this is certainly the sound rule to follow.

### Questions

1. Are all men the sons of God? Is God the Father of all men?

2. Is it possible to regard as truly born of God anyone who has not been 'soundly converted'? Consider the cases of a young child, and of a grown man.

3. Read the present Methodist Baptism Service. Is there any place where it claims too much? or not enough?

*Sermon Fifteen**

# The Great Privilege of those that are Born of God

THIS fine and eloquent sermon covers much the same ground as the previous one, but is in more practical tone. It was probably composed for publication, and placed here for the purpose of modifying the uncompromising statements of Sermon XIV on the complete freedom of the re-born from sin.

1. '*In one point of time.*'

    This statement is natural in one who was accustomed to witness sudden conversions.

2. '*Justification implies only a relative, the new birth a real, change.*'

    There is much truth in this distinction, and the maxim 'God in justifying us does something *for* us; in begetting us again, He does the work *in* us' is admirable as clarifying the position. It is, however, possible to make this distinction too fixed. Some have represented justification almost as a matter of form, a mere change of legal status. Those who speak of God 'accounting righteous those who in fact are not' are in danger of that supposition against which Wesley has already warned us, namely, that in justifying man God is deceived. (Sermon V, II, 4.) If, with Wesley, we say that justification is forgiveness (Sermon V, II, 5) it is certainly something that God does for us, but it is also the first real beginning of a change that God works in us. (See notes, Sermon V, II, 5, pp. 44 ff.). The distinction between justification and the new birth is that they are two aspects of the same thing, i.e., the very starting-point of the Christian experience.

    *No. 19 in *Fifty-three Sermons*

## SERMON XV

> '*The one is the taking away the guilt, the other the taking away the power, of sin.*'

Yes: but for a man to be released from guilt is a first stage toward destroying the enslaving power of sin.

1. '*it implies not barely the being baptized.*'

   See introduction to Sermon XIV.

3. We now come to an analogy, very beautifully worked out, between physical and spiritual birth. Most of the eloquence of Wesley we have so far encountered owes its effect to a connected series of brief yet profound aphorisms, of telling, and at times, of cutting, phrases. For example, paragraph 2 of this sermon is typical of John Wesley. This is the eloquence of a logician. It is therefore interesting to find here a sample of a different kind of eloquence, more imaginative and poetical, that based upon the illustrative story, the parable, the analogy. Yet even here we see the utterly systematic mind at work. The effect is good, and we cannot but regret that the published records of Wesley's preaching contain so few examples of this method.

   > '*The child which is not yet born subsists indeed by the air,*' being supplied with oxygen from that taken in from the air by the mother.

6. '*God is continually calling to him from on high.*'

   This is prevenient grace (see note to Sermon XII, II, 1, p. 105).

8. '*so it is continually rendered back by love, &c.*'

   The one who has been born again will attend upon the means of grace and Christian service, and so will grow in grace. Man is not purely passive in receiving from God the gift of life.

II. 2. *'By sin, I here understand outward sin.'*
This is rather an unhelpful limitation.

*'acknowledged to be such at the time that it is transgressed.'*

Wesley shows admirable insight in bringing in this proviso, the forgetting of which has caused much confusion in the discussion of Christian ethics. The moral law by which God judges any man is not the perfect moral law as it exists in the mind of God. It is such part of that perfect law as the man in question sees at the time to be the moral law, or, we might perhaps say, such part as he may reasonably be expected to see, will he only open his eyes to the light given to his day and generation. Not every lapse from God's perfect will is a sin, though every lapse is evil in its consequences. Sin is a falling short of the standard known to be binding upon one. As the race has opportunity to learn by experience, so that binding moral standard is raised. Thus an action which in one society and in one age was not wrong, may be a sin in another society or in a succeeding age. Another consequence of this principle is that only God can judge sin, for no man can say for certain how much of God's law his brother knows, or how much he ought to know.

4. This paragraph is based on acceptance of the old tradition that David was the general author of the Book of Psalms (apart from those specially attributed to others). This tradition is largely abandoned today, though some Psalms may be by David. Wesley's argument is by no means rendered invalid by this. In any case we can accept the position that David was a great figure in the upward march of Hebrew religion. He can truly be described as a man of God. Note that the quotations are from the Prayer-Book version of the Psalms.

5. We are not *quite* convinced by this argument. If two partners in fruitful Christian work have so decisive a difference in policy that they decide that it is more profitable to the work for them to dissolve that partnership, there is certainly a general suspicion that some sinful temper may have crept in. This is usually the

case in practice. It is not *necessarily* so, however. There is an obvious possibility that such disagreement may at times be perfectly innocent.

6. Wesley is on much sounder ground here. The charitable limitations regarding sin, laid down in our note to II, 2 (p. 125), have to be stretched rather a long way if they are to cover the case of St. Peter at Antioch. It would, however, be illuminating to have St. Peter's account of the incident.

7–10. Here is a masterly analysis of that fatal process, whereby a man who genuinely knows and loves God may fall, and fall badly, if he does not watch and pray. These paragraphs are stored with guidance for the soul that would walk with God. They merit prayerful as well as studious attention.

9. '*the unquestionable progress from grace to sin.*'

The only comment we would make is that for stage (4) to take place is itself the token of some turning away from 'the faith that works by love'. It is hardly possible to admit that the *full* possession of faith is consistent with some degree of actual inward sin, as distinct from temptation. (This dubious position also seems to be required by paragraph 7.) However, even men of the stamp of David, Barnabas, and Peter, are not in fact constantly in full possession of faith. They are frequently found hovering between stage (3) and stage (4), though because they are also habitually found watching unto prayer they rarely sink to stage (5). They *rarely* sink, but there are unhappy exceptions, which lead to the occasional lapses of the saints.

III. 1. '*Some sin of omission, at least, must necessarily precede the loss of faith.*'

This is unhappily expressed. If Wesley be taken literally, his statement is hard to defend. (See note to II. 9, *supra.*) Furthermore too much is built upon the distinction between 'sins of omission', 'inward sins', and 'outward sins'. Some 'inward sins' are farther along the downward path than some 'outward sins'. One would judge that the first stage of sin, here called sin of omission, or inward sin, is the same as that described as 'negative, inward sin' in II. 7. If this be so, the sin which 'must necessarily precede the loss of faith' is neglect of the means of grace. We thus return to the point made in discussion II. 9. To be found neglecting the means of grace is a token of *some* failing in faith. Nevertheless, a grievous and noticeable loss of faith, such as might possibly entrap an upright man into a serious fault, is only likely to set in *after* a believer has neglected 'to keep himself'.

'ἐξελκόμενοι': the word translated 'drawn away' in James i. 14.

'δελεαζόμενοι': the word translated 'enticed' in the same verse.

*'so that we may commit any outward sin whatever.'*

Some have taken this as indicating that Wesley thought that a single lapse into outward sin carries one back to the condition of the unconverted sinner. This would be a very extreme position. It is preferable to suppose that he intended it as a solemn warning that it is possible for one who is normally a firm believer, in his lapse, to sink not merely to trivial faults, but even to heinous crimes. This is unhappily the truth.

3. This paragraph gives the practical, and most valuable, application of the sermon.

*'prevents':*

i.e., 'anticipates'. (See note to Sermon XII, II, 1, p. 105.)

## Questions

1. A man of strong character and great gifts often displays serious faults of character in other directions, e.g., conceit, intolerance, a domineering spirit inconsiderate of the feelings of the less able, even selfish ambition. A man of colourless personality and trivial achievements may be blameless and harmless. Which is more nearly 'the man after God's own heart'? Where does the character of Jesus fit into the picture?

2. A gifted office-bearer in the Church, hitherto highly respected, shocks everyone by being found in some serious sin. Should he be expelled from office? and from his membership as well? Give reasons. Should the Minister be severe with him, or offer him the mercies of Christ? What practical advice should he offer regarding daily life?

*Sermons Sixteen—Twenty-Eight*

# Upon our Lord's Sermon on the Mount

*Introduction.*

The central section of the Standard Sermons is made up of a set of thirteen expositions of the Sermon on the Mount. The reader is urged not to skip them. Several circumstances conspire to tempt one, when perhaps short of time for study, to give these thirteen sermons a perfunctory reading only, for the mere sake of saying that they have been read, yet no more. For one thing, they do not bear as titles the great doctrines of the Christian faith. This may hint that they are of less importance than the others, and this impression is justified in so far that the reader will not find here many doctrinal points that have not already been raised. In the second place, the great scheme of Justification, Sanctification, Perfection, &c., is associated in the mind with the Epistle to the Romans rather than with the Sermon on the Mount. Surely, one will say, we read Wesley for this grand scheme. Finally, it may be objected, much has been learned since the eighteenth century regarding methods of Biblical interpretation. Wesley is therefore out of date as an expositor of the Gospels, much as we reverence his abiding value as a preacher of the Gospel. It is to be admitted that there is some justice in this last plea. Nevertheless, the temptation to neglect these sermons should be resisted, for they merit attention as fully as any in the volume. Sermon XVIII, certainly, is not excelled by any one of the Forty-Four.

Recent years have heard much of Marx's charge that religion is the opium of the people. The enemies of Christianity have maintained that the Church is only interested in getting men to heaven, and that she is not at heart interested in righting the manifold wrongs of the world below. Indeed, the Church has been represented as a defender of the present order, with its economic and social privileges, and as an enemy of progress, her weapon being the promise of a reward hereafter for those who patiently endure injustice now. Whatever may have unhappily been the case with some branches of the Church, on the Continent and elsewhere, or even with some Methodists, Wesley himself emerges unscathed from this base and damaging attack. We know that the great evangelist was also a pioneer of popular education, a builder of orphanages, a provider of work for the unemployed, and keenly interested in political affairs—being both an ardent patriot, and one who was not afraid on occasion to rebuke the foreign policy of the government. Another token of this is that a third part of the Standard Sermons is taken up with the exposition of the great ethical utterances of the Sermon on the Mount. Here is page after page of most pointed and practical instruction in how the Christian ought to behave. Nor is the advice confined purely to personal problems. Wesley deals faithfully with business and economic affairs as well, though in terms of the simpler conditions of his day. Since the beginning, therefore, these things have held a rightful and prominent place in the Methodist pulpit.

Some preachers of 'the social Gospel', particularly in those years before their over-optimistic enthusiasm was dispelled by the awful spectacle of two savage world-wars in a single generation, have grievously erred in diluting the Christian Gospel to an ethical system. Christianity has been equated with 'the Sermon on the Mount', and by 'the Sermon on the Mount' has been intended the spirit of *These things shall be*'. Such preachers have slurred over the dreadful fact of sin, and that man needs a miracle of divine salvation if he is to rise above selfishness and pride. In expounding our Lord's beautiful words of brotherhood and good-will they have forgotten that the background to all is the tremendous fact of God. No one can accuse Wesley of this error. When he preaches on the Sermon on the Mount the doctrines of sin, of the judgement of God, of the saving work of Christ, and of Justification, Sanctification, and Perfection, are always lurking just round the corner. Indeed, these great themes are at times drawn in, as it were, by the hair of the head. There is more than one passage which would almost make one think that the *real* interest of Wesley in the Sermon on the Mount is to find the Epistle to the Romans in every verse. This would be a distortion of the position, but Wesley's approach is certainly the right one.

Finally, these Sermons should be valued as memorials to Wesley's piety and eloquence. Here are to be found some of the most notable examples of his wonderfully powerful style, systematic, logical, and epigrammatic. Here also a great saint and a passionate evangelist lays bare his heart. Again and again we have to read not with interest only, for our instruction, but with reverence and solemn awe.

*Sermon Sixteen*\*

# Upon our Lord's Sermon on the Mount

### DISCOURSE I

3. '*he takes care to refute . . . all the practical mistakes . . . which should ever arise in the Christian Church.*'

   The Sermon on the Mount certainly speaks to every age. We need not, however, suppose that our Lord had, in the days of His flesh, and when bounded by the limits of a human mind, a supernatural knowledge of later events in the history of the Church.

4. 'Οἱ μαθηταὶ αὐτοῦ': i.e., 'His disciples'.

5. '*many have supposed that other parts concerned only the Apostles, &c.*':
   i.e., the moral standard is too high to be applied to *all* Christians: hence the point of paragraph 4. This is Wesley's doctrine of Christian Perfection.

7. '*but never, besides here, did He give . . . a general view of the whole.*'
   Actually much of the Sermon on the Mount is probably an arrangement made by the Evangelist of disconnected sayings of Jesus preserved by the Church.

8. '*Who is he that lusteth?*'
   'To lust' is here used in the old sense of 'to desire'. See the Prayer-Book Version of Ps. xxxiv. 12.

9. '*It is something more than human, &c.*'
   Wesley is profoundly right here. We should not think of our Lord as One Who went about 'pressing His claims'. His stupendous claims were generally implicit. One of the greatest was that He did not hesitate to treat as subject to His

\* No. 21 in *Fifty-three Sermons*

own authority the Law of Moses, which in that day was regarded as God's supreme word to man.

'Ο ὬΝ': i.e., The Being: the One Who IS.

I. 2. It is possible that Luke vi. 20, 'Blessed are ye poor', is the original form. An attitude most typical of the Old Testament Prophets, those forerunners of the democratic ideal, was that God looks with favour upon the poor. The rich are in mortal spiritual peril. (Amos, Isaiah lxi. 1; lxvi. 2.) Jesus carried on this tradition. The peril of the rich man is that he is tempted to organize his possessions so as to make for himself a position independent of God. (Luke xii. 16–21.) The poor man has only God to trust in. He is therefore 'poor in spirit'.

3. *'the love of money is the root of all evil.'*

For the meaning of this text see the Revised Version of 1 Tim. vi. 10.

*'vows of voluntary poverty.'*

Asceticism, i.e., the laying of great store by celibacy, much fasting, coarseness of dress, poverty, and, in extreme cases, self-torture, springs from the feeling that material things are *in themselves* in some way alien to God. This idea is due to traces of Greek, and still more, of Oriental, pagan thought lingering in the Church.

*'tautology.'*

i.e., saying the same thing twice over in different words.

4. From this point on we have a spiritualizing of the text, but essentially a legitimate one, for it reflects the deepest intention of Jesus.

*'if he tells them'*: i.e., 'if he counts them'.

7. *'This some have monstrously styled "the virtue of humility".'*

This is an unhappy phrase, which goes beyond what is reasonable. Wesley is moved to it by extreme care to emphasize that the *only* ground for salvation is faith, and by fear lest some will hope to earn their salvation by their penitence.

9. Wesley is absolutely right here. 'Humilitas' (from which our word 'humility' is derived) in classical Latin means 'meanness, baseness, abjectness'. Similarly, the Greek ταπεινός, translated 'lowly' or 'humble' in the New Testament, in classical Greek meant 'mean-spirited', 'contemptible'. It was under Christian influence that the words changed in meaning. This change in usage was no accident, but reflects a profound change in thought regarding what is to be admired in human character.

12. The lines are from Charles Wesley. See the former *Methodist Hymn-book* (1904), No. 341.

II. 1. *'this triumphant state does not often continue long.'*
This statement reflects the experience of Wesley, and of many of his converts.

3. *'But He now "hides His face and they are troubled".'*
Wesley says this on the strength of a quotation. He is not to be understood as meaning that God actually *causes* the reaction of darkness that may follow a conversion.

The first quotation is from John Donne's 'Hymn to God the Father', the second from Charles Wesley.

5. John xvi. 19–22 refers, rather, to the departure of Christ and the coming of the Holy Spirit.

## Questions

1. The Sermon on the Mount is binding upon all men. Is this true of the letter of the Sermon, or of the spirit only?

2. A pious old lady is supposed to have prayed in the prayer-meeting: 'O Lord, make our young people miserable!' What do you think of her prayer?

*Sermon Seventeen**

# Upon our Lord's Sermon on the Mount

### DISCOURSE II

1. 2. *'discomposed':*
or, as would more usually be said today, 'upset'.

*'Brute philosophers':*
i.e., philosophers who do not feel. Wesley means the ancient Stoics, who taught that the philosophic man should keep his soul serene and unruffled within, and hold himself aloof from all invasion of desire and emotion, either painful or happy.

*'Apathy.'*
This was the name given to this condition of insensibility to pleasure and pain. The Stoics considered it to be the highest condition of life. To call the doctrine of 'Apathy', which has been professed by some of the noblest of men, 'one of the foulest errors of Heathenism' is quite indefensible. However, it *is* an error of non-Christian thought, at any rate when held in an extreme form. The idea that the body, with its desires, is 'the prison-house of the soul', springs from the same root as asceticism, i.e., from the false notion that the opposite to the spiritual is the material, the material creation being essentially alien to God. This error has at times infected the Church. At the same time, there is more than a germ of truth in the doctrine of 'Apathy', for it is a witness to the fundamental proposition that the man of God will be able to view from the standpoint of eternal spiritual principle every passing event, despite the waves of pain or pleasure that these may bring.

3. *'the affections, which the God of nature never designed should be rooted out by grace.'*
This is the sufficient Christian defence against these tendencies. God is the Creator of the material equally as of the

* No. 22 in *Fifty-three Sermons*

spiritual. Natural emotions and desires are to be controlled to good ends, not distrusted and abolished.

5. *'even the harsher . . . passions are applicable to the noblest purposes.*

This is sound religion, and excellent psychology. Thus the combative instinct, so often used in selfish aggression, is by the Christian to be harnessed to give impetus to the attack upon wrong. This the psychologist calls 'sublimation'.

8. *'to prefer the reading of those copies which omit . . . "without a cause".'*

Many of the best ancient manuscripts contain the word, which is, nevertheless, probably a very early addition to the text. Wesley's observations are admirable.

9. There is no real distinction between the Syriac word 'Raca' as a weaker, and 'thou fool' as a stronger, term of abuse. It is a case of Hebrew poetic parallelism.

*'stoning.' 'burning alive.'*

In the times of our Lord barbarous punishments such as these were by humane custom evaded among the Jews. Thus the Mosaic Law requiring stoning to death was regarded as duly observed if the victim were sent to a speedy end by flinging him from a precipice, provided a stone was then placed upon the body.

'Γαὶ 'Εννόμ.'

Put into English letters these words would read 'Gai Hennom', illustrating the derivation of the word 'Gehenna'. 'Gehenna' is in our New Testament translated 'hell' (but see the Revised Version margin). Gehenna, originally the name of the place where the refuse of Jerusalem was burned, and also being a place of ill-omen through ancient association with barbarous pagan rites, was to our Lord's hearers the common name for the place of punishment for the damned.

11. Matthew v. 25–6 is not a description of God's treatment of the impenitent sinner, with God as the Judge, and Satan the executioner (the latter a quite indefensible supposition). The passage is a parable, a simple story from current life to enforce the prudent maxim: 'Make all haste to settle a grievance out of court if you can.' The moral is: 'Always be reconciled to your brother at once.'

13. This paragraph is apt, though unusual in application. 'Blessed are the gentle, for they shall inherit the earth', is probably much nearer in intention to, 'Blessed are the gentle, it is to them that God will give the reins of power when He sets up His Kingdom', than to the more usual, 'Blessed are the gentle, for they will win through in the end'.


II. 2–6. Here is a beautiful, moving, and profound passage. The goal of religion is not merely that men may find a way to live together conveniently, nor is it the hope of heavenly reward. These two opposite impoverishments of the Gospel are passed by, while Wesley shows that the great promise of religion is that men shall know God, shall be made like Him, and shall hold fellowship with Him now and for ever. Only so can the deepest passion of the soul be satisfied.

5. For the hymn by Charles Wesley whence these lines come, see the end of Sermon XXXV.


III. 1. *'concerned for those who are . . . still dead in trespasses and sins.'*
This is surely narrower than our Lord's intention. The Beatitude speaks of every kind of mercy.

2. Wesley here digresses into a long exposition of 1 Cor. xiii, packed with most admirable and practical advice in manner and conversation.

3. *'coals of fire.'*

An interesting and unusual alternative to the rendering: 'coals of fire'='pangs of remorse.'

6. 'οὐ περπερεύεται.'

These words are accurately rendered by the accustomed 'vaunteth not itself'.

*'the ancient Heathen':* i.e., Seneca.

8. *'A late writer':* Addison.

*'it will necessarily appear in all his intercourse.'*

This was certainly the case with Wesley. The polite world doubtless considered it 'very bad form' that Wesley must look upon every time and place as a possible occasion for evangelism, not the hour of Divine Worship alone, but likewise the companionship of the stage-coach and the inn. Wesley flings back the taunt with a novel definition of good breeding.

10. *'It is not improbable, &c.'* to end.

All this is supposition: see note, Sermon XV, II, 5 (pp. 125 f.)·

*'paroxysm.'*

'παροξυσμός':

the word translated 'sharpness', in English letters would appear as 'paroxusmos'.

11. 'οὐ λογίζεται τὸ κακόν':

translated 'thinketh no evil', might more fully be rendered, 'does not keep accounts regarding evil'.

12. True toleration and public spirit can therefore exist only where there is love.

13. What a happy nation would it be where all politicians rejoiced in this way!

14. The rules (1) to (5) are good. (2) is admirable, most practical, most truly 'Wesleyan'.

17. *'This completes the character of him that is truly merciful.'*

Wesley starts by limiting mercy to spiritual works. He ends by stretching it a long way.

The lines are from Prior's poem, 'Charity'.

18. Who can say after reading this that the Methodists thought only of getting to heaven, and passed by the wrongs of earth as of small account?

*'Babylon the Great.'*

The Protestants of that day commonly interpreted 'Babylon the Great' of Rev. xviii as a reference to the Papacy. Modern scientific exegesis shows that the pagan Rome of Nero is intended.

*'Protestant Churches too know how to persecute, &c.':*

though not all ardent Protestants have been as candid as Wesley.

The main reason why, in more violent ages, Rome has shed more blood is that she has had more power.

## Questions

1. Is the life of Jesus an example of 'Blessed are the meek'?

2. 'What warm defender of any cause is clear of these? But is it not necessary 'to land good and hard' if one is to prevail in controversy for the right? A *moderate* policy may generally be the wiser, but can a *moderate* man ever gain a following?

*Sermon Eighteen*\*

# Upon our Lord's Sermon on the Mount

### Discourse III

I. 4. '*If persons as dear to thee as thy right eye, &c.*'

It is probable that in the thought of the Evangelist 'the eye' and 'the hand' of Matt. v. 29-30 represent impure sexual desire. This is appropriate because desire is excited so largely through sight and touch. If this be accepted, Wesley's 'person dear to thee' may rightly be given a particular application. The possibility remains open, however, that 'the eye' and 'the right hand' may stand for *anything* precious (cf. Ps. cxxxvii. 5: Gal. iv. 15), in which case Wesley's exposition would be too limited.

5. '*saving for the cause of fornication.*'

It is as well to bear in mind that the original saying of Jesus, as preserved in Mark x. 11-12, and as attested by Luke xvi. 18, omits this clause. Jesus enunciated the uncompromising ideal. Here we have the modification necessitated by the imperfection of human affairs. There is bound to be a difference between the standard that the State can *enforce* by legal compulsion upon the citizen, and the much higher ideal standard that the Church solemnly *recommends* to her members. A State which cares for the social good of the people will insist that marriage involves far-reaching social obligations, and is therefore not to be dissolved simply because one or both partners has 'changed his mind'. However, the Church is bound to require of the professing Christian who comes to be married in her holy rites that the solemn vow 'for better for worse . . . till death us do part' be taken *seriously*, because a life-long union is of the essence of Christian marriage. The question whether a divorced person

\* No. 23 in *Fifty-three Sermons*

can rightly be married again in Church is a very difficult one, the more so as divorce is now obtainable on other grounds than adultery. It is not always easy to reconcile the duty of witnessing to the Christian ideal with the parallel duty of ministering to those who in the past may have fallen from that ideal. The marriage of a divorced person in Church ought only to be allowed if it is abundantly clear that he (or she) appreciates and accepts the Christian standard, is penitent for any past lapse, and is now in earnest in the Christian way of life. The Church should surely make it plain that those who do not accept the Christian principle of a life-long union should be content with a civil marriage.

'*by parity of reason, &c.*'

In Christian ethics, as opposed to the confused standards of social convention, there is the same high standard for the man as for the woman.

10. This defence of the propriety of a Christian taking a legal oath has as its background the objection of some Reformation zealots, and later, of the Quakers, to taking any oath, on account of the Lord's saying just referred to. Wesley reproduces the stock arguments of current controversy.

'*He was here reproving . . . common swearing*':

i.e., foul and blasphemous conversation.

The teaching of Jesus, summarized in the previous paragraph, hardly bears this out. Our Lord condemned perjury, legal quibbling as to whether particular forms of oath were binding or no, and, above all, that careless standard of truth which assumes that a simple affirmation is not sufficient. If all men habitually spoke the truth there would be no occasion for oaths. Hence ideally oaths are to be condemned, but in an imperfect world they may be necessary in practice.

11. '*But the great lesson.*'

One lesson indeed, but hardly the great lesson.

II. We have here a beautiful and eloquent section, though based upon a stretching of the significance of 'peace-maker' to something far beyond the obvious and original. It is typical of Wesley that he must strive to find as much as possible of the whole Gospel in each Beatitude.

III. 2. Here are some apt comments from the New Testament upon the Beatitudes.

3. Here is a scathing commentary from Wesley's own experience.

5. *'Just in that manner and measure which the wise Disposer of all sees . . . will tend most to His children's growth.'*

It is a very common opinion among the pious that God 'permits' certain evils to run a course allotted according to a wise plan, and then interposes to vindicate the distressed cause of right. Thus the goodness and the sovereignty of God appear to be vindicated. It is, however, very doubtful whether this pious theory will bear dispassionate examination. It is true that God is the Sovereign Lord, and that anything evil that occurs in His world is in a sense 'permitted'. It does not exist in defiance of His will. The only rational explanation of the continuance of evil, that does justice to the goodness of God, is that He would have children, not slaves; those who will do right because they love so to do, and not because it is the fixed law of their nature. God has thus created man with an independent personality, and with a measure of free will. He so values and respects the personalities He has created that He will not annihilate them if and when they use their powers for evil, and mar His plan. Rather than that He will let them go their own way. His purpose is to suffer with them and for them even to the end, until He freely wins them to Himself. If this be so, it would be just as contrary to God's plan for Him to use His sovereign might to curb wicked men in the later and more extreme phases of their evil course, as it would be to do so at the first beginnings. If, for the sake of His suffering saints, it is not inconsistent with the divine plan for God to interfere with man's free course after he has gone a certain distance in persecution, it is difficult to see why His goodness should not prompt Him to interfere at the beginning. Any theory of God 'permitting' evil, apart from the general principle that He respects the free personalities He has created, makes God morally responsible for such evil as occurs.

'*The ungodly are only a sword of His.*'

It has been said: 'The blood of the martyrs is the seed of the Church.' This has often proved true. *Unsuccessful* persecution, say by ruthless bloodshed carried on inefficiently or intermittently, or by the milder process of social pressure, has often resulted in the establishment of the Church. Such persecution drives half-hearted members from the flock, acts as a witness to the sincerity of the remainder, and wins the sympathy of the fair-minded onlooker. Even as this sermon was being written, this was evidently the case with Methodism. If this were the whole truth one might defend the proposition that persecutors are an instrument used by God for the ultimate good of His cause. It is very doubtful, however, whether this view would seem credible to the unhappy victims of severe persecution. Efficient and sustained persecution does result in the annihilation of good and the enthronement of evil. It would be blasphemy to maintain that the Gestapo was the sword of God.

'*when the pure doctrine of Christ began to be planted again*':

i.e., at the Protestant Reformation.

'*a king, wise and good beyond his years.*" Edward VI.

'*a cry of oppression and wrong, &c.*'

This is the sad and sober truth. Under the hypocritical cloak of zeal for rooting out 'Popish superstition' Edward's Ministers of State swept most of the property of the old Trade Guilds, and of the Schools, into their own pockets, and those of their favourites. This was a shattering blow to the social and cultural life of the nation, which was not mended for three hundred years.

'*the cry of those who even then expired in the flames.*'

There were a few martyrs also in this period.

'*Then He sold them into the hands of their persecutors.*'

The reaction to misgovernment under the banner of 'Protestantism' was the natural welcome given by the nation to Mary, who brought the Roman Catholic party to power again. The resultant persecution showed England that 'though the Protestants did not know how to govern, they knew how to die'. It was the savage spectacle of humble and pious men and women in the flames that won the mass of the nation to the new faith.

6. '*loss of business or employment.*'

This was a common lot for the early Methodist. No hope that the populace would accord him a martyr's crown was there to sustain him in his trials. There are times when to live for Christ is as hard as to die for Him.

12. '*your miserable teachers.*'

See Exod. xxi. 23-5; Lev. xxiv. 20; Deut. xix. 21.

There is a striking and rather quaint contrast in this paragraph. First we have the lofty ideal of love toward enemies, brilliantly symbolized in our Lord's startling paradoxes. This is Wesley's most apt conclusion to the discussion of persecution. Then we step straight from Galilee into the commonsense and comfortable England of the eighteenth century. The lofty ideal is given an exceedingly practical application to the mundane business of 'getting and spending'.

13. '*the children of the devil had added the latter.*'

This is too strong. The addition 'Thou shalt hate thine enemy' does not actually occur in the Old Testament, but there are not a few chapters which answer to the spirit of it. Jesus clearly regarded both parts as together representative of Judaism, at any rate at its more commonplace levels.

IV. Here is a moving peroration to a noble sermon.

'*This is the genuine religion of Jesus Christ!*'

The religion of this sermon is an infinite distance above any merely ethical system. It is the religion of the soul that adores the mystery of love divine. Yet who dare say that it is otherworldly, ineffective in its impact on practical affairs, or absorbed with the bliss of heaven to the exclusion of man's life on earth?

## QUESTIONS

1. Would it be fair to Wesley to say that his real interest is not to expound the Sermon on the Mount, but to preach 'Justification by Faith' and 'Sanctification'? What evidence is there in this sermon?

2. 'They see Him in the firmament of heaven, . . . giving grass for the cattle, . . . upholding all things.' (I. 6.) Why then do not all the astronomers and biologists find that their science speaks to them of God?

3. 'The proud, because he is proud, cannot but persecute the lowly, &c.' (III. 4.) Are differences in character and temperament the main, or even an important, cause of the strife of the world?

4. 'They may put confidence in them; for they know their ways are not like other men's. But still they love them not.' (III. 8.) Is this an uncharitable judgement to pass upon the average worldly man?

5. Why ought the Christian not designedly to bring persecution upon himself? (III. 9.)

6. Is it right for a Church to try to forbid its members availing themselves of the legal provisions for divorce provided by the State?

*Sermon Nineteen**

# Upon our Lord's Sermon on the Mount

### Discourse IV

1. 'ἀπαύγασμα τῆς δόξης αὐτοῦ':
    the phrase translated 'effulgence of his glory' (A.V. 'brightness of his glory'), in Heb. i. 3.

    'χαρακτὴρ τῆς ὑποστάσεως αὐτοῦ':
    translated 'very image of his substance' (A.V. 'express image of his person)', in the same verse.

2. '*These are what damps the vigour of the soul.*'
    The thing which makes the Christian religion arduous, so that 'few there be that find it', is that it is a severely ethical religion. There is a deep-seated instinct in man which craves for satisfaction in religious worship. The ceremonial or emotional side of religion is therefore normally a joy, but 'being good' is hard work. Thus the multitude was glad to observe the two minutes' silence on November 11. This was a corporate act of religious (though not specifically Christian) worship The multitude was perfectly sincere in this. Yet few were prepared to translate their emotions into strong ethical resolve, and to give themselves to practical activity for the healing of the nations. The Roman Church certainly has room in her system for the few who are zealous for God and strict in life, but she also makes wide provision for popular festivals which make no necessary stern demand upon the individual participant. Thus the Church has a greater hold on communal life in the typical Roman Catholic country than in the typical Protestant country. In the typical heathen country *everybody* worships, though that popular worship has little ethical content.

* No. 24 in *Fifty-three Sermons*

3. Wesley is now back to the attack on 'stillness', though from a different angle than in Sermon XII. (See introductory note.) There he shows the error of those who would neglect the outward means of grace, here the error of those who would neglect outward good works, the fruit of religion. The two errors are different aspects of the same thing, the religion that is purely inward.

4. Wesley's severe language is explained by the circumstance that the error of 'stillness' proved seductive to some very zealous converts.

5. '*patient*':
   i.e., 'that which *suffers*'. cf. the phrase 'doing and suffering' in paragraph 2.

I. 2. Hence Charles Wesley's lines:

> 'Not in the tombs we pine to dwell,
> Not in the dark monastic cell,
>   By vows and grates confined.'
>   *Methodist Hymn-book* (1904), No. 599, v. 4.

6. '*complication.*'
   A word now almost always used in an evil sense, but here in a good.

7. Here is a word to those disciples who may at times regret having to mix with 'all sorts' in the office or workshop.

9. Hebrews vi. 4–6 refers to the sin of apostasy, of accepting the Christian way, and then definitely renouncing it. None are harder to recover than these; hence the Apostle's severe verdict, which must not, however, be pressed too literally.

III. 1–8. This section clearly reflects arguments with Moravians at the Fetter Lane Society, controversy with William Law, &c.

## SERMON ON THE MOUNT: IV  149

5. '*It does not at all damp the ardour of his thought.*'

This is sound psychology. The great thing which confirms and deepens an inward impression on the heart and mind is to take the appropriate action demanded by it. Thus, 'no impression without expression' is one of the great maxims of teaching. It is good Gospel too.

'*having only one eye of the soul, which moves round on outward things, and one immovably fixed on God.*'

Here is a strange image indeed, from which a little more sense of humour would have rescued Wesley. It is yet a true image for all that.

For the rest of this hymn by Charles Wesley see the 1904 *Methodist Hymn-book*, No. 587.

7. '*what does it avail to feed and clothe, &c.*'

The first missionaries went abroad because they feared that the heathen world was a cataract of souls pouring into eternal damnation, but they were soon found feeding and clothing, teaching, and healing.

'*If these are changed, God doeth it Himself.*'

It is absolutely true that conversion is the work of God, and that no man can of himself do anything to effect this change in his brother. Yet this circumstance is not to be used as an excuse for neglecting evangelism. God's chosen means of speaking to the sinner is through His servants. That God has chosen this method is not that He could not do it without, but for the blessing of His servants, that their faith and love may grow in expressing it.

8. '*Perhaps it did so for this very reason, because you thought you was accountable for the event.*'

There is a world of sound advice in this, particularly in times when evangelism is difficult. How many disciples have been tempted to doubt whether their faith was a real one because they have not been as successful in evangelism as they had hoped! They have needlessly tormented their souls. How many Churches have been tempted to grow disillusioned about the message they exist to preach, simply because this or that mission has not apparently succeeded.

IV. 3. *'Let there be no darkness or reservedness in your conversation.'*

Rightly or wrongly, Wesley felt that this was the case with the Moravians. In a letter of September, 1738, he asks them: 'Do you not use cunning, guile, or dissimulation in many cases? Are you not of a close, dark, reserved temper and behaviour?'

### QUESTIONS

1. Why is there usually a larger congregation at the Harvest Thanksgiving than at the Covenant Service? Which service does more good to the Church? to the community?

2. 'Christianity is essentially a social religion.' (I. 1.) Does Wesley's statement involve the proposition that there is no true, full, Christianity outside the Church?

3. Can a hermit render any service to God? Does his life make any kind of witness to the world?

4. 'I cannot speak for Christ, not even in private conversation. What I do is to try to preach by a good example.' This plea is sometimes a sincere one, but it may also conceal a subtle and dangerous error. What is that error?

5. 'Social, open, active Christians.' (II. 7.) Is to be a 'social Christian' the same thing as to be 'an open, active Christian'? What light does your answer show on the place of the Church in the Christian life?

6. One objects: 'Does not attending to outward things clog the soul?' (III. 4.) In principle we say 'No'. Nevertheless, is it not possible for a believer, or a Church, to be 'too busy'?

*Sermon Twenty**

# Upon our Lord's Sermon on the Mount

### DISCOURSE V

I. 2. *'But the moral law . . . He did not take away.'*

This distinction between the moral and the ceremonial Law was not known to the Jews. There was to them simply 'the Law', God's word to man, in which were mingled elements of religious ceremony and of morality. In the early centuries the Church found herself in the difficult position of having to vindicate the Old Testament as part of the Christian Scriptures, and herself as the legitimate heir of all the ancient promises of God, and at the same time to justify herself for not observing many rites enjoined in the Old Testament, e.g., circumcision, the rules of unclean food, &c. The argument advanced was that there were two parts to the Law, the moral and the ceremonial. It was taught that Christ confirmed the former, and abolished the latter. This distinction became a recognized element in Christian theology, and is hence used by Wesley here. As a matter of historical fact the theory is unfounded. It nevertheless bears witness to an important truth, namely, that Christianity is continuous with Judaism, new and yet not new, and the heir of all that is good in the old Covenant. In particular, Christianity is a strictly ethical religion, and this tradition of ethical monotheism is the main part of that Christian heritage from Judaism. At the same time, the theory may obscure the circumstance that the Christian does not, like the Jew, live a moral life because certain rules are laid down in the Old Testament, and because he feels an obligation to set himself to keep these rules in the strength of his own resolve. The Christian law is the spirit of Christ dwelling in the heart, prompting in freedom and love to do those things which are well-pleasing to God and helpful to man. This

* No. 25 in *Fifty-three Sermons*

was clearly the position of St. Paul, who, in saying that Christ was the end of the Law, did not make any distinction between one part and another. He founded a strict morality solely but firmly upon the reign of love in the heart. Some acknowledgement of this position is made by Wesley in Sermon XXIX, 1-3, where we read that 'the moral law itself . . . stood on a different foundation from what it did before'.

*'contained in the Ten Commandments.'*

Here is illustrated the difficulty in separating the moral and ceremonial elements of the Mosaic Law. The Ten Commandments are undoubtedly one of the world's great historic statements of the principles of moral conduct. As such they are still a light to the Christian's path, and rightly find a place in Christian worship. Yet even the Ten Commandments contain ceremonial elements, which are not literally obeyed by the Church. For example, the prohibition of graven images, if taken in the original and ancient Jewish sense, would forbid all statuary, religious and otherwise. So, also, the Church does not in fact observe the Jewish Sabbath, from Friday sunset to Saturday sunset, as ordained in the Decalogue. Our Sunday, the anniversary of the Lord's Resurrection, is a similar yet new and distinct custom, based upon the tradition of the Church rather than upon the Fourth Commandment. The Second and Fourth Commandments are just as much part of the ceremonial Law as is the rite of circumcision.

*'Every part of this law must remain in force, . . . as depending . . . on the nature of God.'*

The theory of the moral and ceremonial laws in the Mosaic Law may have to be abandoned. It yet remains that there *is* a moral law, and Wesley here states a most profound truth about it. The moral law is valid because it reflects the moral character of God.

3. *'I am not come to destroy, but to fulfil.'*

Jesus looked upon all that was good and spiritual in the religion of His People, upon the essential Judaism, and saw that He was the natural climax of it all. He was the One who was to bring it to its purposed perfection. He was the One who alone could bring to man the power to live up to those noble standards. Thus our Lord taught that He had come to fulfil the Law.

4. '*a religion . . . as old as the creation.*'

Wesley probably has in mind here the now discarded theory that, before the Fall, Adam and Eve were in a state of mental and moral perfection. Living under 'the Covenant of Works' they were, in fact, perfect Christians. (See notes to Sermons V, I, 1-4, pp. 38 ff.; and VI. 1, pp. 55 f.) However, Wesley's comment remains true in this sense, that God is always the same, so that the principles of right are eternal, and those who have sought God in every age have had communion with the same God. Yet, as Wesley would most strongly have held, Christianity is more than the perfect revelation of what God always is. It is the Gospel of the entry of God Incarnate into the world to work our salvation. It is therefore essentially new, as well as essentially old.


II. 1. '*Shall in no wise pass from the Law.*'

The Greek of this phrase, which Wesley gives, is the strongest form of negative. It has not the force of an imperative.

'*till the consummation of all things*':

i.e., until the day when this age shall pass away, and God's new order for the world shall begin.

2. '*Yea, the very same words, considered in different respects, &c.*'

This distinction which Wesley seeks to uphold reflects his fundamental idea that in the Old Testament there are moral precepts and maxims of piety which are entirely in accordance with the spirit of Christianity, while in Christ there is offered a new power to live according to those precepts and maxims. Man is not left any longer to shoulder the responsibility himself.

## SERMON XX

**III. 1.** '*Whosoever, therefore, shall break one of these least commandments, &c.*'

To confess to perplexity, as some have done, because our Lord did not carry out this rule Himself (e.g., in the matter of ceremonial washing, Sabbath observance, &c.), witnesses to lack of apprehension of the spirit of Jesus. Jesus was not a dull and prosaic schoolmaster, whose language never rose above that of bare common sense, and whose main virtue was systematic thoroughness. He was a prophet and a poet, whose appeal was above all to the imagination. He taught not in catechisms, but in parables, which are to be understood as vivid pictures of profound but simple principles, not as mazes of 'hidden meanings' to be tediously unravelled by means of a clue. His teaching is full of daring paradoxes, of sweeping assertions balanced elsewhere by other and opposite ones. We learn from His words not detailed rules, but a spirit. The present utterance is no more to be taken *literally* than are those concerning the other cheek, and locking the door when praying. The *spirit* of it is: 'The ancient religion of our People, the Hebrews, is wholeheartedly to be reverenced as God's authentic word to man.' Such was certainly an important element in the teaching of Jesus, and was quite consistent with the freedom He showed, and with the new and strange things He dared to say and do. Matt. v. 18, 19, 20, are, in fact, three various and vigorous exemplifications of the general principle laid down in v. 17.

**5–9.** We now come to the heart of the sermon, the real practical point.

**6.** Here is the chief condemnation of many of the Clergy, and of some Dissenting Ministers of the day. A few might be 'sinful ministers', but the besetting sin of the day was 'to live an easy, harmless life'.

**7.** '*the highest rank of the enemies of the Gospel.*'

Enthusiasts for evangelical religion can, if they do not watch their steps, run into the error of supposing that 'spiritual experience' is the whole of religion, and that 'being good' does not matter very much in comparison. Thus they can sink into the gross excess of teaching that Christ came to abolish all moral rules, 'because man is saved by faith alone'. This is the heresy of antinomianism. Wesley was troubled with it at times among the Methodists. We have already seen, in Sermons XII and XIX, how Wesley rebuked the error of 'stillness' that kept appearing among some of the Moravians and Methodists. Antinomianism is the extreme and most disastrous development along the same line. It is the neglect, in favour of a religion entirely composed of inward feelings and thoughts, not only of the means of grace and of Christian service, but also of the decencies of life.

9. This is the great Christian answer to the sin of antinomianism.

IV. 2. '*The Pharisees were a very ancient sect.*'

The Pharisees were actually the 'modern development' of Judaism in the times of our Lord. The Sadducees, or Jerusalem Priests, were the conservatives, who accepted as fully authoritative only the ancient books of the Law. They also rejected the doctrines of the General Resurrection, and of Angels, which were both relatively late developments. (Acts xxiii. 6–8.) The Pharisees upheld the claim of the 'tradition of the elders', which had gradually been developed by the Scribes to explain and expand the Law, so as to adapt its ancient rules to changed conditions. They were actually the cream of the nation, those who took the national religion seriously. They were also the dominant party in the times of Jesus, and enjoyed great prestige. Yet many of them fell grievously into the errors of self-righteousness and externalism, which so easily beset those to whom the sum of religion is to be 'zealous of the law in the minutest points'.

3. '*It is not every man that can say this.*'

Wesley most aptly quotes this parable here, and gives the Pharisee his due. The claim was true, and reflected a standard not easily attained. Yet a man has an utterly wrong spirit when he can stand in the presence of God and *make* the claim.

5. '*an entire fifth of all that they possessed.*'

This would not be possible for long! The tithe was paid on income, not on capital. (See Revised Version of Luke xviii. 12.)

6. It is pleasing to find Wesley so much more just to the Pharisees than many commentators.

7. '*particular*': i.e., 'odd'.

'*Are you not an extortioner? &c.*'

Here is a little window into Wesley's famous rule: 'Gain all you can.' (Sermon XLIV, I, 1–8.) Prices are not to be fixed by the automatic law of supply and demand. Wesley adheres to the ancient and salutary Christian rule that for everything there is a 'just price', to be determined by ethical as well as by economic considerations.

8. '*So our Church clearly . . . enjoins.*' See the table of Fasts in the Prayer Book.

11. '*inward as well as outward obedience.*'

This is the essential point. We need not suppose that the Pharisees did not often obey from the heart. To many of them the keeping of the Law was a delight. Yet, however sincere, the Pharisee had to admit that the outward act enjoined by the Law was the *essential* thing. If the motive were altogether good, so much the better, but it was not *necessary* to raise this issue. The Christian, on the other hand, is absolutely committed to the position that even the most perfect outward performance will not avail before God, unless from the perfect motive. Furthermore, the Christian has a deeper sense than the Pharisee that obedience is not possible apart from a miraculous change of heart worked by God.

## Question

'Love, and do as you like': i.e., the Christian's Law is not a system of fixed, outward commandments, but the free impulse of the heart and mind which is filled with the Spirit of Christ. Is this standard suitable for all Christians, or only for the few, select, spiritual, and intelligent? Is it not safer to give the ordinary crowd of well-meaning simple people in the Church a set of rules, written in black and white, and to say: 'This is the Law of God; obey it'?

## Sermon Twenty-One*

# Upon our Lord's Sermon on the Mount

### Discourse VI

**I. 3.** '*synagogue.*'

The word means, 'a leading, or a coming, together', and so, 'an assembly'. In the New Testament it always refers to the local place of Jewish worship.

The trumpet may be purely figurative, or it may be the ram's horn used at the Synagogue on certain occasions.

**II. 4.** ' μὴ βατταλογήσητε ':

'do not chatter', 'do not be emptily long-winded'.

It is characteristic of much heathen (not Jewish) prayer that it consists of the endless and unthinking repetition of some sacred formula or incantation.

**5.** '*It is not so much to move God . . . as to move yourselves.*'

This is undoubtedly the essence of the matter. We pray so that we may know God, and be made the sort of people He can use in His purposes. Prayer is not a means of harnessing God's power to our schemes. It is the means of harnessing ourselves to God's schemes, and to God's power. We ask for things in prayer not because God will not give unless we ask, but because to ask confirms our attitude of dependence upon God, and also because to pour out all the desires of the heart is the natural impulse of one who knows that God is his loving Father. At the same time, there is a sort of exception to this principle. It is a fact that one human personality can influence another by its state of thought and feeling. This is very obvious

\* No. 26 in *Fifty-three Sermons*

SERMON ON THE MOUNT: VI 159

when men are together in a crowd. An example of this is the 'atmosphere' developed in a religious service. For a man to find himself part of a company engaged in fervent prayer may be for him the actual cause of a change of heart and mind. It would seem that the same thing can happen to some extent when the subjects of the experience are not within sight and sound of one another, though how this can be is at present very mysterious. Thus there is a real possibility that the proverbial mother's prayer for her absent son may have a real effect upon him.

III. 5. 'Πατὴρ ἀνδρῶν τε θεῶν τε.'

'Father of both men and gods.' A common title for Zeus in the Greek poets.

6. *'uncreated night':* a reminiscence of *Paradise Lost*, ii. 150.

'ἀπ' αἰῶνος':

'from the beginning of the age', i.e., 'from the beginning of this whole present order of things'. The translation 'from the beginning of the world' is not incorrect, therefore, though the effect is certainly 'from all eternity'.

7. ' *"the Gods created", a plural noun joined with a verb of the singular number, &c.*'

Wesley here gives the Hebrew name for God, as it appears in the first sentence of Genesis, and observes that this word (Elohim) is plural in grammatical form. The idea that this accident of grammar is a mysterious hint at the Christian doctrine of the Trinity is a very ancient notion, but a purely fanciful one. It is an argument similar to the very usual one which has found the Three Persons of the Godhead in the cry 'Holy, holy, holy', of Isaiah vi. 3. Though Elohim is plural in form it is certainly not intended to be plural in sense, hence it is followed by a singular verb. A rough, though not completely accurate, parallel in English is the use of the word 'oats'. This is a sort of plural in form, though the word 'oat' is not much used, yet it is correct to say 'oats is'.

9. *'only an expression of, or petition for, resignation.'*

Wesley is certainly right in finding more than this in the petition. Most probably it is a parallel to 'Thy kingdom come', which phrase we may render: 'May Thy sovereignty over the earth be established.'

11. *'till the love of many waxed cold.'*

Observe Wesley's explanation of the abandonment of the ancient custom of a daily celebration of the Holy Communion. What would he have said of many modern Methodists? It is hardly likely that our Lord had the sacramental bread in mind when He spoke of 'daily bread', for the Lord's Supper was not yet instituted. Such a thought would, however, be very natural to the ancient Fathers of the Church.

The meaning of the word rendered 'daily' is most obscure, but there is no theory better than the one stated by Wesley.

12. *'All our desert, we own, is hell.'*

In a sense this is true, for there is nothing we can do to establish a claim upon God for His blessing. However, human parents cannot bring a child into the world without thereby assuming a moral obligation to give him wise care and kindly attention, for that child is a living, feeling, thinking person. The same principle undoubtedly holds true with God, if we are to imagine Him as good.

13. *'Our trespasses.'*

This is the Prayer-Book version, and so has passed into general use. The translation 'debts' is more accurate.

*'The word translated "forgive", implies either to forgive a debt, or to unloose a chain.'*

The second idea is not in the text, and is brought to the passage by Wesley. It is, however, a profoundly true idea that release from the power of sin is the natural consequence of release from its guilt. See note to Sermon V, II, 5 (pp. 44 ff.).

14. *'And hath He not yet cast you quick.'*

'Quick' is an old word for 'alive'.

The noble paraphrase on the Lord's Prayer is generally assumed to be by John Wesley himself, for the style is his rather than that of Charles. Part of it occurs in the present *Methodist Hymn-book* as No. 47, part as No. 794.

### QUESTION

What is the value in praying for the health of a friend, or of oneself? Consider the cases of one suffering from a nervous breakdown, of one who has had an operation for appendicitis, and of one who has had a leg off.

*Sermon Twenty-Two**

# Upon our Lord's Sermon on the Mount

### Discourse VII

2. '*good works were the cause, at least the previous condition, of justification.*'

However, Sugden quotes Wesley in the *Minutes of Conference*, 1770, as follows: 'We have received it as a maxim that a man is to do nothing in order to justification. Nothing can be more false. Whoever desires to find favour with God should cease from evil and learn to do well. Whoever repents should do works meet for repentance. And if this is not in order to find favour, what does he do them for? Is not this salvation by works? Not by the *merit* of works, but by works as a *condition.*'

At first sight this may appear like a contradiction by Wesley of one of his fundamental propositions. Actually there is an important distinction in the last sentence of the quotation given above. The *effective cause* of man's forgiveness or justification is the unmerited love of a God who pardons the penitent sinner.

Man does not earn his forgiveness by his 'works meet for repentance'. These works are not the *effective cause* of his acceptance with God. Yet God expects them, and looks upon them with favour, because they are the necessary token that the profession of penitence is indeed sincere. Thus good works 'meet for repentance', e.g., a sincere attempt to make amends for wrongs done to one's neighbour, are in a sense a *previous condition* of justification. Sugden gives an illuminating comparison to illustrate the difference between *effective cause* and *previous condition*. 'It is a condition of the explosion of a charge that the gunpowder should be dry; but we should not usually speak of the dryness as the cause of the explosion.' (I. 450.)

* No. 27 in *Fifty-three Sermons*

I. 2. '*indifferent circumstances*':

i.e., circumstances that do not matter either way, that are not of the essence of the business.

3. '*Tertullian*.

He was a famous Christian writer who lived in Carthage, North Africa, from about A.D. 160 to 240. He is celebrated as the one who first coined the formula 'Three Persons, One Substance', to express the idea of the Christian Trinity. He strongly held that to be a Christian required an austere manner of life.

6. '*Epiphanius.*'

He was born about A.D. 310–320, and lived until 403. He became Bishop of Salamis, in Cyprus, and was famous as a zealot for strict orthodoxy.

'*The annual fasts in our Church.*'

See the table at the beginning of the Prayer Book. This time-table reflects the custom of the medieval Church. In more recent centuries fasting has been so little in vogue as a means of grace among Protestants that only an exceptionally strict and traditionalist Anglican would be found seriously attempting to observe all these fasts. We remember, however, that the Wesleys and other Oxford Methodists were just such strict traditionalists. Indeed, this whole sermon answers to the life of 'Oxford Methodism' (The Holy Club), rather than to the Methodism that has gone out to the world.

II. 6. '*and sometimes to rap them up.*'

'To rap' means 'to snatch up and carry away'. A lingering usage of this old verb is the phrase 'rapt attention'.

10. Matthew xvii. 19. The words 'and fasting' are shown by the manuscripts to be of doubtful authenticity.

12. This paragraph presses logic too far. Our Lord lived among people who were in the custom of fasting, and gave them advice

regarding that custom. This hardly involves universal and positive instruction to fast. He did not rebuke their custom, nor have we any real evidence for supposing that He did not observe the chief Jewish fasts. In general Jesus behaved as a pious Jew. He fasted on occasion Himself, though it would not seem that He laid much store by regular or ceremonial fasting. Certainly the disciples, and so presumably their Master, did not keep the frequent fasts of the Pharisees. Thus the Christian who does fast can claim some mandate from His Lord, but hardly a definite commandment.

## Questions

1. 'Fasting is ... an help to prayer.' (II. 6.) Is this true in experience? Do you know anyone who has tried?

2. Why should the 'Catholic' have had much to say about abstinence from food as profitable to religion, but relatively little about abstinence from 'worldly amusements', while the Protestant has often regarded avoidance of dancing, card-playing, the theatre, &c., as necessary to piety, while having little to say about indulgence in food?

3. 'Many of those who now fear God are deeply sensible how often they have sinned against Him, by the abuse of these lawful things.... They abstain, as far as is possible.' (II. 3.) Is this a sufficient reason for our teaching that total abstinence from alcoholic drink is the best standard for a Methodist?

4. Fasting is valuable as the means of breaking an undue dependence upon the merely material. Is not then the man who abandons his hope of professional or economic advance so as to take up Christian work, or who jeopardizes his business or forgoes doubtful profits so that he may fight against social wrong, the one who most truly fasts?

5. Consider II. 7, 8, 9. Is a modern preacher justified in trying to draw practical and detailed guidance for the Christian life to-day from Old Testament stories such as these?

*Sermon Twenty-Three*\*

# Upon our Lord's Sermon on the Mount

### DISCOURSE VIII

1. The long quotation in this paragraph is from William Law's *Serious Call to a Devout and Holy Life*, chap. iv, though Wesley is not very exact in his citation. The *Serious Call* is, despite its forbidding title, a very interesting book, which should be read by all who would understand the times of Wesley.

2-8. '*The eye of the soul is then said to be single, when it looks at one thing only.*'

'Single' rather means 'sound', 'undiseased', and 'evil' means 'diseased', though Wesley's treatment is very effective and edifying.

9. Wesley's observations on the morality of primitive peoples are most interesting. The present sentiments are hardly to be taken as his serious opinion, for he writes in bitter irony. Natural reaction to the vices and artificialities of polite society gave rise in some quarters (e.g., among the forerunners of the French Revolution), to the theory of 'the noble savage'. This was the illusion that the unpolished are also the virtuous. Wesley seems to have gone to America with some inclination to this view. His *Journal* for June 30, 1736, reads: 'I hoped a door was opened for going up immediately to the Choctaws, the least polished, that is, the least corrupted, of all the Indian nations.' That later experience disillusioned him we find from the *Journal* for July 9, 1737, and Dec. 2, 1737 (21-28). These passages should be read as the commentary upon the present paragraph. The failings in sobriety, humility, and charity, of the savage tribes are here made an instrument to flay European civilization. However, Wesley does seem to be largely serious

\* No. 28 in *Fifty-three Sermons*

when he passes on to the subject of the unconscious obedience of the American Indians to the commandment, 'lay not up for yourselves treasures upon earth'. The comparative morality of civilized and uncivilized races presents many problems, and there was little in Wesley's mental background to help him solve them. For example, a primitive tribe may have barbarous marriage customs, and yet the bonds prescribed by those customs may invariably be honoured. A Christian nation has nobler customs, which are yet often broken. It is, however, impossible to deny that the latter is the higher state of development. When the two cultures come into contact the main obvious result is at first frequently a disastrous collapse of the old morality among the simple people, leaving nothing in its place. It would not however be right on this account to try to leave those people for ever in their primitive ignorance. Again, so long as the African seriously believes in his fetishes the vegetable-gardens protected by them will be secure. With the best of intentions the European destroys that superstition, and thieving often starts. This is the growing-pain toward a higher and freer morality. The path must be trodden, though it is beset with pitfalls. This should remind us of the solemn moral obligation of the higher races not to thrust their civilization indiscriminately upon the lower by ruthless commercial exploitation, and to be careful to take the Christian religion to them as well as mines and cinemas. To return to Wesley's point: it is a fact that many tribes, living on a communal basis, and producing only for their subsistence, are splendidly free from our lamented entangling chains of commercialism, with all the economic insecurity and social cleavage produced thereby. As Wesley observes, many of the heathen are largely free from the false and materialistic standards so strictly exposed in the latter part of the paragraph. That primitive societies also have their excellences should teach more fortunate nations a salutary lesson of humility, and of respect for the rights of others.

*'They were bred up by their Christian parents . . . to break it as soon and as much as they could.'*

This is the condemnation of the 'acquisitive society'.

## SERMON ON THE MOUNT: VIII

11. *'provide things honest in the sight of all men.'*

   The word 'honest' has changed in connotation since the translation of the Bible. It there means 'honourable' in the broad sense of the word, not just 'paying twenty shillings in the pound'. (See Revised Version.) What Wesley says is very sound and good. For a fuller account of his views, see Sermon XLIV.

12. Wesley has a right to say this, for he himself abundantly lived up to it.

13. *'the open, speculative Heathens.'*

   Wesley probably here means the Greek and Roman philosophers, rather than the 'Heathen' he has just been writing of, though the point is not clear.

15. All this is very sensible, and very important. The poor, as well as the rich, can set their heart upon the things of earth. The rich as well as the poor, can have treasure in heaven.

16. A perfect example of Wesley's eloquence in denunciation.

18. *'the cloud-topt palaces.'*

   This is doubtless a reminiscence of Shakespeare, *The Tempest*, IV, i. 152: 'The cloud-capt towers, the gorgeous palaces.'

   *'the poor Heathen,'* i.e., Horace.

   The quotation is from his *Epistles*, i. 2. 52. Sugden translates as follows the lines, together with the previous one. 'When a man is under the bondage of desire or fear, his house and his property give him just as much pleasure as pictures to one with sore eyes, or poultices to the martyr to gout, or the music of the lyre to a sufferer from ear-ache.'

19. A magnificent statement of a solemn theme beloved of moralists.

'*Linquenda tellus, &c.*'

These lines are also from Horace, *Odes*, ii. 14. 21. Gladstone translates:

> Earth, home, and winsome wife, thy fate
> Will have thee leave; and not one tree
> Of all, save cypress that we hate,
> O, transient lord, shall follow thee.

20. '*To my new courts, &c.*' From Prior's *Solomon*, II, 53.

'*Amidst our plenty, &c.*' From the Moral to Prior's *Ladle*, 162.

23. 24. The long quotation is from Law's *Serious Call*, CLI, vi.

25. Excusing and defending themselves multitudes have asked: 'Is it not lawful for me to do what I will with mine own?' The Christian answer is: 'These things are not your own. You, with all your powers to work and to gain, belong to God. You are His steward, and you are under a moral obligation to use all your talents and possessions in His service.' There is no 'self-made man'.

26. '*This is the part of a "faithful and wise steward", &c.*'

Wesley here moves into a sphere of economic thought remote from the present day. The issue today is between those who would defend the moral right of the able to amass a fortune according to his ability, and those who would seek to reduce by social legislation any great difference in wealth between one man and another. Wesley is on neither side. He assumes that there is nothing inherently improper in the existence of rich and poor side by side. He also assumes that this difference in estate is not caused simply by the accident that some are more fortunate than others in opportunity and ability. It is ordained by God. A religious man is therefore to continue in the 'proper station' to which God calls him, acting as a steward. He is not called upon to dispose of his possessions, but neither is he to desire to increase them, so as to 'rise in the world'. (See also introduction to Sermon XLIV.)

28. Note that Wesley departs from his usual custom, in that there are no sub-divisions to this sermon.

'*willing "to communicate"*': i.e., willing to share with others.

'*none said that anything was his own, but they had all things common.*' (Acts. iv. 32.)

The first disciples were not Christian Communists in the modern sense. All that is intended is that they were liberal in charity toward one another.

'*No fair occasion, &c.*'

These lines are from a poem by Samuel Wesley, John's elder brother. For the whole poem, see the beginning of Wesley's *Journal*.

## Sermon Twenty-Four\*

# Upon our Lord's Sermon on the Mount

### Discourse IX

4. '*Mammon was the name of one of the heathen gods.*'

This is incorrect. The word was first used by the Jews as a name for money, and was later personified.

12. '*he cannot comfortably serve both.*'

Wesley has traversed familiar ground. He now comes to a very typical application, strikingly epigrammatic, original, and profoundly true.

15. '*Take no thought for your life.*'

The intention of the Greek, and of the translators of the Authorized Version, is better represented by the Revised, 'Be not anxious.' Wesley expounds in this sense (16).

21. Romans x. 3 will hardly bear this construction. The contrast is not the general evangelical one between inward and outward religion. It is the definite historical contrast between 'the righteousness of God', i.e., the new, Christian way of salvation and 'the righteousness of the law', i.e., the old, traditional Jewish way.

'*It is finished!*'

We can only speculate as to the meaning of the awful cry from the Cross. Reverent reserve is most necessary. The most natural sense is, perhaps, that the course of suffering upon which our Lord had set Himself was now fully run.

\* No. 29 in *Fifty-three Sermons*

*'put an end to the law . . . of external rites and ceremonies.'*

That Christ has brought to an end the religion of Law is more obvious in the case of rites and ceremonies. The same thing is true in principle, however, with those commandments of the Mosaic Law which relate to moral conduct. These remain of value as guidance to the soul, but the Christian does not set out to establish himself in favour with God by his own efforts in obedience to them.

23. *'and all these things shall be added unto you.'*

This is another example of a saying of our Lord which is the powerful enforcement of a profound principle by means of an astounding paradox. The appeal is not to common sense, but to the imagination. Thus we mislead ourselves if we try to take it literally. Unhappy experience shows that those who fix their whole heart upon God do not necessarily and invariably find that 'all things needful for the body' come to them. Our Lord Himself might almost be cited as an example to the contrary.

25. *'The jealous God, in the wise course of His providence, frequently suffers this.'*

We can hardly suppose that God at times takes special action to punish the worldly-minded with worldly calamity. If it is consistent with His plan to interfere in this way with the affairs of men on certain occasions, it is hard to understand why He should permit the continuation of the most harmful cases of evil men enjoying the prestige and power of worldly prosperity.

26. *'How easily we are carried away, in a kind of waking dream, &c.'*

Here we see Wesley both as a sound psychologist, and as a wise pastor who well knows 'what is in man'.

*'Do not believe thyself. Thou wilt not do it then, unless thou doest it now.'*

This is plain and salutary advice for every preacher. Take it to heart!

28. '*Live thou today*':

    and also, 'never be triflingly employed' (first Rule of a Helper).

Live as in the light of eternity, but keep your eye fixed upon the present and its actions, rather than upon the future and its dreams.

*Sermon Twenty-Five**

# Upon our Lord's Sermon on the Mount

## Discourse X

6-7. In applying 'Judge not, that ye be not judged', Wesley plainly has in mind the condescension and gibes of the detractors of Methodism, and very hard he hits.

8-12. Wesley is very practical in application here, and he puts his standard very high. There would be few quarrels in the Church if these rules were more observed.

13. This saying has been attributed by some to Seneca.

14. *'tell it unto the Church'*: i.e., to the *assembly*.

    Jesus had the Jewish Synagogue in mind, not the Christian Church.

15. Wesley is perhaps a little too ingenious in trying to find a direct connexion between Matt. vii. 5 and 6. He yet gives some good advice, doubtless born of experience. The best commentary upon this rather difficult text is perhaps the example of Jesus Himself. He gave all men a stirring summons, but if they would not heed he was content to leave them to go their own way. He would not thrust Himself upon men. This course was the mark of His respect for personality.

16. It is a dreadful fact that to face the pointed appeal of the Gospel, and stubbornly to reject it, leaves a man worse than before. There is therefore an occasion for refraining from 'getting at' a man. Yet with this, the servant of the Lord must watch himself lest he make a mere excuse for not speaking when he should. The unbeliever in a congregation is in a

* No. 30 in *Fifty-three Sermons*

different position. The appeal of the Gospel to a particular individual is then less pointed. If a man is careless the message goes 'like water off a duck's back'. There is less risk of hardening him.

*'talk with them in their own manner, and upon their own principles.'*

If a man is in such a condition that it does more harm than good to speak of repentance for sin, and of the grace of God in Christ Jesus, it may be possible to reason with him regarding the ruin that may come to home and health and job through careless moral habits. He may also be open to the appeal that upright individuals are necessary if there is to be a better social order. Thus the way may be paved for the Gospel appeal on another occasion.

*'the rational, honourable, and unjust Epicure . . . Felix.'*

This collection of epithets may appear puzzling. By 'rational' Wesley presumably means that Felix prided himself upon his common sense, which may have been the case. By 'honourable' he must mean 'of high rank', for Felix was not honourable in any other sense. By 'Epicure' Wesley may intend that Felix was an Epicurean philosopher, which would be much more than his due. He may intend the lower sense of 'a person devoted to sensual pleasure', which would perhaps be more just. Felix was certainly 'unjust'.

17. *'inconvenience'!*

    i.e., 'misfortune'. The word was stronger then than now.

22. *'the heathen Emperor.'* Alexander Severus (A.D. 222–235).

*Sermon Twenty-Six*\*

# Upon our Lord's Sermon on the Mount

## DISCOURSE XI

1. '*Enter ye in . . . at the strait gate.*'

It is sometimes forgotten that 'strait' is an old word for 'narrow', and has nothing to do with 'straight'. We have the word in 'The Straits of Dover'.

I. 5. '*the generality of every age and sex . . . are walking in the way of destruction.*'

This grim paragraph, together with I. 6 and II. 2–4, well illustrates the difficulty which some have felt concerning the traditional doctrine of the eternal damnation of unbelievers It is playing with words to say that the majority of ordinary people are believers. We must at all costs adhere to Wesley's strict standard, as here laid down, of what constitutes sin. Thus Wesley's judgement of his age is to be upheld, and is still substantially true today, though our society is less degenerate. Yet the thoughtful man will shrink from drawing the awful conclusion, which Wesley does here, that all who are not Christians indeed, genuinely converted, and with a real experience of saving faith, are on the high road to hell. That great majority of our neighbours which continues to live with many human failings (i.e., *sins*), unconquered, and who in their better moments only rise to the level of 'seeking to establish their own righteousness', are nevertheless for the most part 'decent people', very generally lovable, and with many possibilities of good in them. The Lord, who warned all these that they were on 'the broad way', yet loved them, and counted them His friends. A kindly instinct wells up in the heart of those who go to comfort the bereaved, which unless one's

\* No. 31 in *Fifty-three Sermons*

mouth is stopped by the memory of open and grievous faults, prompts the assurance that all is well with the dear departed, even though he was not a *Christian*. That assurance turns the work of Christ into an irrelevance in human affairs, yet it has so much to defend it. Surely death will bring to 'the generality of every age and sex' not eternal damnation, but stern discipline, and the hope of better things if they respond aright to the awful and searching experience of meeting face to face that God with whom they have so long trifled. This would seem to be the true way to make necessary modification of the unbending sternness of Wesley's statement.

II. 1. '*securely*': i.e., 'without anxiety'.

6–8. Here is reflected, as in a mirror, the bitter prejudice and opposition encountered by the prophets of strange and wonderful truths.

9–10. Here, likewise, is the portrait of a Methodist, as he was seen by the world. There was, however, at least one Methodist of whom it was *not* true to say: 'They are not able to reason either strongly or clearly.'

III. 1. '*strive as in an agony*.'

The point of this rendering is seen when we remember that the verb translated 'strive' in Luke xiii. 24 would in English letters be written 'agonizo'. The meaning actually is 'strive as an athlete strives in a contest'.

2. '*for* ἄρξησθε ("ye begin") *seems to be only an elegant expletive.*'

This is incorrect. The word 'begin' is to be given its full meaning. As Sugden observes, 'it implies the inception of a plan that is never consummated; the plea and effort of these people is cut short by the answer they receive from the lord of the house.' (I, 540.)

4. *'you must be singular, or be damned!'*
   This phrase became a Methodist proverb.

6. *'Abstain from all appearance of evil':*
   i.e., 'abstain from every species of evil'.

*Sermon Twenty-Seven**

# Upon our Lord's Sermon on the Mount

Discourse XII

I. 2. *'prophets . . . are . . . not those who foretell things to come, but those who speak in the name of God.'*

This is a sound point, though often forgotten. A right understanding of the prophetical books of the Old Testament shows that they do not forecast future events in detail. The prophets spoke to their own day, and of events of their own time. Where they do deal with the future it is in *general* terms only, the theme being, 'God rules the world; therefore, those who trust and obey Him will be wonderfully carried through all the vicissitudes of life, to the accomplishment of His purpose; those who disobey Him will work their own ultimate ruin.' It is important to remember that this principle holds also in the case of apocalyptical prophecy, e.g., the latter half of Daniel. The Church early began to apply secondary meanings to many Old Testament passages, and in particular, to read them as forecasts of events in the life of Christ. An early and most striking example of this process is recorded in Acts viii. 26–40. The process was naturally stimulated by the frequent ignorance of the Church in bygone days concerning the original and historical meaning of much of the prophetical writings. Here was a way to 'make sense' of them. These secondary applications are frequently so apt, and so spiritually beautiful, that they are abundantly justified from the point of view of piety, though not of historical scholarship. A prophet is an *inspired* preacher, as distinct from a well-meaning person who merely repeats what he has learned from others. He is a preacher with a new message for a new age, a message wonderful and compelling and manifestly straight from God. The incorrect usage is illustrated in the phrase: 'So-and-so is a good weather-

* No. 32 in *Fifty-three Sermons*

prophet'; the correct in the statement: 'Wesley is the prophet of Methodism.'

II. 5. *'They should be very sorry to see one who means so well, hurried into any extreme, &c.'*
We overhear some eighteenth-century clergyman, a thoroughly well-intentioned and honourable gentleman, yet one who has no real conception of the religion of the heart, expostulating with a Methodist.

III. 2. *'What are the fruits of their doctrine as to themselves?'*
It is not always easy to apply this rule. The background of this sermon is clearly the position of the Methodist Society in its original condition as a community forming an integral part of the Church of England. The guidance is intended for the Methodist who, attending his Parish Church, finds that his Parish Priest is (i) of an unworthy manner of life, or (ii) erroneous in doctrine, or strongly opposed to the particular doctrinal emphasis of Methodism. The burning problem was provided by case (ii). The real condemnation of the religious life of Wesley's time was not so much that there was a certain number of thoroughly black sheep in the fold, though this was unhappily the case. It was that religion had very widely sunk to a cold respectability. Multitudes of parsons hardly realized that their office was to lead men into communion with God. They thought of themselves as upholders of conventional morality, of social decency, and of patriotic virtue. Many a bitter opponent of Methodism was personally of an upright character, and according to his lights, faithful in his ministerial duties.

3. There is difficulty here also. Many a man has been soundly converted by a preacher who has later been exposed as a man seriously compromised in his private life and character. The blessing has come from the sound doctrine, not from the false

man. However, the words of our Lord are certainly the plain and general rule, and the main substance of Wesley's sermon is good advice.

6–9. Here we come to the practical point of the sermon, in those days a matter of pressing importance.

6. *'For many years I have been almost afraid to speak, &c.'*

Wesley's candour does him great credit. He shows himself as one who dearly loves and loyally cleaves to the Church that he judges. This should be the attitude of every reformer. Here are happily united broad sympathies and zeal, qualities all too often sadly disjoined.

*'The Scribes and Pharisees sit in Moses' seat.'*

Rightly understood, this text is most apposite. Our Lord plainly regarded the Jewish nation as the People of God, and cherished His place in the community. He loved to join in their worship, though He can never have listened to a Rabbi who was not infinitely His spiritual inferior. In spirit He was loyal to the ordinances of the Jewish religion, for all His freedom in dealing with details. All this is a mark that Jesus looked with faith and affection to the ideal, the pure and spiritual Israel, as the true and essential Israel, even while He flayed in words that will never be forgotten all that was base and unworthy in the nation round about Him. The present text, together with such as 'Think not that I came to destroy the law or the prophets', &c., plainly answers to this attitude. Our Lord's example is the Christian's guidance in those trying situations which are bound to arise in the life of him who is more zealous for truth and right than his fellow-worshippers. Wesley in his day faced the same issue as Jesus, and here shows forth some of the virtues perfectly displayed in his Lord.

8. *'the validity of the ordinance does not depend on the goodness of him that administers, &c.'*

Certainly the universal Church is right in this teaching. *No one* is 'good enough' to lead the people in the celebration of the central act of Christian worship. The Holy Communion administered by an unworthy celebrant is in principle a means of grace still. It should be found so in fact by those who have a faith robust enough to look behind the offence of the minister to the faithfulness of the Lord's promise. However, it is clearly most unhealthy for the Church that the offence should be there. The unworthy minister should therefore certainly be prevented from functioning.

*'experimentally':* i.e., 'in experience'.

*Sermon Twenty-Eight**

# Upon our Lord's Sermon on the Mount

### Discourse XIII

I. 1–5. This section briefly covers the same ground as Sermon II, 'The Almost Christian'. The reader may well feel that Wesley stretches too far his description of him who has built his house upon the sand. He includes some people to whom it is hard to deny the name of a genuine Christian. The same was seen in Sermon II. All is made plain if it is kept firmly in mind that Wesley is taking the greatest of pains, even to the point of overstatement, to place it beyond cavil that no man, however sincerely good, is a Christian unless all his goodness flows from a profound experience of faith in Christ.

Notice the modest and gracious spirit of the last sentence of paragraph I, 1. This will have been an addition made when the sermon was prepared for publication.

II. 2. Here is a philosophy of life in a nut-shell.

*'this is the end of man, to glorify Him who made him for Himself.'*

This is a reference to the profound and inspiring opening to the Shorter Catechism of the Westminster Assembly, one of Presbyterianism's great words to the world. The first answer in the Catechism is: 'Man's chief end is to glorify God and to enjoy Him for ever.'

III. We are now back again on the theme of the 'Almost Christian'

1. *'right opinions, which, by a gross abuse of words, I have called faith.*

Wesley does well to say this. From the earliest times the Church has been conscious that one inherent part of her way

* No. 33 in *Fifty-three Sermons*

of life is a certain body of opinion about God and Christ. It was therefore quite natural that the phrase 'the faith' should come to be attached to these opinions. Thus it is deeply entrenched in Christian tradition that 'the faith' means 'sound belief about God, the Lord Christ, man, salvation, &c.' This usage cannot now be expelled, though it is an unfortunate one. Confusion between 'faith' and 'the faith' has been the occasion for multitudes to suppose that it is the teaching of the Church that man is saved by orthodoxy.

2. '*it is the least part of the religion of Christ.*'

This may seem an over-statement, but it is true in principle. The Christian experience is not simply a *means* to an end, the *end* being good conduct from a sincere motive. Man's 'chief end' is not merely 'to be good', but 'to glorify God and to enjoy Him for ever'. 'Being good' is an inherent and necessary part of true religion because one who is the child of God *must* show the fruits of it. Thus sincere goodness must *always* be a part of the religion of Christ, but not the *greatest* part.

4. '*Then go and learn what thou hast so often taught.*'

This may seem a paradox, but many preachers would testify to its truth. There was a day in Wesley's own life when he needed this advice himself. 'Immediately it struck into my mind, "Leave off preaching. How can you preach to others, who have not faith yourself?" I asked Böhler whether he thought I should leave off or not. He answered, "By no means." I asked, "But what can I preach?" He said, "Preach faith *till* you have it; and then, *because* you have it, you *will* preach faith." ' (*Journal*, March 4, 1738.)

*Sermon Twenty-Nine*\*

# The Original, Nature, Property, and Use of the Law

THIS sermon covers, though in a more systematic and detailed way, ground already traversed in Sermon XX. The two following sermons also have a similar theme, namely, to show that the Gospel contains and enforces the principle of moral law. That four sermons are devoted to this topic, as well as Sermon XII to the kindred subject of the place of the means of grace in the Christian life, well shows the great importance Wesley attached to this matter. Against the excesses of 'stillness' (see introductory note to Sermon XII), and of antinomianism (see note to Sermon XX, III, 7, pp. 154 f.), Wesley felt himself under strong controversial necessity to assert that an upright character, good conduct, and the diligent cultivation of the practical devotional life, are inherent parts of the Christian way.

To most modern Christians this proposition may seem so obvious as hardly to need defence. This is because religion today is not usually in a state of revivalistic fervour. It is just at those times of outstanding 'revival', when evangelical religion shows its greatest glories, and when souls are in transports of enthusiasm for the converting power of the Gospel, that the temptation chiefly presents itself to fix the eye *exclusively* upon the joy and peace of an 'experience'. Without meaning any harm, believers can allow the practical accompaniments of faith to sink into obscurity. Any preacher who finds that God blesses him with conspicuous success in evangelistic work should be on his guard against this subtle temptation, for it can still make itself felt today. He should be advised by Wesley to give an adequate and emphatic place in his preaching to the claims of the Church, and of an upright and socially useful life.

\* No. 34 in *Fifty-three Sermons*

2. *'What! the law of Rome only, or the ceremonial law? No, surely; but the moral law.'*

In the present text St. Paul is certainly writing of the Mosaic Law, and not of the legal system of Rome. For the supposed distinction between the moral and ceremonial law in the Law of Moses, see Sermon XX, I, 2. We cannot uphold this sharp distinction, but it is important to realize that the essential argument of this Sermon is not overturned thereby. St. Paul taught that in the Gospel the whole system of legal religion, moral and ceremonial, is done away. Man is not called to justify himself in the sight of God by his own effort in obedience to God's commands. The moral life of the Christian is the fruit of the Spirit working in the heart. Thus to the Christian the foundation of morality is not any system of fixed, external, moral commandments, but the free and spontaneous impulse of a heart filled with the love of God. Nevertheless, the heart needs to be guided and enlightened on that free course by knowledge as to what are the demands of a moral life. The discoveries of all those, of every age and place, who have sought for right and truth have their place in this education. Next to the character and words of Christ Himself the loftiest passages of the Old Testament, and of the Christian Apostles, certainly have pride of place among these educators. However, this free principle of Christian morality by no means does away with the tremendous fact that there is a moral law binding upon all men of every age and circumstance. This eternal law of right is, as Wesley observes, nothing less than the reflection of God's eternal character, mirrored in the soul of man. The relation of the Gospel to this moral law is, firstly, that many have had some knowledge of the moral law, and a few much knowledge, but only in Christ is that law seen to perfection; and secondly, that in Christ God offers to man power to obey that law, which obedience is above even the noblest of men apart from Christ.

*'the flesh ... that is, of corrupt nature.'*

See Sermon VIII, I, 2, with note, p. 69.

3. *'the moral law itself . . . stood on a different foundation from what it did before.'*

Before the advent of Christ man had to obey the moral law by his own effort. This was moral and legal religion. In Christ man obeys by the grace of God. This is moral religion still, but not legal religion. St. Paul described this change as the end of the Law. Wesley has the same intention in mind, but prefers to speak of placing the moral law on a different foundation, because he wishes to make it abundantly plain that the Gospel requires strict morality.

I. 1. Wesley is on sound ground here. God, being good, must have declared His moral law, to the degree in which it could be understood, to every imaginable thinking being capable of morality. Whether thought travels back to the Patriarchs of Bible story, or to the angels of heaven, this principle still holds good.

2. It is interesting to observe that Wesley regarded even the angels, who have never needed redemption, as capable of moral development. This is an unusual but profound thought. That moral agents have to grow in grace is not simply the consequence of a fall into sin. It is also the consequence of God's plan that the perfection found in one stage of development, in the seed or in the child, should gradually give place to the perfection found in another stage, in the flower or in the man. This plan runs through all creation.

4. This paragraph presupposes the theory of the Original Righteousness of Adam and Eve.

*'being reconciled to man.'*

The New Testament describes man as reconciled to God, but never God as reconciled to man.

II. 2. By 'the law' in the present text St. Paul means the whole Mosaic system, moral and ceremonial, but it is obvious from the chapter that he mainly has in mind the moral commandments. There are two sides to St. Paul's teaching regarding the Law of Moses. Including the ceremonial commandments, the Law was from God, and therefore in principle 'holy, and just, and good'. Nevertheless, the Law was inadequate to keep man from sin, for the restraint even of a righteous law produced only rebellion in sinful hearts. In practical outworking, therefore, the religion of the Law was a part of man's bondage.

3. *'the streaming forth . . . of His glory.'*

For this, see the first part of Hebrews i. 3.

4. *'the ancient Heathen.'*

Wesley here gives a reminiscence of Plato, *Phaedrus*, 250, D

III. 4. *'the Apostle, speaking in the person of one who was convinced of sin, &c.'*

St. Paul is speaking of his actual self. The moving passage, Romans vii. 7–25, is a piece of idealized autobiography. In the first half of v. 9 the Apostle refers to his own happy days of early childhood, before he was old enough to be bound by the Law, in the second part to the time when he came of age under the Law. In vv. 7, 8, 10, 11, his bitter reflection is that the stern prohibitions of God's righteous Law stirred up his sinful heart to perverse rebellion. He then goes on to describe his tragic position as a man morally impotent, a divided self, tormented by unfulfilled aspirations, borne down by guilt and self-despising. From this impasse Christ had delivered him. These experiences explain St. Paul's attitude to the Mosaic Law.

*'Sin, taking occasion by the commandment':*

or, as it might well be rendered. 'Sin, making the commandment a strategic base of operations.'

It is important to remember that St. Paul blames himself, and not God's holy law, for this tragic effect (vv. 12–14).

## SERMON XXIX

5. *'essential or accidental.'*

   An 'essential' is that without which a thing would not be what it is. An 'accidental' is something connected with a thing, which is yet not an essential. See note to Sermon I, III. 3, pp. 7 f.

6. *'curious'*: i.e., interesting as a matter of speculation.

7. Wesley's answer is sound so far as it goes. The statement that a thing is right because God wills it is correct in principle, but open to the possible misunderstanding that God is an arbitrary tyrant. This misunderstanding is prevented if one prefers to say that God wills a thing because it is right. However, one must not speak as though God were bound by some necessity outside Himself.

9. *'a considerate person'*: i.e., 'a person who stops to consider'.

IV. 1. This paragraph reflects Wesley's own experience as a believer, and as an evangelist. The way to reception of the Gospel was opened by a knowledge of the strictness of God's moral demands, a sense of the awful fate laid up for those who did not fulfil them, and a realization that apart from Christ God's demands could not be met.

2. *'I give up every plea beside, &c.'*

   For other verses of this Wesley hymn see the *Methodist Hymn-book*, No. 344.

3. *'It has yet a farther office, namely, to keep us with Him.'*

   What Wesley presumably means is that it is helpful to the spiritual growth of the Christian believer constantly to be reminded by the great fact of moral law that God is a righteous God, who requires righteousness in His children—and so in paragraphs 4–7.

*'Closer and closer let us cleave, &c.'*

For this hymn, by Charles Wesley, see the *Methodist Hymn-book*, No. 712.

4. *'deriving'*: i.e., 'conveying', 'transmitting'.

7. *'the love of God in Christ endears the law to me.'*

Some of Wesley's statements in paragraphs 3-7 about the place of law in the Christian life may seem a little puzzling to some. This sentence explains his intention. The man whose heart is filled with the love of God will earnestly desire to know and to do all the righteous will of God. This all-important truth is at once simple and profound. The moral of the whole sermon is: 'Christianity is an ethical religion.'

8. *'thou . . . that rankest it with sin, Satan, and death'?*

i.e., the Antinomian.

10. *'abhor sin itself, far more than the punishment of it.'*

An admirable and spiritual maxim, which is the very antidote of all legalism.

### Questions

1. Wesley regards the preaching of the Law, i.e., the enforcement of the inflexible moral demands of God, and of the awful consequences of neglecting them, as the normal way in which men are convinced of their need of Christ. Do modern preachers still find this to be the case? If not, what is the reason: a greater degree of moral carelessness in the average hearer? a decline in the fear of hell-fire? a greater emphasis upon God as a kind and forgiving Father?

2. Are careless and sinful men likely to be brought to penitence by sermons on the forgiving love of God in Christ, or will this only happen to 'one in an age'? (IV. 1.)

*Sermon Thirty*\*

# The Law established through Faith

### Discourse I

IN this sermon the relation of morality to the Gospel is explained with admirable clarity.

1. '*But now the righteousness of God without the law*':

or more accurately, 'apart from the law', i.e., the righteousness (or salvation) of God has nothing to do with the religion of law.

'*propitiation.*' See note to Sermon V. II. 5 pp. 44 ff.

'*that He might be just, and yet the justifier of him which believeth, &c.*'
See note to Sermon V, IV, 1, pp. 47 f.

I. 6. '*which is, in the strongest sense, preaching the law.*'

We are reminded by Wesley's argument how much this most important subject has been obscured by confusion of terms. One has used 'preaching the law' in one sense, one in another. If by 'preaching the law' is meant, with Wesley, sternly reminding men of the moral demands of God, and warning them of the consequences of disobedience, then St. Paul preached the law. So will all true evangelists. Those who use the phrase 'a preacher of the law' as a term of reproach (I. 1), may do so because they have fallen into the grievous error of obscuring the strictly ethical nature of Christianity. Against such this sermon is rightly aimed. Some, however, by 'a preacher of the law' mean one who teaches that man must earn acceptance by God through his own efforts in obedience to God's law. i.e., 'Justification by works'. If this definition be accepted the

\* No. 35 in *Fifty-three Sermons*

reproach is upheld. It is hence most important that every preacher should think clearly upon this point, and make his thought clear to his hearers.

7. The reader of Acts will notice that when St. Paul preached to Jews his main argument was: 'The resurrection and the Prophets prove that the crucified Jesus is nevertheless the Messiah.' When he preached to a pagan audience, as at Lystra and at Athens, he started off on the familiar Jewish ground: 'There is but one true God, the Creator, who is the righteous Judge of the earth.' The distinctive Christian message could not be preached without this foundation.

II. 2. Here are some pointed and necessary warnings. Multitudes who have rejoiced in the evangelical experience have fallen in some degree into these errors. The extreme of antinomianism is an *open* offence. The *partial* error may pass unnoticed.

3. See notes to Sermons V, I, 1-4, pp. 38 ff., and VI, 1, pp. 55 f.

5. '*they are the Pharisees who make the Antinomians.*'

Here is a true word indeed, and a particular example of one of the great laws of human life. That those who revolt against an error so commonly go to the other extreme is one of the most fertile causes of disorder in this world. Always one should seek the golden mean.

III. 3. '*the grace of God ruling in his heart, and causing all his works to be wrought in love.*'

This is the very heart of the matter. The moral law to which a Christian is subject is not an external law of fixed (written) moral commandments. It is a law written on the heart, prompting the Christian to all that is right in a spirit of freedom. However, the moral law is not any the less strict, binding, and exacting, because it is a law of freedom.

4. 5. '*Has it not infected you? &c.*'

Who can answer these searching and practical questions?

7. '*let it be an invariable rule, "I will do nothing now I am 'under grace', which I durst not have done when 'under the law' ".*'

This is an admirable rule, but hard to apply in many cases, because so few modern Christians have passed through a distinct stage of conviction of sin, living under the religion of stern duty, before they came to the freedom and joy of the Gospel. One way to adapt the rule is to ask oneself: 'Why should I, an enlightened and free evangelical Christian, be less strict in life, less devoted to the institutions of my Church, less generous to the good cause, than so many folk I know, whose religion seems impossibly narrow, legalistic, or institutionalized?'

## QUESTIONS

1. 'Not only the declaring the love of Christ to sinners, but also the declaring that He will come from heaven in flaming fire.' (I. 10.) Judging from these published sermons, taken as a whole, would you say that Wesley's typical method of awakening the careless was to 'dangle them over the pit,' or to speak of the Cross, and of the joy of communion with God?

2. A preacher resolves 'to offer Christ in every sermon'. Is he in danger of finding that 'by constant repetition' the glories of the Gospel 'lose their force, and grow more and more flat and dead'? (I. 12.) If so, what would you prefer as topics to give variety: threatening with hell-fire? practical instruction on personal morals? lectures on the obligations of Christian citizenship? enforcement of duty to the Church?

*Sermon Thirty-One*\*

# The Law established through Faith

## Discourse II

I. 1. 'καπηλεύοντες.'

This verb (from 2 Cor. ii. 17) means, in the first place, 'to make merchandise of'; and so, as a secondary meaning, 'to adulterate (for the purpose of trade)'.

'*cauponize*'; i.e., 'to keep a little shop'.

3. '*one of their most eminent Rabbis*';

i.e., Rabbi David Kimchi, who lived at Narbonne from 1155 to 1235.

Wesley is not altogether fair to Judaism. It is the natural and inevitable tendency of any system of legal religion or morality, based upon obedience to fixed, external commandments, to regard the outward act of obedience as the thing that *really* matters, whatever be the merits of a right motive within. It is not surprising that much popular Judaism has fallen here, as has some popular Christianity. However, true Judaism has risen above this.

II. 1. '*Faith will totally fail; it will be swallowed up in sight.*'

This idea is very common in Christian thought. It is largely a matter of what is meant by different words. If faith be in some way the opposite to sight, as in the above quotation, it will obviously have an end in heaven. If faith be the attitude of a needy soul clinging to the Saviour, that soul has only to be finally confirmed in perfect love, and faith has played its part. However, in its fullest sense faith is the outgoing of man

\* No. 36 in *Fifty-three Sermons*

in heart and mind and spirit to God, in an attitude of loving trust. We cannot imagine the perfected ever passing beyond this sort of faith.

'*Its nature and its office still the same, &c.*'

These lines are from Matthew Prior's poem, 'Charity'. For a more exact quotation see Sermon XVII, 17.

4. '*For then his reason's eye was strong and clear, &c.*'

An inaccurate quotation from Sir John Davies' 'Nosce Teipsum', iii. (1599).

6. '*faith . . . leads to . . . the establishing anew the law of love in our hearts.*'

This is the sound and practical aim of the foregoing involved and speculative argument. Wesley correctly treats the law of love as, for the Christian, the equivalent of the moral law. The preaching of faith is the road to love. Therefore it is the road to moral law. Thus faith establishes the law.

III. 3. '*For there is no motive which so powerfully inclines us to love God, as the sense of the love of God in Christ.*'

Here is the heart of the Gospel. This principle is the great foundation alike of religious devotion and of morality.

*Sermon Thirty-Two**

# The Nature of Enthusiasm

THIS great sermon answers to Wesley the pastor, rather than to Wesley the prophet. It shows Wesley the pastor at his best. Here is a sermon packed with practical and spiritual good sense. As it stands it speaks to a day that is gone, yet it still has many a valuable message for the disciple, and for the preacher, of today.

The word 'enthusiasm' is an interesting example of a word that deteriorated in meaning with the passage of time, and then, as is unusual in such cases, later became re-established in a good sense. By original derivation in the Greek the word meant, 'possession by the divine'. Plato introduced it into the language of philosophy to denote the direct intuition of the divine, by the indwelling of God in the soul, as it occurs in prophets, mystics, poets, and philosophers. Used at first in English in the Platonic sense, 'enthusiastic' soon fell to mean 'fanatical'. Thus Shaftesbury wrote in 1711: 'Inspiration is a real feeling for the Divine Presence, and Enthusiasm is a false one.' Thus 'enthusiast' was a standard term of abuse to be applied to a Methodist. Misunderstanding and misrepresentation of the doctrine of the Witness of the Spirit provided ample opportunity for the damaging charge, and we have to admit the possibility that now and again a few of those who exulted in the new evangelical experience did actually step over the line into 'enthusiasm'. Wesley had many attacks to answer, and this sermon is part of a long controversy. As the nation gradually assimilated the Methodist witness, and the chilly atmosphere of eighteenth-century religion was thawed, it became more widely realized that a Christian might have a rapturous experience of the presence of God in his heart, and yet not be a madman. This is doubtless one influence that has helped since Wesley's day to re-establish the word 'enthusiasm' in a good sense.

* No. 37 in *Fifty-three Sermons*

1. The eighteenth-century background of this sermon is admirably painted in a few bold strokes.

2. '*And it is no compliment which the men of the world pay you herein.*'

   Wesley means: 'it is no mere neat retort they make; they really mean what they say'. Wesley's sense is not: 'they are being rude to you'.

6. See note on introduction to this Sermon, p. 195.

7. '*uncouth*': i.e., 'unfamiliar'.

9. '*a late eminent writer*':
   Shaftesbury. See his 'Letter on Enthusiasm'.

10. Wesley shows an exact and a just mind in first making recognition of those who use the word 'enthusiasm' in its original and good sense (8, 9), but he is abundantly justified in taking it for the purpose of this sermon in its then usual sense, as a term of reproach, and often of scurrilous abuse.

11. '*madness rather than of folly, &c.*'

    A premiss is that which is laid down before the argument starts. Wesley's distinction here is: a fool may be level-headed; the place where he starts may be sound. He comes to the wrong conclusion because he cannot think straight. A madman may be able to think straight, but he cannot fail to arrive at the wrong conclusion because the things he takes for granted at the beginning are all wrong. He has an unbalanced mind. As Wesley sees it, the objection to the Methodist was not that he lacked intellectual ability, but that his mind had been overthrown by a strange delusion.

13. '*those who imagine they have the grace which they have not*':

    i.e., those whose 'experience' is a mere wave of emotion, and not a real change of character, mind, and will. It is important to realize that Wesley dismisses all such as 'enthusiasts'.

14. *'reveries':* i.e., 'fantastic notions'.

16. 17. Wesley hits back with force here. The man whose Christianity is a mere conventional Churchmanship, that is, the one who is foremost to denounce Methodism as 'enthusiasm', is plainly told that it is himself who is the poor deluded soul, for ever supposing that he is a Christian.

18. The 'gifts' mentioned here, and in the following paragraphs, are some of the very things which it was alleged were the fantastic pretentions of the Methodists. Wesley forcibly disowns the charge by implication, admitting that one who claimed such things would indeed be an 'enthusiast'.

20. *'particular directions from God.'*

    The Rev. Thomas Church had in 'Remarks on the Rev. Mr. John Wesley's Last Journal' (1744), pointed as a chief instance of Wesley's 'enthusiasm' to his occasional custom of casting lots or opening the Bible at random (after prayer), to seek decision in doubtful questions. Wesley's defence was that he never did this unless the most careful thought had failed to point what was best to be done. This answer agrees in spirit with the present paragraph. In the ordinary issues of life the God-given faculty of intelligence is sufficient, and when sufficient is to be used. There may, however, be graver matters in which a Christian may rightly seek special guidance from God. This is a common-sense outlook. Nevertheless, we have some sympathy also with Mr. Church, for few people today would regard the casting of lots or 'Bible-pricking' as reasonable ways in which to seek this special guidance.

21. *'of old times.'*

    Wesley here faces a difficulty. In the circumstances of life in his own day Wesley regards the claim to have received divine guidance by means of visions, dreams, &c., as evidence of an unbalanced mind. The Bible, however, is full of visions and dreams. He had therefore to assume that God had changed

His method with the passage of time. It is probably preferable to say that human mentality has changed with the advance of the race in culture. For a single example, among a people where everyone as a matter of course takes stories of angels seriously a vision of angels is far more likely to be seen by an individual than in a society like ours, where most ordinary people greet the story of an angel with instinctive scepticism. We can well imagine that to a generation which, on account of its mental background, was in the habit of seeing angels, God would choose to communicate His revelation by this method. To a different generation He would speak by a different method, for God always speaks to men through what they already know. Wesley is thus right in treating Biblical visions, dreams, &c., more seriously as divine revelation than similar alleged phenomena in the eighteenth century. In an age of reason visions are likely to be seen mainly by abnormal types of person.

24. 25. What magnificent common-sense piety is here! In all cases where man can be guided by reason and experience Wesley places his trust in the power of reason and experience. Excluded is every attempt to discover the will of God by methods which would save man the trouble of thinking, and relieve him of responsibility for his actions. Nevertheless, the thinking Christian is deeply conscious that he is in the hand of God. As he thinks, so he constantly prays that God will inspire every faculty by which he may learn of reason and experience. All human self-sufficiency in the presence of God is hence also excluded.

26. *'would it not be better to say, "I want to know . . . what will make me most useful"?'*

Wesley is absolutely right here. Currency is depreciated by making it too common. So also great words are emptied of their meaning by being used of trivial matters. By this abuse of language men impoverish their power to express their deepest feelings and thoughts, and ultimately also their power to think and feel deeply. The sanctimonious person whose speech is habitually larded with pious clichés is guilty of much more than a lapse in good taste. The request 'I want to know what is the will of God' should be reserved for a worthy occasion, when one is confronted by a serious moral choice. Wesley's connexion of this matter with the Third Commandment may at first sight seem an unduly severe judgement, but the connexion is there. The wrong in 'taking the name of the Lord in vain' is not merely disrespect to God. It is rather that one is ruining one's power to use aright those sacred words which, when used aright, are the means of lifting one up to God in worship. This is the crucial example of a general principle.

27. This level-headed paragraph, coming as it does from the pen of a great evangelist, is surely an eye-opener for many a well-meaning but uninstructed soul.

28. 29. Wesley is profoundly right here. God rules the whole creation by law, and before that law there are no favourites. The Christian man, therefore, should not look for divine deliverances from calamity, specially granted because he is righteous, and withheld from the wicked. However, this rule of law by no means excludes the idea of divine providence. God's whole law is wise and good, and, in the truest sense, providential. There are thus no particular providences, in the sense of exceptions to God's law, yet every particular blessing that comes to man under the wise rule of God is a particular providence.

*'even in the sins of others, I see the providence of God to me.'*

For example, the rise of Nazidom was a compelling demonstration of the inherent corruption of every State organized apart from moral law. This ghastly development was certainly not decreed by the providence of God, but occurred wholly in defiance of God's plan for the world. However, this compelling demonstration had a very salutary effect upon many who beheld it, opening their eyes to the evil lying hid in some aspects of the life and thought of other nations. For them this was providential.

## SERMON XXXII

'*universis tanquam singulis, &c.*'

This seems to be intended as a quotation from St. Augustine. See Sermon LXVII, 26 (*Works*, VI. p. 323, 3rd Edition).

31–2. Here is the just and awful condemnation of 'enthusiasm', of fanaticism.

33–9. Here is a cogent summary to a sermon which must have amazed many of the detractors of Methodism, supposing them to have read it.

### QUESTIONS

1. The Netherlands, Belgium, and France fell to the Germans, but at Dunkirk and in the Battle of Britain this country was saved. Is the man who regards this remarkable deliverance as a special and miraculous providence of God an 'enthusiast'?

2. A preacher goes into the pulpit trusting 'for a message to be given him'. Is he an 'enthusiast'? Would you hold this rule for one man, with one set of gifts, and another rule for another, with different gifts? What then of leading in public prayer?

3. Is it possible to understand the Bible without a good commentary?

4. On what grounds, if any, do you object to the printing of the letters 'D.V.', i.e., 'God willing', on the announcement of the time and place of a service or meeting?

5. May a Christian rightly speak of (divine) guidance to spend his half-day gardening rather than golfing? or to take some flowers to his wife on her birthday? or to go to the boss and ask for a rise? or to send his child to this school rather than that? or to speak about Christ to a man in the same railway-carriage? or to offer himself for the Mission-Field?

*Sermon Thirty-Three*\*

# A Caution against Bigotry

MUCH is rightly heard today of the necessity of living down old quarrels in the Church, of Christian co-operation, and of Church reunion. The sympathy of Methodism to these most worthy causes is pledged beforehand in this noble and moving sermon, which merits the careful attention of all our people. It is also interesting as containing Wesley's defence of the Methodist custom of allowing laymen to preach.

2. '*Has not the power of doing this been withdrawn from the Church, for twelve or fourteen hundred years?*'

The answer to this is, 'Yes, and No.' The peasants of Galilee and Judea in Bible times, in common with many other simple peoples, described what we should call mental disorder as 'possession by a devil'. It is well established that mental disorder can often be cured by appropriate psychological treatment. In the case of a sufferer who seriously believes that his mental or nervous affliction is due to devil-possession, exorcism, or the invocation of the name of God over him, to cast out the devil, will often prove to be the natural and appropriate psychological treatment to work a cure. Thus there were many exorcists among the Jews, and it is natural to see our Lord as the supreme example of this healing power. As the mental background of belief in devil-possession has declined, so has the scope for exorcism, though psychological treatment of mental disorders by other methods appropriate to the mind of the times continues with growing success. There is, however, still scope for 'casting out devils' among the primitive peoples of Africa, the East, &c.

\* No. 38 in *Fifty-three Sermons*

## SERMON XXXIII

I. 1. *'the devil dwells and works, &c.'*

To the Biblical writers the natural explanation of the powers of darkness which so manifestly blight God's world was in terms of personal demons, with a personal Devil as their king. Objection can be raised to this system of thought, but at the very least, not greater than can be raised to other explanations of the power of evil in the world. The matter in any case remains largely a dark mystery. However, it is pure presumption to assume that humans are the sole thinking, feeling, personal beings created by God. There is nothing unreasonable in a belief in purely spiritual beings, such as angels. If these are free moral agents there is nothing to exclude the dreadful possibility that some of these might fall, as men have done, and become devils. The problem of evil is not hereby solved. It is but carried a stage farther back. Some sort of explanation is however provided for the manifest and tragic fact that evil in this world is organized in an all too intelligent and resourceful conspiracy, and likewise for such natural evil as seems to be unconnected with human sin, such as loathsome diseases and parasites, the birth of hideous monstrosities and of idiots, and possibly, also, of calamities such as earthquakes. No Christian need hesitate too much in following the Bible to speak of the Devil as a person, though these theories are by no means a necessary part of Christian belief.

3. Wesley obviously did not realize that the phenomena described in the New Testament as 'devil-possession' (e.g., epilepsy) were still with him in the eighteenth century, but he is right in ascribing to the decay of superstition the obvious difference in this matter between the times of our Lord and his own day.

4. Lapland had the reputation for being the home of witchcraft

4–6. Wesley cunningly adapts his theme to make some telling thrusts at his familiar audience.

6. *'secure':* i.e., free from anxiety.

7-8. As is generally the case in these matters, there are two sides to the picture. Latin literature bears witness that there were many virtuous and public-spirited Romans, and also many a dark and tragic blot upon their society.

8. *'before Caesar's return from Gaul':*

i.e., while the State was in the throes of revolution. Conditions were hardly normal then.

9. Moved by enthusiasm for the present theme, Wesley has travelled far from his early dream of 'the noble savage'. (See Sermon XXIII, 9, and note, pp. 165 f.) He now flies to the other extreme.

10. The story of European colonization is nowhere a very pretty one, but it is only fair to observe that there are degrees even here. The British slave trade was atrocious, but the Spanish regime in South America more so. However, in general, Wesley's candour is most praiseworthy. Though the best of patriots, he avoids the common error of excepting one's own nation from the catalogue of international wrong.

II. The systematic mind is at work here. For a brief analysis of 'our unhappy divisions', this admirable section would be hard to beat.

1. We start with the most natural, the most inevitable, and in a sense the least blameworthy occasion of division in the Church, that is, the geographical. For the ex-Wesleyan and ex-Primitive Chapel in a single village to be well content to continue in their separate ways is an unnatural and grievous sin. For a Church in Wales and a Church in Lincolnshire to take no thought for one another is less so, and much less again if the one is in New York and the other in Abyssinia.

## SERMON XXXIII

**2.** '*particularly observable in our own countrymen.*'

As the French traveller observed, in England there are a hundred religions, and only one sauce. What would Wesley have said of modern America?

'*upon points of no moment.*'

It is illuminating to find that Wesley, the zealous Churchman, had the insight to see what is unfortunately too little realized even today, namely, that many of the divisions of British Christianity are not founded upon any substantial difference of religious principle. It would have been interesting had he gone into details. Nowhere is this more the case than with the past divisions of Methodism, which have been clearly due to the instinct of individualism, and not to any doctrinal difference.

**3.** '*Nor does it appear that the difference which then began was ever entirely removed.*'

The 'difference' is the matter of the circumcision of Gentile converts, and of their incorporation into the Jewish nation: see Acts xv. 1-31. What Wesley says is essentially correct. St. Paul and the Gentile party certainly carried the day for the Church as a whole, but the Epistle of James is witness to the continuance, within the Church of a party which regarded Christianity as a section of Judaism. On the wider issue, likewise, it is easy to look back with longing, and to view through rose-coloured spectacles 'the early, pure centuries of the undivided Church'. A little historical knowledge, however, will show that within the ambit of that most impressive world-wide unity there was room for many genuine differences of opinion, and, unhappily, for not a few bitter quarrels. Here is a more serious and intractable cause of disunity than geography and the instinct of individualism: the existence of communions which suspect one another's orthodoxy 'even in several subjects of importance'. In his last sentence Wesley gives an instance of such a dispute much to the fore in his day, namely, the issue between Calvinist and non-Calvinist theology.

A CAUTION AGAINST BIGOTRY

4. '*that Liturgy which we approve of beyond all others*'*:*
the *Book of Common Prayer.*

'*he may, from a principle of conscience, refrain from . . . the ordinances of Christ.*'
Wesley presumably intends the Society of Friends (Quakers), who do not observe Baptism and the Holy Communion at all.

'*a difference . . . as to the manner of administering those ordinances, or the persons, &c.*'
Wesley probably mainly has in mind the Baptists, who insist on Baptism by total immersion and on the admission to the sacrament of those alone who can make a personal confession of Christian faith (i.e., adults).

5. Wesley here writes of the Roman Church. Considering the standard of the times in which he lived, it is a most moving and unusual spectacle of Christian charity to find a zealous Anglican extending the obligation of toleration alike to Calvinists, Lutherans, Friends, Baptists, and to Roman Catholics. We must not be too hard on Wesley because, when faced with actual public controversy about the position of Rome, he at times found it hard to live up to the lofty standard here acknowledged. The acid test of toleration is whether it can be extended, as with Wesley here, even to those whose views one conscientiously considers to be dangerous errors.

'*utterly false.*'
This is too severe a judgement, and one hardly compatible with the view that Roman Catholics fill the place of Christian disciples who 'follow not with us'. One may feel forced to maintain that some parts of Roman doctrine are utterly false, and that many other parts are doubtful, and yet admit the Roman Church to be a part of the universal Church. If their whole doctrine is utterly false this admission cannot be made at all.

'*dropped one whole commandment of God*':
i.e., Thou shalt not make unto thee a graven image'.

This common objection obscures the circumstance that, while the Ten Commandments are a valuable guide to the conscience of the Church, they are not binding upon her in a literal, Jewish, or *legal* sense. (See note to Sermon XX, I, 2.) Though one would not defend all Roman customs with regard to images, it must be maintained that the Church is in principle completely free to decide, under the guidance of the Holy Spirit, what sort of religious apparatus is most helpful to devotion.

6. Wesley is profoundly right here. The deepest and bitterest cause of division in the Church, and the hardest to be healed, is 'the human element'. Because of this, one party and another are all too often separated not only by 'an honest difference of opinion', but also by suspicion, and even hatred. Men can easily mistake sinful pride, prejudice, and self-will for zeal for the truth of God.

7. We close with a level-headed proviso.

III. 5. Here is a very practical application of a great theme. Wesley hastens to the defence of his lay preachers. In 1739-40 Thomas Maxfield, the first Methodist lay preacher, had started his work. Wesley at first seriously considered stopping this as an irregularity. His mother's wise counsel was: 'Take care what you do with respect to that young man, for he is as surely called of God to preach as you are. *Examine what have been the fruits of his preaching*, and hear him also yourself.' Wesley adopts the test proposed first by his mother.

7. '*an outward call*':

i.e., an official sanction by the Church. The letter of Methodist law, not always very regularly observed, which admits only accredited preachers to our pulpits, would make the outward call for all practical purposes a necessity.

'*never was so unhappy a quotation.*'

Wesley protests too much. We may rightly be chary of applying Old Testament precedents to the Christian Church, but so far as it goes the argument from Heb. v. 4 is to be upheld. True, this text refers to the work of a priest, and not of a preacher, but Aaron was the officer of a religious society appropriate to ancient times, while a Methodist Local Preacher is the same in modern days. Then as now, one who leads public worship must be appointed by the Church, though if he is to do any good he must also have an inward sense of mission prompting him to the task.

9. '*By setting them to construe a sentence of Greek, and asking them a few commonplace questions?*'

The slovenly standards of churchmanship so common in those days had affected methods of examination of candidates for ordination. The examination was often perfunctory in the extreme, as Wesley rightly objects.

'*as is still done by most of the Protestant Churches of Europe.*'

This continental custom of a year's probationary preaching before ordination was one of Wesley's regular arguments in vindication of the position of a lay preacher.

10. '*and yet the Bishop will not ordain him.*'

Wesley actually made efforts, unhappily unsuccessful, to obtain episcopal ordination for some of his preachers. Had this been granted, the final breach between Methodism and the Church of England might never have occurred.

IV. 3. '*Am I not sorry that God should thus own and bless a man that holds such erroneous opinions?*'

Here is a test of open-mindedness indeed! Who can lightly claim to feel no pang when he sees men brought to God by the preaching of a Church about whose doctrine he has misgivings, rather than by that of his own?

4. '*Arian, Socinian.*'

These are alternative names for those we now know as Unitarians.

'*Deist.*'

A Deist is one who believes in the existence of God, but not in any supernatural revelation from God. Thus, according to a Deist nothing is known of God save what may be seen of Him in His creation by the use of reason. God is also represented as One who has created the world, and then retired from it, leaving it severely alone to proceed according to its own fixed laws. This leaves no possibility of a supernatural redemption. Deism was very widespread in Wesley's day, and was a main enemy of the Gospel, even though many Deist positions have some truth in them. The Deists largely passed as Christians, and many of them were excellent men, but their teaching completely emptied the Gospel of its vital content. For practical purposes Deism was not unlike the 'Scientific Humanism' of today.

6. '*Think not the bigotry of another is any excuse for your own.*'

Here is another searching test for Christian charity. Wesley has the right to propose it, for who ever was an object of more bigotry than he, and a more unjustified object?

'*a great man.*' Wesley means John Calvin.

## QUESTIONS

1. The adherents of a sect appear to be good and sincere men. Does this prove that their views are correct? Does it prove that they are actually advancing the work of God?

2. Is it humanly possible to be open-minded and tolerant without sapping one's own zeal for one's own way? or to be an enthusiast for the reunion of the universal Church without insensibly compromising one's single-minded loyalty to one's own communion?

*Sermon Thirty-Four**

# Catholic Spirit

THIS sermon covers similar ground to the last, though here the emphasis falls more upon questions of the organization and worship of the Church, than on questions of doctrine and preaching. The choice of text is not a happy one. A reference to the context will show that the speaker in it is Jehu, an officer in the army of Joram, king of Israel. He was a zealot for Jehovah-worship, who conspired with Elisha the prophet to raise a rebellion against the royal house of Ahab. By a policy of alliance with pagan Tyre this dynasty had compromised with Baal-worship. Jehu has just killed Joram, Jezebel, seventy members of the house of Ahab, as well as forty-two of the royal house of Judah, and is now on the way to organize a massacre of the priests of Baal. He falls in with the Rechabites, under their chief Jehonadab. These Rechabites were rigid devotees of Jehovah, who had pledged themselves to the life of nomadic shepherds, after the manner of the old, pure, desert days, because a settled agricultural life in Canaan seemed inextricably bound up with pagan cults. (For this, see the illuminating passage from Jeremiah, quoted in this sermon, I. 1.) The Rechabites were thus 'total abstainers' not only from wine, but from civilization. Jehu knows that these men are likely allies in his rebellion, and this verse is his successful invitation to join with him. Thus a text which pre-supposes that the way to deal with a false religion is to slay those who profess it, is quaintly adapted to preach the virtues of toleration.

5. *'as mixed a character as he was.'*

This is just. We need not necessarily doubt Jehu's sincerity as a reformer, but he lived in an age of gross darkness.

* No. 39 in *Fifty-three Sermons*

I. 2. *'to drive furiously.'* See 2 Kings ix. 20.

*'abound in his own sense'*: i.e., 'have full liberty of his opinions'.

4. *'although every man necessarily believes that every particular opinion which he holds is true . . . yet can no man be assured that all his own opinions, taken together, are true.'*

The confusion here lies in the words 'taken together'. It is an example of the common fallacy of speaking of the general class as though it could actually exist apart from the sum total of particular individuals, e.g., of speaking of 'humanity' as though it were a thing existing apart from 'men'. It is rare to find Wesley in a lapse of logic. What he intends to say is: 'although no man ever adopts a particular opinion unless he holds it to be true, yet no man can ever be assured that all his powers of thought are beyond possibility of mistake.' This is an obvious truth.

5. *'invincible ignorance.'*

This term, much used in medieval theology, denotes ignorance which the man in question has not the power to overcome. It is not a term of abuse, as has often been supposed, but is a charitable way of allowing that some men are not truly to blame for some of their errors. Their blindness may not be wilful, but due to a deep and permanent defect of mental equipment, due perhaps to heredity, perhaps to upbringing. Thus theologians have sought to explain why some apparently good and sincere men will, most mysteriously, not be convinced of manifest Christian truth. The term thus describes a very common tragedy of human affairs.

10. *'every follower of Christ is obliged . . . to be a member of . . . some Church.'*

Here is an important truth, though one often neglected in modern times. To join with a congregation of Christian worshippers is no 'optional luxury' in the Christian life. It is part and parcel of the thing itself. There are many good people,

## CATHOLIC SPIRIT

and some indeed who are Christians in a restricted sense of the word, who remain outside what they choose to disparage as 'organized Christianity'. Nevertheless, to be a Christian in the truest and fullest sense of the word definitely involves association with the Church. This is New Testament doctrine. It is there assumed as a matter of course that all converts join the Church.

'*one . . . who is born in England ought to be a member of . . . the Church of England.*'

This is an ancient Anglican proposition, for use in controversy with Dissenters, and also to define the relation of the Church with other Protestant national Churches, in the German states, Scandinavia, &c. We may perhaps say that if a national Church were *truly* national, and so broad in sympathy that believers of every temperament and experience could make themselves happy within her if they would, then this argument would hold. One who dissented from such a national Church would display himself a mere sectarian, a rank individualist going his own way for no sufficient reason, and lacking the essential Christian virtue of Catholic spirit. In so far as national Churches have fallen below this ideal, so far has dissent from them been morally justified.

'*private judgement, on which that whole Reformation stands.*'

This is true, in the sense that the Protestant Reformation took place because men undertook to defy ecclesiastical authority in the name of private judgement. However, it should not be assumed from this that in the Protestant Churches private judgement remains the sole guide to religious conviction. Those who have tried to live in this way have fallen inevitably into an anarchy of errors, for no man is wise or good enough to live to himself alone. Protestant and evangelical Churches also have organs of authority, the Bible and the great Creeds, their own particular tradition and doctrinal standards, as well as the counsel of one's fellow-believers. This authority should always be reverenced by those who would know the truth. However, the Church should always seek to administer this authority by persuasion, and not by compulsion. The ideal is that the individual should not accept this authority in an unthinking or in a slavish spirit, but freely, willingly, and from personal conviction of its validity. Thus 'private judgement' always stands alongside Church authority.

11. '*in the same posture and manner that I do.*'

The Presbyterians sit to receive the Holy Communion, while the Anglicans kneel.

'*sureties for the baptized*': i.e., the godparents.

The Anglican Church incorporates infants into the Church on the promise of parents and friends that the children shall be brought up as Christians. The godparents confess the Faith on behalf of the child for whose Christian nurture they are assuming a measure of responsibility. Thus they are 'sureties'. The Methodist Church proceeds upon the same principle, but is more realistic in that her Order for Baptism of Infants emphasizes this suretyship as resting mainly upon the parents and the whole local Church. The Baptists maintain that formal incorporation into the Church by Baptism should wait until the person to be baptized can himself confess the Faith (i.e., as a converted adult).

12–18. In allowing broad sympathy to flow out across barriers of creed, organization, and liturgy to fellow-believers, Wesley by no means shows himself indifferent to the circumstance whether these are believers indeed. He requires of them all a very high standard of Christian experience and moral character. Indeed, he goes so far as to assume that they enjoy the Witness of the Spirit (12), that they are rightly devoted to the principle of Justification by Faith and not by Works (13), and that they enjoy assurance in their experience (14). In strict logic this would seem to involve that only sound Evangelicals can be regarded as sheep of other folds. Wesley can hardly intend to compromise his own lofty standard of Catholic spirit in this way. We have to keep in mind the wise qualification at the end of (18), 'if thou art but sincerely desirous of it', which at any rate partially solves the contradiction. However, Wesley is certainly right in essentials. It should be the ideal of the Christian to cultivate broad sympathies toward various types of believer, while at the same time strictly excluding the error of supposing that it does not greatly matter whether one's brother is a believer or no.

II. 2. '*I believe the Episcopal form of church government to be scriptural and apostolical.*'

It is interesting that Wesley should have allowed this statement to go out to the world unmodified.

'*Independent*': i.e., Congregational.

'*Let all these smaller points stand aside.*'

Here is the hard core of all doctrinal division between Church and Church. Those commonly called 'Catholic' would emphatically repudiate the suggestion that the manner in which the sacraments are administered is in any sense a 'smaller point' of the Christian Faith.

5. This is the way to deal with heretics.

III. 1. The word 'Catholic' means 'universal'. The Catholic Church is the whole company of genuine Christians, of every age and place, as distinct from any local or temporary body. A Catholic Christian is one whose principle is to count his loyalty as extending in the fullest sense to every part of the Catholic Church, and not merely to some local company in which he happens to have an interest. The opposite to 'Catholic' is thus 'sectarian'. All true Christians are Catholic, for this Catholic spirit, being in essence nothing other than the expression of Christian love for all the fellow-members of the Body of Christ, is the characteristic of true morality and churchmanship. It is a great misfortune that in the course of controversy the noble term 'Catholic' has come to be used as the counterpart to 'Protestant', and is upon the lips of the multitude generally synonymous with 'Roman Catholic'. A good Methodist is a true Catholic, and should make good the proud claim.

*'latitudinarianism.'*

In the proper, historical sense of the word a Latitudinarian was one who accepted Anglican forms of Church government and worship, without regarding them as essentials. However, the word was commonly used in a debased sense, as of one who was inclined to think that all religions are equally good. It is in this sense that Wesley used the word.

2. *'both scriptural and rational.'*

Notice how Wesley does not hesitate to place these terms together. Scripture and reason are joint pillars of Christian truth. This represents the truest Christian tradition, which has not regarded reason and revelation as opposed forces. They are rather complementary to one another, for God's endowment of reason and His gift of a revelation of Himself are alike necessary if man is to see God.

3. *'congregations';* i.e., Churches.

#### QUESTIONS

1. How often has it been asked: 'What of Christians outside the Church?' Why does not the New Testament answer this question?

2. Is separation to form a new religious communion ever right, or, at best, only the best of a bad job?

3. Is expulsion a right measure with which to combat spreading error or unbelief within the Church? Would you have a different rule for private members and Church officers?

4. 'You need not even endeavour to come over to me, or bring me over to you.' (II. 1.) Is it possible to carry this out, without disloyalty to the truth? Compare II. 6.

5. How can a man love those he does not know? (III. 4.)

*Sermon Thirty-Five**

# Christian Perfection

WE come at length to another sermon on one of 'our doctrines', for Methodists have always regarded the preaching of 'Christian Perfection' as an important part of the distinctive witness of our Church. The real intention of Wesley's teaching was very simple. No limit was to be set upon the power of God's redeeming grace, even in the life of the humblest believer. Therefore God called all men, without exception, to the highest standard of Christian experience and moral life. No man had sunk so low that God could not enable him for this high calling. Hence the obligation to seek this calling rested upon all, and none could rightly excuse himself from it. With Justification, or forgiveness, there began a progressive change of character, worked by the indwelling Spirit of God. This process was Sanctification. It was the emphatic teaching of Wesley that the Christian should seek and expect that this process should come to a glorious climax, and, normally, to a sudden climax. This was the experience of 'Entire Sanctification'. The believer had then attained to Christian Perfection.

The error that Wesley laboured so hard to overthrow by this teaching was that only the select few can hope to attain in this present life to the rapturous experience of immediate communion with God, and to an heroic moral stature. It was widely supposed that these things were reserved for the Church of the apostolic age, or in more modern times, for select souls born with a special religious temperament, or possibly and more generally, for those in religious orders, clergymen, etc. The most that could be expected of ordinary people, possibly of humble gifts and slender education, men who had to earn their living out in the world, was that they should go to Church when they could, and attain to a respectable standard of honesty and conventional morality. Against all this Wesley insisted as

* No. 40 in *Fifty-three Sermons*

an essential part of the Gospel that the gate to the highest was open to all, and that all must press in. He was abundantly justified in this, and it is lamentable that this teaching is not as prominent as it ought to be in Methodist pulpits. It will be observed that the preaching of Christian Perfection has a similar intention to the doctrine of the Witness of the Spirit, i.e., that God can speak straight to the heart, and raise faith to the level of abounding peace and joy, full assurance of salvation, and real inward victory over sin. The former is the principle 'the highest is open to you all' applied with the Christian's character and moral life mainly in mind, the latter the same principle applied particularly to his piety and religious experience. The two stand or fall together.

The objection may quite reasonably be raised that a single standard, and that a most elevated one, cannot rightly be applied to all men alike. They are so varied in spiritual aptitude. A few have inherited great gifts, or are fortunate in the opportunities they enjoy. Many have inherited characteristics which are the source of grievous temptation to them, and they may have to spend all their days in a narrow circle, possibly borne down by sordid surroundings. How can they all rise to the heights? This was, indeed, one of the main objections Wesley had to meet. It was claimed that he was asking too much of human nature; that he made Christianity far more difficult than Christ had intended. This was a variation upon the slander we have observed so often, that Wesley was a fanatic, who carried things beyond all due measure. Wesley's sufficient answer was in his definition of Christian Perfection as Perfect Love. He followed his Lord in teaching that God judges a man not by how many spiritual talents he has been given, but by the use he makes of them. God, who looks upon the heart, can see an utterly sincere intention of walking with Him, and a complete opening of the heart in desire toward Him, when these things are there. He can make allowances for natural defects of temperament and understanding, and for the lingering power of temptation; for all those things, in fact, which frustrate the perfect practical outcome of that intention. No Christian need feel himself condemned before God, and excluded from the fullness of blessing, because some defect of nature must remain with him until the day when he receives the reward of a higher perfection in heaven. Yet all the time God demands, and offers, nothing less than this complete opening of the heart toward Himself, this overmastering affection which expels all other affections. Christian Perfection is thus not perfect moral performance, and complete likeness to God. That is a perfection reserved for heaven. It is Perfect Love. So, in his 'Plain Account of Christian Perfection' (*Works*, Vol. XI, p. 371), Wesley claims that his famous description of 'The Character of a Methodist' is the description of a perfect Christian: 'one who loves the Lord his God with all his heart, with all his soul, with all his mind, and with all his strength,' &c. Here is a standard, and the only conceivable standard, which can fairly be applied to all sorts and conditions of men. By contrast, Wesley avoided the use of the phrase 'sinless perfection' for the entirely sanctified. It did not make sufficient recognition of those inherent limitations of the human constitution from which we cannot rightly hope to be released in this life. The believer to whom has been granted the gift of entire sanctification will not have anything in his life for which he feels guilt, but there will remain many things which remind him that, compared with the glorious perfection of Jesus, he is a lowly and unworthy creature. 'Sinless perfection' is therefore too presumptuous a term.

To apply this standard in detail, at once excluding easy-going views as to what is involved in Perfect Love, and making due allowance for human limitations, is a task requiring no little judgement. This is the task of the present sermon, together with XXXVI, on 'Wandering Thoughts'; XXXVII, on 'Satan's Devices'; and XLI, on 'Heaviness through Manifold Temptations'. That the background of these sermons is controversy and misunderstanding is seen in the circumstance that they deal mainly with the negative side. The aim is to show what Christian Perfection does *not* involve, and to 'make allowances'. Sermon XXXV is also largely taken up with a very complicated argument to show that the Bible justifies and requires the preaching of this doctrine. As it stands, therefore, the sermon on 'Christian Perfection' is most disappointing as an evangelical statement of a great Methodist theme. The main value is controversial. The reader will, however, find plenty of splendid *positive* statements scattered through the Standard Sermons, e.g., in the Sermons on the Sermon on the Mount.

The ideal principle of Entire Sanctification is plainly laid down in the 'Plain Account of Christian Perfection' (Wesley's *Works*, Vol. XI, p. 379). 'They are freed from evil thoughts, so that they cannot enter into them, no, not for a moment. Aforetime, when an evil thought came in, they looked up, and it vanished away. But now it does not come in, there being no room for this, in a soul which is full of God.' All believers have true victory over temptation, but for the Perfected there is a more secure victory beyond this. Such is Wesley's utter faith in the expulsive power of a new affection, even the love of God shed abroad in the heart. On p. 393 of the same we further read: '(1) That Christian perfection is that love of God and our neighbour, which implies deliverance from all sin. (2) That this is received merely by faith. (3) That it is given instantaneously, in one moment. (4) That we are to expect it, not at death, but every moment; that now is the accepted time, now is the day of this salvation.' On (4) Wesley records the following from the *Minutes of the Second Methodist Conference*, 1745 ('Plain Account', p. 387). ' "Q. When does inward sanctification begin?" "A. In the moment a man is justified. ... From that time a believer gradually dies to sin, and grows in grace." "Q. Is this ordinarily given till a little before death?" "A. It is not to those who expect it no sooner." "Q. But may we expect it sooner?" "A. Why not?" ' We see here that Wesley trusted that God normally gave the believer this complete victory over sin, but that it might have to wait until the moment of death. A reason for this in many cases was that so many Christians had been taught not to expect this gift, and so did not seek it. This is manifestly Wesley's charitable attempt to bring all sincere believers within his scheme. We may entertain some reserve about point (3). The reason for this insistence that the climax of the process of sanctification is a *sudden* glorious gift is that it is a *gift*, received by simple faith, and not

## CHRISTIAN PERFECTION

something attained by man's own effort, and therefore attained gradually. However, this does not make quite enough allowance for a principle of which Wesley has already shown himself aware in Sermon VIII, 'The First-fruits of the Spirit' (I, 3 and II, 5-13). Justification is likewise a gift received by faith, and therefore in ideal theory is instantaneous. There is, however, a certain discrepancy between the ideal and the actual. A Christian does not normally pass in one bound to perfect and continuous 'saving faith'. There are 'ups and downs' until he is confirmed in the new way. Surely this is also the case with the gift of entire sanctification. In a sense Wesley admits this, speaking of a work of grace preceding and *following* Christian Perfection. As so often, the general principle Wesley lays down is somewhat too rigid, but the provisos he admits show admirable understanding of the practical affairs of the Christian life. At the same time, there is real value in the idea of the gift as a sudden one. It is a very common thing for all manner of psychological processes gradually to work up to a sudden climax, to a moment of realization or decision. This is certainly true of the process of conversion, and surely also of the later growth of Christian experience. The phrase 'the second blessing', so frequently associated with 'Entire Sanctification', would not have remained in use so long had it not corresponded with reality. Christians of many years' experience have indeed been aware in their lives of new, sudden, and glorious moments, which have for ever lifted them on to a higher plane. The criticism of the phrase 'the second blessing' is not that it speaks of a sudden change, but that it assumes that the adult Christian is to expect only one such outstanding moment of enlightenment. It is surely more common to experience several. One should also guard against supposing that the holiness of the entirely sanctified is of a different kind from that of the ordinary believer, so that there are two kinds of Christian. The one is but the fullness of the other.

A useful summary with which to close the discussion of this important matter may be made from Wesley's 'Brief Thoughts on Christian Perfection'. (*Works*, Vol. XI, p. 446.) '1. By perfection I mean the humble, gentle, patient love of God and our neighbour, ruling our tempers, words, and actions. I do not include an impossibility of falling from it.... And I do not contend for the term *sinless*, though I do not object against it. 2. As to the manner. I believe this perfection is always wrought in the soul by a simple act of faith; consequently, in an instant. But I believe a gradual work, both preceding and following that instant. 3. As to the time. I believe this instant generally is the instant of death.... But I believe it may be ten, twenty, or forty years before. I believe it is usually many years after justification.'

1. *'The very sound of it is an abomination to them.'*

Wesley may have in mind: (i) those who objected that he was a fanatic, or (ii) the Continental Protestants, who rejected the term 'Perfection' at the Reformation. The ancient tradition of the Church had been largely dominated by the ascetic theory of Perfection. This was the conception of a double standard. 'Evangelical precepts' applied to all the faithful, 'Counsels of Perfection' only to those called to be saints, i.e., in practice, those who embarked upon 'the religious life'. For example, it was an evangelical precept that a man marry, live faithfully with his wife, and bring up Christian children. It was the counsel of perfection that he enter a monastery to live a celibate life. The Reformers felt that this involved the notion that a man is saved by the degree of zeal he shows for the institutions of the Church. The cardinal principle of Justification by Faith was thereby compromised. Thus the followers of Luther came to restrict 'Perfection' to that which may be expected only in heaven, and to condemn talk of *present* Perfection as reflecting a lack of realization for the utter unworthiness of man in the sight of God.

I. 4. *'the children of God do not mistake as to the things essential to salvation.'*

The assumption lies to hand here that the faith by which a man is saved is something other than orthodoxy (cf. Sermon

I, I, 4). It is all too easy for a simple believer to hold mistaken theological views, even on essential points.

5. The Christian therefore needs the collective wisdom of the Church to help him to understand the Bible (cf. Sermon XXXII, 27).

7. *'let us not give that soft title to known sins.'*

Here is the practical issue, how to assure a man that God indeed fully receives him, without making him think lightly of sin.

To his list of imperfections Wesley might well have added that 'invincible ignorance' and even more, that 'invincible prejudice' he treated of in Sermon XXXIV, I, 5 (with note, p. 210).

II. This section is largely a closely-reasoned argument to show that the doctrine of Christian Perfection as Wesley understood it accords with the New Testament. His choice of passages doubtless reflects many an hour of controversy. Though we need not defend every particular piece of exegesis, Wesley is certainly right in his main conclusion. The ground has largely been traversed already in Sermon XV.

The beginner may be excused if he feels puzzled by some of the involved arguments which follow. This intricate manipulation of texts is made necessary by the assumption that the divine inspiration of the Bible involves the notion that every single phrase and every single word is by itself a message straight from God. If each separate text is of the fullest divine authority, it is obviously impossible to imagine that any text from one part of the Bible can fail to fit exactly with any text from another part. They must all in some way fit into a single divine plan. Hence we find stretching, and adapting, and special explanations, in order to overcome 'difficulties'. The fact is that the Biblical writers were not human typewriters, moved automatically by the finger of God. They were real men, inspired by God dwelling in their hearts and minds. Some had a more perfect knowledge of God than others. They were not always perfectly successful in expressing themselves, any more than are writers today. Some found natural one way of putting a truth, or one emphasis, some another. Thus we learn the truth of God from these inspired writings by looking chiefly at the general picture, by making allowances for the personality of different writers, and by correcting details by comparison with the whole. Thus we are not to be perturbed if odd texts appear to contradict the general sense, and if others are obscure in meaning. These are things to be acknowledged, not explained away at all costs.

4. *'He that hath suffered in the flesh hath ceased from sin.'* (1 Peter iv. 1, 2.)

This may either mean: 'the man who has endured persecution for Christ's sake may be trusted to do right in all things'; or, 'the Christian is united to his Lord in all things; in His death, by taking up the cross and following Him, in His resurrection, by sharing in His victory over sin.'

8. *'discovered':* i.e., 'disclosed'.

*'we cannot measure the privileges of real Christians by those formerly given to the Jews.'*

This is a sound conclusion. Revelation is progressive, and we do not today accept without question the standards even of Abraham or David.

10. *'There is no man that sinneth not.'*

Solomon here speaks of human affairs as he found them. From this point of view his statement is still true.

14. Wesley is a little too emphatic in demolishing this argument. If St. Peter and St. Paul did actually on occasion commit sin, it is likely that the same will be true of all lesser Christians.

However, even if every Christian that has ever lived has actually sinned, this by no means does away with the fact that God calls all men to the highest, and has opened the way to it, so that there is no excuse for anything less. This is the essence of Wesley's witness. He is quite right to say that the sin of St. Peter and St. Paul (or, indeed, of all Christians), does not make a fall into sin a *necessity* for any individual.

16. '*the ancient Fathers inform us*,' doubtless on the basis of surmise.

    '*this thorn was given . . . fourteen years before.*'
    There is no evidence for this.

17. At one moment the Apostle refers to human affairs in general, and speaks of himself as part of the race, with a 'we'. At another he shows himself conscious that the Christian is apart from the human race, dwelling on a higher place. There is a formal contradiction in word, but not a real one in sense.

18-20. Wesley is a little too ingenious in trying to show that there is no formal contradiction between the verses he quotes. However, he had the heart of the matter in his statement: '*but let no man say, I need it not.*' 'If we say that we have no sin, we deceive ourselves': here is the practical. It is only right that even the best of men should so speak when he finds himself in the presence of the holy God. 'Whosoever is born of God doth not commit sin': here is the ideal. The Christian is in principle freed from sin, though unhappily the actual falls behind the ideal. As with St. James, there is a formal contradiction, but no real one.

21. All that Wesley has been saying so far applies to the new convert and to every believer. The bare minimum in the Christian life is to receive power to cease from actual sinful words and deeds. It is worthy of note, also, that in Sermon XV, II, 7-9, Wesley has already allowed a modification even of this minimum. If a believer does not 'keep himself' by watching and prayer he may

fall into outward sin. His discipleship is not entirely annulled thereby, because he can be restored. Thus on conversion a man is ideally delivered from the power of definite sinful habits, but the ideal may not become the actual all at once, or without 'ups and downs'. However, according to the teaching of Wesley, even the ideally perfect conquest of these definite sinful habits is only a beginning. There has also to be built up in the believer an entirely new mind and spirit, the deepest, strongest, most spontaneous, and most constant instinct of which is to cleave to all that is good. Such a mind is no longer tempted to trifle with every sinful thought that presents itself. The practical outcome of this is that the victory over outward sin, over actual sinful habits of word and deed, is now finally consolidated. The territory won is now a secure possession, no longer, as at first, disputed by the ejected enemy. This change is entire sanctification, the attainment of Christian Perfection. To put the matter in everyday language: if by the grace of God, one persists in good habits of thought, word, and deed, these become 'second nature'.

24. As Sugden observes (II, 170): 'The distinction between evil thoughts and evil tempers is a very fine one. An evil thought is a thought of sin dwelt upon and pondered over with pleasure; an evil temper is a desire to carry out in act the thought of sin. Thus, a man has injured me. I may allow myself to think with satisfaction of some way of revenging myself upon him, though without any intention of actually doing so; that is an evil thought. Or I may plan some scheme of revenge with the desire and intention of executing it: that is an evil temper.'

26. '*displacency*'*:* i.e., severe displeasure.

27. '*but not till death; not in this world.*'

Wesley has so far laboured to eliminate misunderstanding of his doctrine. He now faces the common objection to it.

'*The Promise of Sanctification.*'

Verses 1, 3, 7, 8, and 14 of this beautiful poem form Hymn 562 in the *Methodist Hymn-book*. Verses 23, 27, and 28 form Hymn 570.

v. 17. '*Wash out my old original stain.*'

Original Sin, called here 'the original stain' by Charles Wesley, represents all that in our human nature by which we are morally inferior to God's original design for us. The *practical outworking* of Original Sin is that we generally find it easier to choose evil than good. Thus we have to be ever on our guard against temptation. The effect of entire sanctification would be to remove that tragic and fatal bias toward evil. One possible, though rather extreme, way of describing entire sanctification is therefore to speak of washing out Original Sin. The elimination of Original Sin would presumably restore man entirely to the state God planned for him in this world. This would be the utmost conceivable degree of sanctification.

QUESTION

'The nearer to Perfection a man is seen to be by his friends, the more certain he will be to disclaim Perfection for himself.' Would you agree to this proposition? Is it consistent with Methodist doctrine? Why did Wesley not claim to have attained to Christian Perfection himself? What of St. Paul? (Phil. iii. 12), St. James (Jas. iii. 2), St. John (1 John i. 8). What of Jesus ? (Luke xviii. 19).

*Sermon Thirty-Six**

# Wandering Thoughts

WESLEY laid it down that the entirely sanctified Christian is not perfect in freedom from inward mental infirmities such as 'weakness or slowness of understanding, dullness or confusedness of apprehension, incoherency of thought, irregular quickness or heaviness of imagination'. (Sermon XXXV, I, 7.) Wesley has mainly in mind, of course, the effect of these things upon the religious rather than the intellectual life. We may perhaps suppose that it was this 'infirmity' that St. Paul had in mind when he wrote: 'we know not how to pray as we ought' (Rom. viii. 26). In the present sermon Wesley gives this point special attention.

2. It has been said, 'The modern man is not worrying about his sins.' This is a sermon for those who *are* so worrying. There are few among us who seriously doubt our eternal salvation, few who shipwreck our religious life through undue concern that we cannot fix our minds upon God with utter intensity. It is good to remember that there are such people, and were there a revival of zeal for religion there would doubtless be more.

I. 1. *'thoughts that wander from the particular point we have in hand.'*

This is the ordinary regular meaning of 'wandering thoughts', but Wesley places a special religious interest first. This, rather than the general question, is the mental infirmity that concerns him.

2. This paragraph reflects Wesley's very serious view of human nature.

* No. 41 in *Fifty-three Sermons*

4. *'While men, like fiends, each other tear.'*

This is a quotation from Charles Wesley's hymn 'For Peace' (1758). The reference is to the Seven Years' War. Great Britain, in alliance with Frederick of Prussia, was fighting France, Austria, and Russia.

There follows a very human picture of the busy Wesley sitting down to his sermon-preparation, and exasperated with himself because his mind is distracted by the 'war news'. How would he have got on today?


II. *'usefully':* i.e., practically.

1. *'he is an Atheist':* i.e., not perhaps in principle, but in practice.

3. *'the corruptible body, &c.'*

Quoted from the Apocrypha, Wisdom ix. 15.

4. *'preternatural':* i.e., beyond the ordinary course of nature.

*'delirium.'* It is hard to defend Wesley's strange use of this word.


III. 1. *'His particular providence over all things.'*
See Sermon XXXII, 28.

4. *'then commence sinful.'*

An old meaning of 'to commence' is 'to set up as' (e.g., in an occupation).

5-7. This is a most important paragraph. In section II. 3-7 Wesley has traced out with admirable insight, though at times in terms on an antiquated physiology, the ways in which the body limits the free flight of the mind and spirit. However, he now goes on to show that this limitation is not *in itself* sinful, though it may be the occasion for temptation to sin. Thus, although the spirit is limited in its powers so long as it is joined to the body, it is not thereby defiled, or bound to sin. In a religious and moral sense the body is *not* 'the prison-house of the soul'. This is a vital truth, though one that has often been forgotten in the Church. Hence men have sometimes mistakenly afflicted the body in hope of nourishing the soul, or have fondly hoped that the mere fact of death will bring them nearer to God.

6. '*They are troublesome . . . but they are not sinful.*'

To be 'troubled' in this way is apparently consistent with Perfect Love (see end of 7). It is, however, a little difficult to reconcile this statement with the one we have already noticed in the 'Plain Account of Christian Perfection' (Wesley's *Works*, Vol. XI, p. 379). 'They are freed from evil thoughts, so that they cannot enter into them, no, not for a moment. Aforetime, when an evil thought came in, they looked up, and it vanished away. But now it does not come in, there being no room for this, in a soul which is full of God.'

*Sermon Thirty-Seven**

# Satan's Devices

HERE is another sermon, and more eloquent than the last, for 'those who are worrying about their sins'. The 'allowances' that are to be made in preaching Perfection are viewed from another aspect. In Sermon XXXVI the theme was the natural limitations of the human constitution, in body, mind, and spirit. Here Wesley faces the tendency of the earnest believer so to repine over the slowness of his spiritual progress as to hinder that very progress for which he craves. In many walks of life it can happen that the good is the enemy of the best. Men attain so far, and then compromise. At times, however, the converse may be true. The best, which is not immediately attainable, can be the enemy of the good, which is. A practical observation for the preacher who would avoid arousing these harmful repinings is: in preaching Perfection lay the emphasis on the practical message, that God calls all alike, i.e., *you*, to the highest. Be a little reserved about the theory of an instantaneous change which should, ideally, lift the believer clear from every troubling thought.

1. '*the subtle god of this world.*'
   See Sermon XXXIII, I, 1, with note, p. 202.

2. '*Although these blessings are inconceivably great, yet we trust to see greater*':
   The argument runs: 'We have been justified, forgiven, restored to fellowship with God, released from complete slavery to sin. All this is unspeakably glorious, yet we are confidently expecting a complete and secure victory over the power of sin, so that temptation is no longer a stumbling-block to us. We look for the day when the love of God shall so perfectly fill the heart as to drive out all contrary affections, and

* No. 42 in *Fifty-three Sermons*

we walk before Him in even joy.' Thus Wesley defines those to whom this sermon is addressed, believers who are pressing on to entire sanctification.

5. *'retort'*: i.e., hurl back.

I. 1. *'If we knew we must remain as we are, even to the day of our death, we might possibly draw a kind of comfort . . . from that necessity':*

The objection Wesley has in mind is as follows: 'If we could feel that Perfection is something reserved for heaven we might enjoy a confidence that we are right with God, even though the remains of sin continue in our hearts for the whole course of our life. However, your teaching that we must *now* press on to Perfection is likely to shatter our confidence, because, while we know we are justified, we also know we have not attained to this other great blessing.'

*'we are assured . . . that unless sin be all done away in this life, we cannot see God in glory.'*

Taken strictly, this statement would involve the assertion that only those who are entirely sanctified can hope for eternal salvation. This rigid proposition would be quite indefensible, and also inconsistent with what Wesley has already said: (i) that it is the justified who are saved; (ii) that the Christian must be tolerant. Wesley presumably eliminated this difficulty by his theory that believers are usually entirely sanctified at the moment of death. Another explanation, more in line with the main stream of Christian tradition, is outlined in the note to Sermon XXVI, I, 5, pp. 175 f.

2-4. Satan's suggestion is: 'You admit you are not entirely sanctified. How then can you be sure you were not suffering from a delusion on the day when you felt you knew your sins were forgiven?'

10-11. Wesley is right here. In the religious life, as in other affairs, man should not be so absorbed with petty day-to-day details as to forget the great issues. At the same time, there is also to be avoided the opposite error of the theorist who can never bring himself down to earth.

13. '*Why are His chariot-wheels so long a-coming?*'
Here is a strange liberty to take with Judges v. 28.

14. Wesley is absolutely right here, and what he says is most important. One of the greatest obstacles to the spread of the Gospel is prejudice caused by misunderstanding, often wilful misunderstanding, of sound teaching. The preacher should constantly be on his guard to avoid occasion for this, particularly by refraining from extreme and one-sided statements.

'*the accidental abuse*':
i.e., the abuse which may be associated, but is not of the necessary essence of the thing.

II. 2. '*careful for nothing*': i.e., anxious, worried.

3. '*not as something that must be, or thou wilt go to hell, but as what may be, to lead thee to heaven.*'
What admirable counsel is this! How much happier and healthier would the Church have been had evangelists always succeeded, as Wesley did, in laying the emphasis upon the gracious note of God's destiny for man, and offer to him, and not upon 'awful threatenings'.

5. '*You may therefore the more cheerfully endure, as yet, the burden of sin that still remains in you.*'
This certainly does not mean that the Christian is to think lightly of his lapses. The 'burden' that is to be endured is not compromise with sin. It represents: (i) the inevitable and natural limitations of the human constitution in body, mind, and spirit; (ii) the circumstance that the complete change, in principle wrought once for all in Christ, requires time and discipline to be worked out fully in actual practice.

*Sermon Thirty-Eight*\*

# Original Sin

THE great Christian doctrine of Original Sin is an attempt to find an explanation for two dreadful facts of experience: (i) that human nature has a bias toward evil, so that to choose evil is generally easier than to choose good, while the line of least resistance in human affairs is always toward evil; and (ii) that sin is universal in the race. It would be impossible to give a strict proof that there are no rare exceptions to the latter proposition, for we have not an account of the life of every man that has ever lived. However, the noblest and best of men have always been acutely aware that their own natures are stained with sin, while, on the other hand, those who have been inclined to claim sinlessness for themselves have been seen by their companions as far from perfect, and as merely deluded We may safely assume from this that all men are by nature sinful. These two propositions are closely connected, because the universality of sin is a token that the moral weakness of any particular individual is due to inherent defect, and not merely to the accident that he happens to have made a bad choice. If one had a penny that *always* came down 'tails', out of millions of tosses, one would become convinced that this was not chance, but that there was something about the penny that made this happen. So, if even a minority were found to be sinless, it might be said that those that had sinned had done so entirely on their own individual responsibility. That *all* have sinned cannot be an accident. It must be due to something inherent in human nature as we know it.

This universal inborn defect is called Original Sin. This venerable term suffers from a serious defect, in that it involves the use of the word 'sin' in two distinct senses. The sermons on Christian Perfection, &c., have opened our eyes to the important distinction between temptation and sin. There may be very

\* No 44 in *Fifty-three Sermons*

ORIGINAL SIN 233

regrettable defects of constitution, which are the occasion of sore temptation, but there is no actual sin until the temptation is dallied with in the mind. If this distinction is made into a general proposition we may say that 'Original Sin' is *not* sin in the proper sense of the word, i.e., a definite sinful feeling, thought, or act, for which God holds one accountable. It rather describes that regrettable defect which is the occasion of temptation, and which makes man so weak before temptation that he will commonly find it overwhelming unless he be fortified by the grace of God. However, we can hardly hope after so many centuries to drive out from theology the term 'Original Sin', on account of this unfortunate ambiguity. We must content ourselves with making it understood.

Some observations on the story of the Creation and the Fall in Genesis i–iii, and on Wesley's ideas regarding the same, have already been made in Sermon V, i, 1-5, with notes, pp. 38 ff. The traditional theory to explain the dreadful fact of Original Sin has been that Adam, the first father of the whole race, depraved his nature by his sin. This depravity has been inherited by all his children. Wesley naturally accepted this theory. The choice of text and treatment in this sermon, however, shows what part of the subject he considered to be of practical importance to the Gospel preacher. The subject of this sermon is not this theory. It is: (i) the demonstration of the fact of the universality of sin; (ii) the assertion of the doctrine of Entire Depravity, i.e., that the inborn effect has gone so far as to turn every part of human nature entirely from good to evil. The modern preacher would be wise to take this choice as a hint. The important and practical aspect is that all men are in dire need of salvation. We must agree with Wesley that a firm witness to this is an essential part of the necessary foundation for preaching the Gospel, even though we may entirely disagree with him as to the interpretation of the story of Adam and Eve. Those who accept the established modern scientific doctrine of evolution would widely agree in propounding their theory of Original Sin somewhat as follows: There came a day when, as they developed, some individuals of a tribe of beings somewhat similar to ourselves in body and in inherent mental powers first awoke to a sense of right and wrong. The first moral urge would probably be a very rudimentary one indeed, perhaps a dim sense that one ought not to scramble for as much food as one can eat, but to make room for the old and weak as well. Nevertheless, this lifted man from the non-moral animal stage to the level of moral responsibility. Here was one of God's great and mysterious creative acts, the initiation of spiritual life. Since then man has been disciplined by being summoned to face first one moral choice, then another. The difficulty in that first choice was the same as that which confronts the race to-day: namely, that 'Time makes ancient good uncouth'. What in the previous subhuman, non-moral stage had not been sinful, but merely natural and animal, was now challenged by the voice of conscience. Morality had to start by flying in the face of deeply entrenched personal habit and social custom. So it has continued ever since. It is not surprising that the first weak stirrings of conscience did not lead to immediate and complete victory over ancient habit. Thus sin was born, with its consequences of sinful habit and guilty conscience. These consequences constituted the 'bias' which made further good choices hard. Thus the presence of a universal and inborn moral defect may be accounted for. However, the Gospel stands upon the fact of sin, not upon any evolutionary theory.

The reader must bear in mind that the background of this sermon is bitter controversy. Wesley faced those who minimized the fact of sin, and in effect taught that man does not need the grace of God to be saved. In his natural and great anxiety to overturn this disastrous error Wesley also errs in overstating his case. He so blackens human nature that, had one only this sermon to read, one might be excused for supposing that Wesley was a severe and morbid fanatic. However, we well know otherwise, and will make allowances for the ungracious spirit of this sermon, remembering that what Wesley is trying to say is a matter of the greatest importance to the preacher.

*Text.* Gen. vi. 5. Wesley's treatment of this text is another example of the error that comes of laying all possible weight upon a single text, as though by itself it were of all-sufficient divine authority. (See opening note to Sermon XXXV, II, pp. 221 f.) The writer of this chapter can hardly have intended it to be taken in a strict and literal sense, for he immediately goes on to describe a family that was an exception, the house of Noah. Wesley had a method of modifying the sombre picture he paints in this sermon of the *entire* depravity of the human race. This was through the doctrine of Prevenient or Preventing Grace ('preventing'='that which goes before'); see Sermon XII, II, 1, with note, p. 105. The celebrated comment on John i, 9, 'This was the true light, who lighteth every man that cometh into the world' in Wesley's *Notes on the New Testament* runs as follows: 'who lighteth every man . . . "By what is vulgarly termed natural conscience, pointing out at least the general lines of good and evil. And this light, if man did not hinder, would shine more and more to the perfect day." ' A further definition is given in Sermon LXXXV, III, 4 (*Works*, Vol. VI, 512): 'No man living is entirely destitute of what is vulgarly called natural conscience. But this is not natural: It is more properly termed, preventing grace. Every man has a greater or less measure of this.' Thus Wesley would not say that man was by nature a mixture of good and bad. He preferred to teach that by nature man was entirely evil, but that God's grace was at work in all men, even those who made no conscious response to it. This is much the same in practical effect, but this way of putting the matter serves to emphasize the truth that whatever is good in man is the gift of God. The present sermon says very little indeed of Prevenient Grace, and thus, when taken alone, presents a one-sided view of Wesley's doctrine of human nature.

It is interesting to observe that among the Jews there was more disposition to find the origin of sin in the passage Gen. vi. 1–7, whence this text comes, rather than in Gen. iii, which has received so much attention from the Church.

1. '*The writings of many of the ancients abound with gay descriptions of the dignity of man.*'

This is true, if one makes the right selection. The other side, the universal wickedness of the race, was however a theme by no means unknown to the classical writers. (See Sermon XXXIII, I, 8.)

2. Wesley has much justice on his side here.

'*not a few persons of strong understanding, as well as extensive learning.*'

Wesley probably mainly has in mind Dr. John Taylor, a learned Presbyterian Minister of Norwich, and a man of Unitarian leanings. In his '*The Scripture Doctrine of Original Sin Proposed to Free and Candid Examination*' (1740), he denied the effect of Adam's sin on the whole race, and allowed that, while men were degenerate, they still had the power to do their duty before God if they would. To answer this book Wesley wrote '*The Doctrine of Original Sin; According to Scripture, Reason, and Experience*' (1757).

4. See Sermon V, I, 1-5, with notes, pp. 38 ff.

I. 1. '*The earth then retained much of its primaeval beauty, &c.*'

There seems nothing to warrant this in the old Hebrew Flood-story.

4. '*It cannot indeed be denied, but many of them, perhaps all, had good motions put into their hearts.*'

Wesley is so carried away by his theme that this recognition of his teaching regarding Prevenient Grace appears somewhat grudging. However, if the statement be taken seriously it is a considerable practical modification of the severe 'No, none at all'.

II. 3. '*From the things that are seen we inferred the existence of an eternal, powerful Being.*'

Here is another important modification of the doctrine of the entire depravity of man. Loyalty to the established tradition

ORIGINAL SIN 237

of Christian theology demanded of Wesley the admission that important truths about God and religion are to be learned from evidences in the natural world, through the exercise of the divine gift of reason. However, from the point of view of a saving religious experience, Wesley is absolutely right in emphasizing that there is a world of difference between an acknowledgement in principle of the existence of God and an 'acquaintance' with Him. Certainly man cannot come to this 'acquaintance' by the exercise of his natural faculties alone. It is the work of divine grace.

4. The story of this barbarous experiment is told by Herodotus (ii. 2), of Psammetichus, King of Egypt.

*'Such is natural religion, abstracted from traditional.'*

Wesley is doubtless correct in claiming that such children would have no religion. The difficulty is that children brought up with an artificial care that they should never be influenced by the religious and moral ideas of other people would not be normal children. It is dangerous to argue that what would be true of such imaginary figures is true of the race. It is a token of the universality of religion, even though it be but of gross superstition, that such artificial care would be necessary to secure a child absolutely devoid of acquired religious ideas. This universality of religion indicates that there is in man a natural and inherent instinct to find for himself some object of religious trust and devotion. Some modern circles have, indeed, consciously repudiated the Christian religion as a superstition, or as a beautiful myth. Experience however shows that in such circles there is generally a turning after a time, sometimes to new and false religions such as Christian Science and Theosophy, sometimes to make a religion of some political theory or leader, sometimes to superstitions like Spiritualism, or even the carrying of mascots. Human nature will not be denied for long. That our nature is like this is a mark that God has made us to seek after Him. That 'traditional religion', at least of some sort, is found practically everywhere, is a token of the reality of 'natural religion'.

6. Superstition is simply religion at a very low level of reason and ethics. The same instinct that finds satisfaction in true religion is seen in action also in superstition, but working apart from knowledge of what is right and wrong, and of the laws which govern the working of the natural world around us. The universality and power of superstition among simple and ignorant people is a token of the utter naturalness of nobler religion among more fortunate people.

8. *'I will sit upon the sides of the north.'* (Isaiah xiv. 13.)

This has nothing to do with Satan, for the passage refers to the King of Babylon.

*'Because I had a mind to it.'*

Wesley is unduly severe in condemning such an answer as necessarily involving the ignoring of the claims of God. There are multitudes of affairs and choices in life, either of no particular moral significance, or where action is dictated by long-established moral and religious habit, in which even the most devout believer hardly has occasion to inquire of his soul: 'What is the will of God for me?' The Christian often simply has to 'make up his mind' like other men, though 'the mind of Christ' is doubtless there as a powerful influence in the subconscious background. To try to turn *everything* into a conscious religious choice would be to turn religion into an obsession. Wesley has already condemned this attitude as 'enthusiasm' in Sermon XXXII, 20.

9. *'Sensual appetites, even those of the lowest kind, have, more or less, the dominion over him.'*

Wesley seems to have sexual desire mainly in mind here, to judge from the lines quoted (of uncertain source), in which 'love' is used in the sense of sexual desire, together with the reference to the sin of adultery. It is unfortunately true that many men of good breeding and education have gone sadly astray in matters of personal purity. However, as elsewhere, Wesley over-blackens his picture, in a not very lovely paragraph.

ORIGINAL SIN 239

10. The verses are from Prior's 'Lines to the Hon. Charles Montague'.

11. *'the old, vain Heathen.'*

   A not very respectful epithet for Cicero. The Latin is apparently an inaccurate quotation of De Officiis, i. 28, 29.

III. 1. *'no man is born, &c.'* Horace, Sat. i. 3, 68.

2. It is surely an extraordinary and indefensible exaggeration to elevate the doctrine of Original Sin, particularly as stated in this severest manner, into the fundamental point of distinction between Christian and non-Christian religion. The practical outcome of the doctrine, namely, that all men are in dire need of salvation, is indeed one of several essential elements of the Gospel. It is, however, only one of several, and one shared with some other religions.

   *'shibboleth':* see Judges xii. **6.**

3. 'Θεραπεία ψυχῆς.'

   'The healing of the soul.' The phrase is of Plato: *Gorgias*. 464. B.

4. Thomas Hobbes of Malmesbury, the great philosopher, lived 1588-1679.

   *'Outward reformation, if their supposition be just, is indeed the one thing needful.'*

   Wesley is absolutely right here, and his judgement illuminates the whole importance of this subject. Some take an over-optimistic view of human nature, ignoring the enslaving power of inward sin. Such are logically bound to dilute the Gospel to a call to man to follow, in his own strength, the good advice and good example of Jesus. Only those who see the need of a miraculous work of salvation can be trusted adequately to preach the Gospel of Grace.

## Questions

1. Does modern preaching suffer through saying too little about Original Sin? Is it better to preach the doctrine without using this term?

2. 'That which is sinful in a man cannot be original to his nature; that which is original cannot be sinful.' Do you agree?

3. Is it possible to explain every morally harmful institution, and every evil habit of thought and feeling current among the people, as the corrupt survival of what was at one time right, or at least, not wrong? Or does this explanation fail to make evil positive enough?

4. Does unsaved man bear the image of the Devil, or the *defaced* image of God?

5. 'Neither grand nor beautiful objects please any longer than they are new.' (II. 10.) Is this true?

6. Consider paragraph II. 11. Should the servant of God have a regard for his good reputation among his neighbours? If so, why? What is he to do when he knows that some good action is almost certain to be misrepresented to his discredit?

7. 'The one acknowledges that many men are infected with many vices; . . . the other declares that all men are "conceived in sin".' (III. 1.) Which judgement do you prefer?

*Sermon Thirty-Nine**

# The New Birth

THIS sermon covers much the same ground as Sermons XIV and XV, though Wesley is more emphatic in guarding against possible misunderstanding of the doctrine of Baptismal Regeneration. The sermon was frequently preached; on a number of occasions the previous sermon on Original Sin was taken as the morning subject, with this to follow.

1. '*the former . . . which God does for us; . . . the latter . . . which God does in us.*' See Sermon XV, 2, with note, p. 123.

   '*We first conceive His wrath to be turned away.*' See note to Sermon V, 1, p. 38.


I. 1. For Wesley's ideas regarding the Image and Likeness of God in Adam, the Original Righteousness of Adam, and the Fall, see Sermon V, I, 1-4, with note, pp. 38 ff.

2. '*he was not made immutable.*'

   The ancient traditional theory was that the 'Image of God' in Adam consisted of those gifts and powers, such as reason, by which man is superior to the animals, and to the rest of creation. This 'Image' was a part of man's very nature, and so could not be lost. The 'Likeness of God' was a supernatural gift of grace, which raised man to moral perfection, and to full communion with God. This was not part of human nature, and was forfeited at the Fall. Wesley, however, does not employ this distinction. He extends the 'Image of God' to include the gift of spiritual grace, speaking of the 'Image' as chiefly the moral image (I, 1). The traditional theory bears witness to the undoubted fact that the chief effect of sin is not to rob man of his gifts, but to sap his moral power to use those

\* No. 45 in *Fifty-three Sermons*

gifts aright. However, it is fanciful to see this distinction in Gen. i. 26: 'Let us make man in our image, after our likeness.' This phrase is an example of Hebrew 'parallelism', i.e., saying the same thing twice in varied form, as a means to poetical effect. This is a mode of expression common throughout the Bible. The 'Image' is the same as the 'Likeness', and denotes that by which man has 'dominion . . . over all the earth', and by which he can speak with God.

3. In Sermon V, I, 5, Wesley teaches that man became liable to physical death at the Fall. The present statement may indicate that Wesley changed his mind later, though this is not a necessary conclusion. The view that man became mortal, and *liable* to death, even though he did not die *there and then*, is a very natural construction to place on Gen. ii. 17.

II. 3. Wesley's account of the incorporation of Gentile proselytes into the community of Israel by Baptism is worthy of attention. This custom was really a particular example of the very natural use of ceremonial washing as an outward sign of cleansing from sin. Another particular example was the baptism of repentant Jews by St. John the Baptist. Thus the infant Church had already to hand in her Jewish background the raw material for Christian Baptism. This was united with the Lord's teaching about a baptism with the Holy Spirit. Such is the origin of a Sacrament which was the outward mark of conversion, of turning from sin to God in penitent faith, of joining the Church, and of a New Birth to a new life.

Compare Sermon XV, I, 2-10; II, 1.

4. '*He "feels in his heart", to use the language of our Church.*' This is from the Homily for Rogation Week, Part III.

III. 2. '*For you will all drop into the pit together, &c.*' This outburst reminds us both of the reality of hell to Wesley, and of the relative rarity in his work of the appeal to fear of

THE NEW BIRTH 243

hell. This surely is the true Christian emphasis, for Jesus Himself on occasion spoke with dark foreboding of the unspeakably dreadful consequences of persistence in sin, yet never made this theme central to His message.

3. *'the poor, ungodly poet':*

i.e., Juvenal. The citation is from Sat. iv. 8.

IV. 1. For a note on the relation of Baptism to the New Birth, and on Wesley's views regarding the same, see the introductory note to Sermon XIV, pp. 115 ff.

*'The judgement of the latter':*

i.e., the Dissenters or Nonconformists. As the Independents (Congregationalists) and Baptists, being organized congregationally, had no single definite standard, Wesley quotes the Presbyterian Larger Catechism as representative of non-Anglican opinion.

2. *'they do not constantly go together.' 'I do not now speak with regard to infants.'*

Wesley does not intend to propound one theory of Baptism for infants, and a contradictory one for adults. It should be remembered that the 'Catholic' tradition in the Church, that Baptism and the New Birth do go together, has been mainly formed with the custom of Infant Baptism as the background. The interest has been to emphasize the spiritual necessity of uniting every soul from infancy onward with the Church, and to explain the spiritual blessings which potentially belong to the child through incorporation into the saving fellowship of the Church. When Wesley looks at the matter from this aspect he affirms his allegiance to traditional Anglican theology. There is, however, always another aspect, which confronts Wesley with a separate problem, not theological but practical and evangelical. The present paragraph does not open with a theoretical judgement upon the case of a sinful and unbelieving adult who, in that condition, goes through the outward form of Holy Baptism. What we have, rather, is pointed and practical advice to an adult who, baptized as an infant, shows no sign in his present life of fulfilling the gracious promise then made.

3. *'an eminent writer.'*

William Law, who in 1739 published *The Grounds and Reasons of Christian Regeneration.*

Wesley is needlessly severe on Law's work. There is, however, a useful theological distinction between the New Birth as the first instantaneous moment of a process, and sanctification as the continuation of that process.

4. Here is the practical issue ably dealt with. The sinner is resisting conviction of sin. He tries to make of the traditional language of his Church a cave of refuge. Wesley faithfully drags him out into the healing light of day.

*'And where lies the uncharitableness now? &c.'*

In controversy with his ecclesiastically minded expostulant Wesley turns back the objection in a neat debating point 'Without the New Birth this sinner is damned, we agree. How then can you deny me the right to offer the New Birth to him here and now, simply on the ground that he was baptized year ago?'

*'What! would you have me deny my baptism?'*

Wesley's answer would have been "No". Had such a baptized sinner been converted Wesley would certainly not have asked him to be re-baptized, and present Methodist usage would agree with this attitude. Rather would Wesley have rejoiced that the promise made in infancy was at length being fulfilled. The Baptism had remained a real one in principle all the time, even though in practice it had lain dormant.

*'eight days old':*

A very usual custom, because the Jews performed circumcision on the eighth day.

*'Do you say, "Nay, but I do no harm to any man," &c.'*

Here we come to another portrait of the 'Almost Christian'.

## QUESTIONS.

1. 'Except he be born again, none can be happy even in this world.' (III, 3.) Is this true?

2. 'Nor is it an objection ... that we cannot comprehend how this work can be wrought.' (IV, 2.) Does it then not matter whether we try to frame a theology to give a reasoned exposition of the things of God?

*Sermon Forty*\*

# The Wilderness State

IN this and the following sermon we come again to some of Wesley's wise pastoral advice to the convert. The theme of both is how the natural effects of the frailty of the human constitution may be distinguished from unfaithfulness and inward sin, so that the Christian may be mentally prepared to bear the former with patience, without falling into compromise with the latter. This is a most important topic, which Wesley always handles with spiritual insight and common sense.

The first subject of the present sermon is the wave of nervous depression which very commonly sweeps over the new convert, after his first joyous experience. Wesley had great understanding of the spiritual problems of those who found that faith in Christ had not brought that constancy of joy and emotional exaltation which they had perhaps expected. He had been through the experience himself, as reference to the *Journal* for the half-year following his evangelical experience of May 24, 1738 will show. On that day he found triumph over sin, but not joy. Next day he wrestled with fear. On May 26 his soul 'continued in peace, but yet in heaviness because of manifold temptation'. On May 28 he woke 'in peace, but not in joy'. By June 4–6 he had increasing joy. On Oct. 14 he was still examining himself, finding a real work of grace in his heart, yet many things which caused him deep regret. On Jan. 4, 1739, Wesley examined himself again, and affirmed that he was not a Christian, on the ground that he did not *feel* love to God, and had no *abiding* joy in the Holy Spirit. It is worthy of note that all this did not prevent him from beginning and pressing on with his powerful work as an evangelist, in which he was already finding much success. This was indeed a good example for every preacher. Many an evangelical Christian has been held back through waiting upon his 'feelings', but not so

\*No. 46 in *Fifty-three Sermons*

Wesley. In time he emerged from 'the wilderness state'. His practical advice on a most important but often neglected subject springs from experience, and merits respect.

The discussion of this 'wilderness state' is associated in Wesley's mind, and in this sermon, with a kindred theme. The mystical writers of the Church had discovered that those who enjoy a deep experience of God are at times likely to be overtaken by periods of spiritual coldness or sorrow. This has been called 'the dark night of the soul'. The Mystics have also found that great spiritual blessings can come to those who endure these periods of darkness in patience, without yielding to the temptation to forsake Christ. On this account they have commonly taught that God leaves the soul in darkness for a time, as a means of discipline, and even that the blessings of the darkness are greater than those of the light. When he is full of peace and joy the believer walks by 'luminous faith', when he goes into darkness the believer is forced to walk by a higher faith, 'naked faith', i.e., faith unsupported by all that sense of joyous triumph and of God's presence that helps human frailty along the path of life. This notion ran quite counter to Wesley's doctrine that the highest privileges for every believer were conscious communion with God, abounding victory over sin, the Witness of the Spirit bringing Full Assurance, and the experience of Perfect Love. Thus there is introduced a controversial element to the sermon. We may rightly admit that there are valuable elements of truth in the mystical doctrine, but Wesley has more robust common sense on his side.

Allowance must be made for the circumstance that Wesley had to face these problems without the light cast upon them by modern psychological investigation. It is now realized that an experience which produces a wave of emotional exaltation is by the natural law of the mind likely to be followed by a wave of nervous depression. 'Nervous energy, when directed vigorously in a certain way, completely expends itself, and must then have a period of recuperation.' (Starbuck, *Psychology of Religion*, p. 357.) The moral of this is that the convert should be encouraged to fix his attention upon his changed principles and moral will, *not* upon his 'feelings', as is so natural. He should look outward to the finished work of Christ, and not inward to his heart.

I. 1. '*It properly consists in the loss of that faith which God has wrought in their heart.*'

This may seem rather a sweeping statement. Its truth depends on what is meant here by 'faith'. If the convert lets go his underlying will to cleave in allegiance to Christ, his conviction that Christ can be the Saviour of men, and his desire to have Christ in the heart as the conqueror of sin, then he has obviously ceased to be a Christian at all. Wesley hardly means that the loss of faith has gone as far as this. The faith which is lost rather seems from the context to be the Witness of the Spirit, and 'the light of heaven'; i.e., a joy and peace in that allegiance, a distinct sense that the Saviour is *my* Saviour, and an experience that He *even now* conquers in my heart.

2. '*They have not now that zeal for the souls of men.*'

Yet Wesley was sustained in this moment by his strong sense of duty, and continued to preach.

II. 1. '*I dare not rank among these the . . . will of God.*'

This is a first point of departure from the doctrine of the Mystics.

(i.) Paragraphs 2–10 describe ways in which darkness of soul may be due to sin yet remaining in the heart of the disciple.

5. The way to avoid, or to recover from, depression, is to continue steadfastly witnessing to the right.

(ii.) (iii.) However, the darkness may be due to things other than sin. There may be infirmities or natural limitations for which the believer is not morally responsible. It is important that he learn to distinguish the one from the other, for these latter require a combination of teachability and patience, rather than penitence. Wesley will help the disciple to know himself.

(ii.) 2. The work of some Mystical writers had had unfortunate effects among the Methodists, as we have seen (introduction to Sermons X, XII). Wesley was on occasion engaged in hot controversy. We are not surprised, therefore, to find that he makes too unfavourable a judgement upon the Mystics of the Roman Church. In fact, Wesley himself must often have walked by what the Mystics have described as 'naked faith', during the six months of frequent fighting and fears which followed his own great evangelical experience.

III. 1. *'To give comfort, is the single point at which they aim, &c.'*

Wesley's words may seem somewhat harsh, but in principle he is right. Some converts who fall into darkness require a stern call to penitence and restitution, if they are indeed in earnest in the Christian way of life, and *not* a redoubled emphasis that 'love only seeks to forgive and forget'. With others, again, it may be otherwise.

*'the title, which has been ignorantly given to others':*

i.e., to the Methodists, by their detractors.

2–14. The sermon closes with faithful advice in detail, adapted to different cases.

## QUESTIONS

1. What is the meaning of St. John xx. 29?

2. Would you allow to be a healthy Christian one who rarely, if ever, enjoyed 'luminous faith', but who frequently found himself wandering in the 'Wilderness State'?

3. Does triumphing in God lead to the temptation of pride? Are Christians purified from pride by 'darkness and dryness'?

4. The Church accomplishes her greatest work in times of revival, but valuable lessons may also be learned from times of spiritual adversity, e.g., the present welcome movement to live down 'our unhappy divisions' largely springs from the adversity and misfortunes of the Churches. Do you think that it is God's plan that there should be periods of adversity as well as of revival and success, or is it simply that God does the best He can with imperfect and sinful servants?

*Sermon Forty-One*\*

# Heaviness through Manifold Temptations

WESLEY here goes farther into the problem faced in the last sermon. Nervous depression and loss of joy in a believer is systematically divided into that which is due to sin, and that which is due to other natural causes. The former Wesley calls 'darkness', the latter, 'heaviness'. This is certainly a helpful distinction, and one of much assistance to the Christian who would know himself.


II. 2. *'heaviness.'*

In old English this word was commonly used in the sense of 'sorrow'.


III. 1. *'Pain is perfect misery, . . .'*

The quotation is from Milton, *Paradise Lost*, VI, 462. The lines actually run:

> 'But pain is perfect misery, the worst
> Of evils, and excessive, overturns
> All patience.'

*'the soul sympathizing with the body.'*

The word 'sympathize' is here used in its true and original sense of 'to suffer together with'.

2. We can hardly suppose that God 'appoints' disease. To Jesus disease was something existing in defiance of the will of God. The healing of the sick was eminently the outward mark of God's work in the world. (Luke vii. 18–23.)

\* No. 47 in *Fifty-three Sermons*

*'Faith no more hinders the sinking of the spirits (as it is called) in an hysteric illness, than the rising of the pulse in a fever.'*

Wesley is here not very far from the matter as it is viewed in the light of modern psychological knowledge. The human mind and nervous system work according to natural laws just as certainly as does the body. If nature makes a state of nervous depression inevitable, as it may at times, faith can no more overcome the effect than she can a purely bodily illness. It is then idle to talk about the effect in terms of 'sin', even though the symptoms may be similar in appearance to the results of inward sin. At the same time, nervous and mental illness can be treated, just as can bodily disease, and *the* great preventive and curative treatment is a strong religious faith in a good, wise, and all-powerful God. Thus there is a sense in which faith *can* often hinder 'the sinking of the spirits'.

3-4. Here is a beautiful picture of Wesley's sympathy with the unfortunate and bereaved. No one was better armed than he to bear with fortitude 'the slings and arrows of outrageous fortune'. He had a constitution naturally possessed of great self-control, and to this was added a strong religious faith. Such fortunate souls often find it hard fully to sympathize with their less heroic brethren; not so Wesley, however.

3. *'But what shall they do who have none of these? &c.'*

Many comfortable Christians have talked airily of the great spiritual benediction that may exist in homes of grinding poverty. So it may, for God has many triumphs of grace. Wesley, however, knew the life of the poor. He doubtless also remembered the acute financial anxiety that had often dogged his childhood home. He certainly did not look upon the lot of the poor through rose-coloured spectacles, but could plainly see that their insecurity, physical misery, and degrading surroundings were the occasion of 'manifold temptations', which may assail the strongest faith. Therefore his heart burned for the poor, in particular for the exploited poor.

'*I laugh at the stupid Heathen.*'

Juvenal, Sat. iii. 152. The lines may be rendered: 'What unhappiness is harder in poverty than that it makes men liable to be laughed at.'

4. '*He would have our affections regulated, not extinguished.*'

Here Christian morality rises above Stoicism, and likewise the ascetic ideal.

'*nature unreproved may drop a tear.*'

From 'The Parish Priest', a poem by Samuel Wesley, junior.

6. How often has it been said that sorrow and adversity drive men and women to God? It is so, if they have triumphant faith, for faith grows when it is greatly exercised. However, the reverse is often true. Sorrow and adversity also bring the occasion of great temptation, and there are many casualties in the battle. Multitudes have been driven into unbelief, bitterness, and selfishness by their misfortunes.

7. For this, see the latter part of the introduction to Sermon XL, and Sermon XL, II, 1.

'*to play at bo-peep with His creatures.*'

A reminiscence of S. Badcock, *Remarks on Dr. Kenrick's Observations.*

8. '*the words of a late writer.*'

Madame Guyon, the celebrated Mystic. (See her *Life*, an edition of which Wesley himself published in 1776.)

9. '*which uses to precede justification*':

i.e., 'which is accustomed to precede justification'.

Wesley is a little too dogmatic in his attempt to fit the Christian experience of Madame Guyon to his familiar scheme of prevenient grace, conviction of sin, justification, and sanctification. We have to admit that many Mystics of deep Christian experience have found themselves 'in the desert' for a time, but we may rightly claim with Wesley that this stage is not invariable and necessary, and that those blessed with the highest degree of faith may escape it, p. 258.

IV. 2. Compare this with section III, 6, and note, p. 253.

V. 4. Here is seen the practical outcome of Wesley's distinction between 'darkness' and 'heaviness'. Here, likewise, is the summary of the whole prolonged discussion of the spiritual state of those who are pressing on to Perfection. (Sermons XXXV, XXXVI, XXXVII, XL, XLI.) The Christian will inevitably be assaulted by many things which hinder him from walking with God in constant and increasing exultation and triumph. Some of these are due to inward sin yet remaining. The Christian must be watchful to repent of these, and to flee from them to Christ. Others are due to the natural limitation, bodily, nervous, and mental, of the human constitution, and to the 'changes and chances of this mortal life'. These are the 'growing pains' of the Christian life. They are to be endured in faith, yet without self-accusings, as a discipline from which much is to be learned. How important it is, then, to distinguish the one from the other!

*Sermon Forty-Two**

# Self-Denial

THE volume of Standard Sermons closes with three more of Wesley's excellent sermons on Christian conduct. We are reminded that Wesley was first, and by nature, a moralist; afterwards, and by grace, an evangelist. To the end of his days he was never more at home than when giving practical instructions to those who already believed. Wesley's eloquence, his powerful literary style, and the remorseless hammer-blows of his logic, are never seen to better effect than when he engages upon such themes. The permanent value of these practical sermons is not only in the instruction they give, though this is often very sound. They should be treasured also for the picture of Wesley, the man. The one who, by inborn nature, is a severe moralist, and to whom Duty, 'stern daughter of the voice of God', is all in all, is not thereby a Christian. If by miracle of grace he comes to a full evangelical experience of salvation he will become perhaps the noblest, and certainly the most useful, of all the servants of God. Wesley was such a one.

4. *'So mystical a manner.'*

We have seen that Wesley often had to take up arms against such errors as 'stillness', the neglect of the means of grace, Antinomianism, and rank individualism. This led him into hot controversy with men who were frequently described as, or who claimed to be, 'mystics'. The effect of this was that the word 'mystical' became for Wesley a term of reproach, as here. This is, however, a misrepresentation of a great word. A Mystic is properly one who has a deep sense of complete union with God in the inmost depths of the soul, and to whom that inward union, and not anything connected with the outward life of the Church or society, is the main part of religion. The Jesus of history, and the Lord of the Creeds, take a place of secondary

* No. 48 in *Fifty-three Sermons*

importance to the Christ in the heart. (A mystic who *repudiates* the Christ of historical fact, and the Church, may indeed be a mystic, but he is hardly a *Christian* mystic.) If the student would be presented with a clear picture of a genuine Christian mystic, let him read the story of that great Indian Christian of modern times, Sadhu Sundar Singh (e.g., in *The Sadhu,* by Streeter and Appasamy). Mysticism is thus one side of genuine religion. It is impossible to imagine any deep religion of the heart without some measure of mystical experience. The Gospel according to St. John is largely a mystical book. The Wesley hymns, likewise, are full of mysticism. Charles Wesley's lines:

> Eager for Thee I ask and pant,
>   So strong the principle divine
> Carries me out with sweet constraint,
>   Till all my hallowed soul is Thine;
> Plunged in the Godhead's deepest sea,
> And lost in Thine immensity;

('Wesley's Hymns,' 374, v. 3)

are typical of the language of the Mystics. It is perhaps because so many of the typical devotional writers of the Church have been of the mystical school that Wesley, in the present paragraph, allows a prejudiced judgement upon what had been written before his time on 'self-denial'.


I. 1. *'having unawares inbibed strong prejudices against it'?*

i.e., they are contaminated with Antinomianism.

Here the controversial issue with those who professed lax Christian ethics is united with the practical interest of the sermon.

*'look upon the whole body of Predestinarians.'*

Logically a Calvinist who believes in Predestination, i.e., that man's salvation depends wholly upon the sovereign choice of God, and not at all upon man's co-operation, should be open to the danger of Antinomianism. One who believes that his own action has no part in his salvation, and moreover, feels himself to be in the grip of irresistible divine grace, so that he *cannot* go to final perdition, will surely be slack in his moral duties. So Wesley seems to have argued. This is, however, a case where logic leads one quite astray. The foundation of Calvinism was not a theoretical judgement upon human free-will, but a practical issue of piety. All was based upon the instinct to magnify the unspeakable majesty of God by giving everything to Him and nothing to man. The God of Calvinist theology was thus a severe task-master rather than a loving Father. The result of this was that Calvinism was a religion of stern duty, and bred men of rigid morals. Indeed, its besetting failing was not Antinomianism, but the opposite one of legalism. On the other hand, Antinomianism, moral laxity on account of the mercy of God, has been the error which has battened upon the warmer and more rapturous types of evangelical religion. A parallel case is the paradox of Communism. Communist theory teaches that all economic and social change proceeds automatically, according to the evolutionary world-process. Logically this should produce political apathy. Men should sit and wait for the inevitable change to happen. Actually, a vivid faith in the reality of this world-process has prompted Communists to be most active in their efforts to change the economic and social order.

'*Ranter.*'

A sect of Antinomians who appeared about 1644 went by this nickname, long before it was attached to the early Primitive Methodists.

2. '*And we see the reason thereof, because we are creatures.*'

This is a valid reason why the will of God should be the rule of man. God is the Sovereign Lord. A reason still more profound, more morally valid, is that God's will is good and wise.

6. This is the important point. 'Self-denial' is no trivial matter. It is something great and wide. To go without some small luxury so as to provide the wherewithal to fill the Missionary Box may be a sincere expression of the spirit of self-denial.

Nevertheless, things like this are only the smaller matters of the law. To get into the habit of speaking of 'self-denial' as though it were essentially the foregoing of small pleasures is utterly to degrade the word. Self-denial is nothing less than saying 'No' to self, to self-will, to self-interest, to self-esteem and pride, and even to self-preservation, whenever saying 'Yes' to God demands this. Wesley's explanation here agrees with the sense of the text. The self-denial of which Jesus there speaks is nothing less than preparedness at the call of God to set foot, in company with Himself, upon a path of life which will certainly lead to hardship, and quite possibly to martyrdom.

7. *'A cross is anything contrary to our will.'*

In this text our Lord was clearly speaking of a literal cross, crucifixion being representative of the cruel and violent deaths that await martyrs. The metaphor of 'taking up the cross' answers to the common custom of making the condemned man carry the cross-beam to the place of execution, where the upright would probably be a fixture. Wesley's extension of the meaning represents the common usage of devotional literature. This usage is legitimate, inasmuch as 'not My will, but Thine be done' was the very spirit that took Christ to a real cross. The difficulty is, however, that it is all too easy to debase the term 'a cross' by applying the metaphor of the great and grim to that which is merely inconvenient and annoying.

14. Self-torture, which has often accompanied certain types of Christian devotion, has been sadly deflated in reputation by modern psychological research. It is now seen not as a mark of extreme zeal for the spiritual, but as a morbid condition arising from the perversion of the sexual instinct.

II. 4. *'they do not attain faith, because they will not "deny themselves".'*

Taken in the strictest sense, this statement would compromise the fundamental doctrine of Justification by Faith. As it stands it reads as though faith were something earned by man on account of the merits of his sincere repentance, rather than the gift of God which produces a change of heart. It was on just this notion that Wesley based so much of his piety in the days before his evangelical experience. We are reminded that this sermon, in its original form at least, dates from this period. This text was first preached from on February 20, 1738. When he first penned these words Wesley doubtless meant them in the strict sense. In the enthusiasm of his evangelical experience he at first denied that good works done before conversion were in any way acceptable to God: e.g., Sermon I, 2; Sermon VI, III, 5. More mature reflection caused him to modify this unduly rigid judgement, and he came to admit that good works 'meet for repentance' might be a *previous condition* to justification, though not the *effective cause* of it. (See Sermon XXII, 2, with note, p. 162.) It is doubtless in this modified sense that Wesley would have the present paragraph to be understood. As such it is a most salutary truth.


III. 2. '*even bodies of men, who were once burning and shining lights.*'

Wesley has in mind the Moravians. He could forget neither the unspeakable blessing that had come to him through their preaching of faith, nor yet the harm wrought in the Methodist Society by the excesses of 'stillness', and even of Antinomianism.

'*Abnegationem omnem proculcamus, &c.*'

This appears to be a conflation of two statements made by Count von Zinzendorf, the Lutheran patron and protector of the Moravians, in his Latin conversation with Wesley in Gray's Inn Walks, September 3, 1741. (See the *Journal* for that date.)

'*that great, bad man.*'

Here Wesley plainly allows the heat of controversy to prejudice him. He should have said of Zinzendorf, 'that great, *good* man,' even though some of his opinions were open to serious question. The present strong repudiation of self-denial is a case in point. The intention is to affirm Justification by Faith:

the way to God is not through any self-imposed discipline of stern self-denial, but by repose upon the gracious promises of a pardoning and delivering God. However, this intention is expressed in so extreme and paradoxical a form as to be an affront to common sense, while the simple and uncritical would certainly misunderstand it to their own ruin. For his part, Wesley was certainly right in rejecting such opinions and modes of expression, though he did less than justice to many of those who were responsible for them.

## QUESTIONS

1. Is it true to say that it is 'more easy to forgo pleasure, than to endure pain'? (I, 7.) Why do so many persist in seeking pleasure in ways which they know will probably bring ultimate pain?

2. If we can allow that God *gives* a cross. is it right to use 'such means to remove the pressure as Christian wisdom directs'? (I, 12.)

3. Which reflects the deeper view of the nature of Christianity?

> 'Some softening gleam of love and prayer
> Shall dawn on every cross and care'
>
> (*M.H.B.* 927, v. 5)

or,

> 'My spirit to Calvary bear,
> To suffer and triumph with Thee.'
>
> (*M.H.B.* 457, v. 2.)

4. Do you approve of the phrase 'Self-denial Week'?

*Sermon Forty-Three**

# The Cure of Evil-Speaking

THE occasion of this sermon, packed with practical advice, seems to have been an outbreak of gossip which took place at Bristol in the beginning of 1752. At this time John and Charles Wesley, and eleven of their preachers, joined together in signing a document pledging themselves to conduct corresponding to the rules of this sermon. The only general comment to be made is that the advice presupposes a community living at a very high level of Christian fellowship. Such plainness of speech would place an unbearable strain upon any ordinary human society. It could not fail to produce open quarrels if practised among those who were not completely prepared to accept, for the good of their own souls, rebukes that might be most wounding to self-esteem. At the same time, a Christian in earnest ought to be able to face this strict social discipline. The advice as such is ideal. A lesson in this matter is to be learned from Methodist history. The early Band-Meeting corresponded to this standard of plain dealing, Christian brother with brother. So long as the Revival continued at white-heat this institution contributed to the health of Methodism. It did not, however, endure nearly so long as the less arduous fellowship of the Class-Meeting. The background of the sermon is certainly the life of the Christian in the Church, not his life in the world. The sins to be rebuked are mainly those faults of temperament, behaviour, and speech, which mar the life of the Church, rather than the open sins of worldly men. There is also an allied problem which Wesley does not face here. There may be occasions when, if scandal be already in circulation, it will be the invidious duty of some responsible person who knows the true facts to allow them to be known, for the sake of the reputation of innocent persons or of the Church, or simply to kill garbled versions and evil surmisings. This may involve making state-

* No. 49 in *Fifty-three Sermons*

ments which are not to the credit of some individual whom one cannot usefully first approach.

3. *'It gratifies our pride, to relate those faults of others whereof we think ourselves not to be guilty.'*

This is the subconscious mainspring of nearly all gossip. Hence evil-speaking is a sin, and not a mere 'failing'.

I. 1. *'Love can bow down the stubborn neck, ...'*

This verse is from a beautiful hymn printed in part as No. 387 in the present Hymn-book.

3. *'Only beware you do not feign the want of opportunity, in order to shun the cross.'*

This warning is necessary, for nothing is easier than to deceive oneself.

6. Wesley is stern with a natural and common human failing, but he is entirely justified. Those who speak of evil must make sure that they do so for the benefit of the one who is at fault, and not to gratify themselves.

7. There is ample moral justification for the general legal obligation of the citizen to assist the course of justice by disclosing to the police serious offences or intended offences. The Christian citizen ought not to shirk this invidious public duty. At the same time, he certainly ought not to be an habitual tale-bearer in trivial matters.

III. 1. *'tell it to the Church.'*

The original sense of our Lord's words would be: 'tell it to the Synagogue'. The later application to the Christian Church is both natural and legitimate.

THE CURE OF EVIL-SPEAKING

'*That whole body of people in England with whom you have a more immediate connexion*': i.e., Methodism.

'*It remains that you tell it to the elder or elders of the Church.*'

In terms of modern Methodist discipline this means: inform the Minister, who should, if the gravity of the case merits it, lay the matter before the Leaders' Meeting.

3. It is a little difficult to say what Jesus meant by: 'let him be to thee as an heathen man'. The intention probably is: 'If he hardens his heart, and insists, let him go his own way for a time.' Jesus respected human personality, and did not attempt to domineer over or to thrust Himself upon those who would not freely yield themselves to Him. At the same time, He diligently sought the wanderers, making Himself the Friend of publicans and sinners. Wesley's rendering is thus entirely in accord with the spirit of Jesus.

'*But have no friendship, no familiarity with him; no other intercourse than with an open Heathen*':

i.e., if opportunity offers, seek to bring him to Christ, but do not open your heart to him as is proper in the fellowship of Christians.

5. '*who are in derision called Methodists.*'

The name had not yet risen from a nickname to a title of honour.

'*Julian.*'

The Roman Emperor Julian, surnamed by the Christians 'the Apostate', reigned A.D. 361-3. He was brought up a Christian, but on ascending the throne declared for the ancient religion of the Empire, and made a short and most unsuccessful attempt to revive its glories. In his Epistles he ascribed the success of Christianity to the liberal charity of the Christians, even to the pagan poor. The phrase 'See how these Christians love one another' does not belong to him, but to Tertullian, **Apologeticus, 39.**

*Sermon Forty-Four**

# The Use of Money

NOT one of the Forty-Four Sermons is more interesting or more topical than this. For one thing, it is a wonderful piece of self-revelation by Wesley. Here is a picture of his character and life, as well as a fine example of his style. For another, it is fascinating to see how so great a Christian faces the economic problem of society. Here is a matter which today is bound to occupy much of the thought of the intelligent Christian. The unprogressive and obscurantist plea is that it is the sole business of the Church to hold prayer-meetings, and to 'get people saved', with the inference that 'the social Gospel' has no place in the Methodist pulpit. That plea is for ever ruled out of court by the inclusion of this fine sermon in our Standard of Methodist preaching.

At the same time, the reader is warned against trying to find in this sermon a charter of Christian Socialism. If a Christian today attacks the purely individualist conception of the economic order he probably does so as a Socialist. It is therefore hard for us to remember that Wesley makes this same attack, but does so as a High Church Tory. Christian economic and social thought of the Middle Ages had seen the feudal society of those days as something ordained by God. The modern conception of the various forms of society as based upon natural economic laws was then unknown. It was held that the duty of the State was to enforce the moral law declared by God through the Church. Church and State were to go hand in hand in regulating 'just prices' and conditions of work, and in preventing 'usury' (i.e., unlawful interest) and the making of profit by holding goods to await a rise in the market. It goes without saying that practice often fell sadly below precept. There is certainly no occasion for looking upon 'Merrie England' through rose-coloured spectacles. The seventeenth-

* No. 50 in *Fifty-three Sermons*

century High Church Toryism of Wesley's upbringing represents the last remnants of the ancient Christian tradition in this country, as it slowly melted away before the rising power of modern commercial society. Wesley's teaching implies that a man's status in society and his material estate are things ordained by God. (See Sermon XXIII, 26, with note, p. 168.) The King, for example, owed his position to a divine calling, not merely to the convenience of a human political constitution. What was true of the Head of the State was in principle also true of the lower orders. Wesley would not, with the modern individualist, have regarded a man's position and wealth as the reflection of ability and enterprise. This would have been condemned by him as an excess of human pride. At the same time, he would have repudiated the modern Socialist doctrine that the State ought to abolish great differences of wealth and social rank. These differences were part of God's plan for the world. Each man was to accept his God-given position in a spirit of responsibility, using it to the glory of God. He was to employ his possessions, whether great or small, as God's steward. This explains how Wesley can, in the present sermon, forcibly repudiate the conceptions of 'economic competition' and 'free enterprise', yet without betraying any indication that he thought it wrong that some should be rich and others poor. He speaks not for the collective society that may succeed the institutions of capitalist industrialism, but for quite a different collective society that preceded those institutions.

This sermon should remind one of the timelessness both of the Christian spirit, and of the problems of human nature and conduct. Wesley spoke to an age quite different from our own in economic circumstances. He spoke from pre-suppositions quite foreign to the mind of today. Yet his advice is relevant to the present time. The love of ease and luxury is still, as in every age, the enemy of the spiritual life. Soulless and rapacious commercialism can defile any social system. Thus no reordering of the political machine will of itself solve the problem of human sin. Successive centuries demand successive changes in the social and economic structure. As a citizen the Christian is called to interest himself in these matters, and to work to secure ordered progress. At the same time there remains to him his own particular task; to uphold the battle for the spiritual as against the materialistic view of life, for ethical considerations as against counsels of expediency. This issue must be joined afresh in every age, and in every human heart. In speaking so effectively to his own times Wesley speaks to our own, and to every age.

The immediate occasion of this sermon is interesting. In 1744 London was thrown into a state of alarm by the news that the Young Pretender, Prince Charles Edward Stewart, grandson of the exiled James II, was in France making preparations to invade the country, in an attempt to recover the throne. Friday, February 17, was proclaimed as a national day of fasting. Wesley improved the occasion by preaching to his people from this text. He records: 'And God opened their hearts, so that they contributed near fifty pounds, which I began laying out the very next hour in linen, woollen, and shoes for those whom I knew to be diligent and yet in want.' Ten days later another thirty pounds was collected, making a very substantial sum for those days. There was, however, a more fundamental reason for the constant preaching of this sermon, and for its publication. The period saw a rapidly growing commerce, and the first beginnings of factory industry, together with the rapid progress of agricultural enclosures. It was thus a time of increasing opportunity for material advancement for the able, though of increasing insecurity for the weak. The sober and frugal Methodist, possessed of a strong sense of purpose in life, was just the man to seize his opportunities. The nineteenth-century association of Wesleyan Methodism with a substantial middle class was thus already on the way. Wesley was very troubled at the spiritual consequences of the growing wealth of many of his people. In the *Minutes* of 1766 it is lamented that 'many Methodists grow rich, and thereby lovers of the present world'. In Sermon CXVI, 16 (*Works*, Vol. VII, p. 289), we read: 'I am distressed. . . . The Methodists grow more and more self-indulgent, because they grow rich. . . . And it is an observation which admits of few exceptions, that nine in ten of them decreased in grace, in the same proportion as they increased in wealth.' As always, Wesley took a balanced view. He did not hate the good things of life as such, for he knew they could be the means of great good if used aright. What he did hate was the selfish abuse of them in luxury and licence. He enjoined application and diligence in business, but was unsparing in his attack on covetousness.

1. *'namely, in this respect, that he used timely precaution.'*

This is probably the point of the parable, which is very obscure in meaning. The unjust steward was confronted with a sudden crisis, and had the good sense to make up his mind quickly as to what was to be done. The moral of the story presumably is: 'You who hear the Gospel face a crisis also. Now is the time to make an all-important decision; see you do not shirk it.' It is a blemish on the sermon that it is connected with this very difficult text, and with a text that has little to do with the subject matter.

2. The first two quotations are from Ovid, Met. i. 1. 141, and then 140.

*'One celebrated writer.'*

Horace, here addressed with more respect than usual.

The quotation is a part of the Odes, iii. 24, 47. A reference to the context would have reminded Wesley that what the poet is actually saying is quite in line with the sermon. Deploring the evil effects of the love of wealth, Horace bids the wealthy dedicate their gold to the public service, or, if they will not, at least throw it into the sea, lest they ruin themselves

*'the use of it would be superseded.'*

This does not at all follow. Even a completely communal State would find money a great convenience as a means of exchange.

I. 1. *'Some employments are absolutely and totally unhealthy, &c.'*

Wesley's outlook is enlightened, yet limited. He does **not** face the necessity that someone has to engage in these occupations, even if the Christian be prudent enough to avoid them.

2 *'defrauding the king of his lawful customs.'*

Smuggling was then widespread in coastal areas, and was frequently hardly accounted wrong by the people. Wesley fought a long battle against it.

*'I am convinced . . . I could not study . . . mathematics.'*

This is a very interesting testimony. By contrast, Sir Isaac Newton, England's greatest mathematician and scientist, was a deeply religious man. Wesley himself was certainly not averse to scientific study, but was interested in medicine and electricity.

3. *'gaming.'*

The worldly-wise condemn gambling because one may lose more than one can afford. Wesley condemns it because one may win. This is the profounder moral standard, for the essential wrong of gambling is the desire to gain from one's neighbour on account of mere chance, and not for some service rendered. Gambling expresses and feeds the spirit of 'something for nothing', which is the very opposite of the ideal of stewardship.

*'such interest as even the laws of our country forbid.'*

An act of Queen Anne limited interest to five per cent. This law was a vestige of the repeated but very partially successful medieval attempts to forbid 'usury', or unlawful interest. Defined in modern terms, 'usury' was interest on capital pure and simple, as distinct from gain arising from laying out land or goods to useful production, i.e., very roughly, 'unearned income' as opposed to 'profits'.

*'thereby all pawnbroking is excluded.'*

Wesley's objection in principle would presumably be that pawnbroking involved 'usury'. He doubtless also had in mind the practical objection that the pawnbroker's shop was a temptation to improvidence among the hard-pressed poor.

THE USE OF MONEY 269

*'we cannot . . . sell our goods below the market price.'*

Wesley did not, therefore, believe that the fair price for goods was that fixed automatically by free economic competition. He adhered to the ancient Christian theory of the 'Just Price', imposed upon commerce by ethical considerations.

4. This is indeed a magnificent paragraph. We have often heard Wesley plead like a Jeremiah or reason like a Paul. Here he thunders against wickedness in high places like an Elijah or an Amos. Wesley was not a total abstainer. That ideal was unknown in his day. We can, however, judge what sort of stand he would take today regarding the drink problem.

5. The medical profession had not then the same standard of honour that it has today.

6. In view of the later rigid ban among Methodists upon the theatre, and other 'worldly amusements', it would have been illuminating had Wesley been a little more explicit upon this point. He writes as though he were unwilling to say outright that the opera and theatre were sinful in themselves, but he certainly sounds as though he were suspicious that they were in fact likely to be *'natural inlets to sin'*. The theatre was, of course, at a lower moral level then than now. Wesley would have agreed that Shakespeare, at least, could *'profit the souls of men'*, for he left behind him his copy of the plays, with manuscript annotations. His successors destroyed what would now be a priceless relic.

7. Here Wesley's stern sense of duty is applied to commerce and industry.

8. *'men run on in the same dull track with their forefathers.'*

Wesley may not have believed in 'free competition', but he certainly believed in 'enterprise'. He himself was one of the pioneers of the cheap popular Press

II. 3. '*in costly . . . books*':

i.e., sumptuously bound editions. Wesley was far too good a scholar to have condemned those books which are costly on account of their contents.

7. '*Moloch.*'

This was the god of the Phoenicians, and was worshipped with a dreadful rite of human sacrifice. A fire burned in the hollow idol, and infants were thrown in.

7. 8. Wesley's advice, though hard to carry out, is most sensible. It is surprising that parents so often let affection get the better of common sense, and leave money to children who will be the worse for it.

III. 1. '*You may as well bury it . . . in the Bank of England.*'

Banking as we know it, where money deposited is usefully employed to finance industry and commerce, was in those days only beginning to arise in this country as a system. However, even then Wesley was somewhat out of date in speaking of a bank as though it were merely a glorified strong-box. Nevertheless, Wesley's argument is not affected thereby. He is not discussing the merits of banking, but urging that a Christian should not try to accumulate wealth for himself. The grand aim of diligence and frugality is that one may be a generous benefactor.

'*Having, first, gained all you can, and, secondly, saved all you can, then "give all you can".*'

We come at length to the completion of Wesley's famous three-fold rule. It is repeated by Wesley in many places. His own conduct is one of the best possible examples of the rule put into practice. Regarding 'gain all you can'; his book concern was a most successful enterprise. In Sermon LXXXVII, II, 7 (*Works*, Vol. VII, 9), he says: 'Two-and-forty years ago, having a desire to furnish poor people with cheaper, shorter, and plainer books than any I had seen, I wrote many small tracts, generally a penny a-piece; and afterwards several larger. Some of these had such a sale as I never thought of; and, by this means, I unawares became rich.' In his later years Wesley made up to £1,000 a year, which would be worth several times that today. As for 'save all you can'; Wesley lived a life of rigid economy and self-denial, though his person was always notably neat and tidy. In the same sermon (II, 6), he claims: 'I save all I can, not willingly wasting anything, not a sheet of paper, not a cup of water. I do not lay out anything, not a shilling, unless as a sacrifice to God.' This was the sober truth. When it came to 'give all you can'; Wesley's example was heroic. He wrote as follows of an Oxford Methodist, modestly not mentioning that it was himself when a young Fellow of Lincoln College: 'One of them had thirty pounds a year. He lived on twenty-eight and gave away forty shillings. The next year, receiving sixty pounds, he still lived on twenty-eight, and gave away thirty-two. The third year he received ninety pounds, and gave away sixty-two. The fourth year he received a hundred and twenty pounds; still he lived as before on twenty-eight, and gave to the poor all the rest.' The result was that in later years he could write in grim humour to the commissioner of taxes that his valuables amounted to 'two silver spoons, one in Bristol, the other in London'. In his closing days he wrote in his Diary for August 1, 1790: 'As my sight fails me much, I do not purpose to keep any more accounts. It suffices that I gain all I can, I save all I can, and I give all I can, that is, all I have.—J.W.' At his death he had given away some £30,000, and left only his furniture, £6 for the bearers at his funeral, and a little loose cash.

The three-fold rule is sound economics as well as sound ethics. Diligence and enterprise are certainly necessary if society is to enjoy an income sufficient for a civilized standard of life. To reduce luxury and waste diverts that income into socially useful channels. Finally, generosity is the secret of continuing economic prosperity in society. The basic cause of economic depression, and the tragic paradox of scarcity in the presence of plenty, is the desire of the individual to *accumulate for himself*.

So long as there is 'business confidence' those who have withdrawn money from current consumption will find that there are plenty of channels of profitable investment for their savings. So long as they invest, this money is fully returned to circulation by being spent on new industrial plant, &c. The public continues to have purchasing power sufficient to keep the factories and shops busy, and there are 'good times'. If this 'confidence' is disturbed, possibly by some relatively small and accidental circumstance, those with savings may feel that they are not likely to *accumulate* by investing them. The construction of new industrial plant, new houses, &c., falls off. This causes unemployment in certain trades, and in turn reduces the amount of spending money in general circulation. 'Confidence', i.e., expectation of gain, further declines. There is a more widespread curtailment of new investment. This makes things worse, and a slump sets in. Could every individual with savings which he was not at the moment able profitably to invest be trusted always to '*give*' them, i.e., to expend them fully on socially useful institutions or industries, without hope of personal gain, the seed of a 'cyclical depression' would never be sown. There would be continuous economic stability. Furthermore, all the varied proposals to cut this vicious circle, whereby a government might embark upon a policy of securing 'full employment', pre-suppose one thing. This is that there be sufficient enlightened public spirit, i.e., sufficient *generosity*, to place the public good before sectional interest.

There is one important proviso to 'give all you can'. The giving of alms to individuals may easily become degrading to the recipient, and also to the giver, particularly when done regularly and on a large scale. The way to 'give' a large sum is certainly to found or support some social institution that exists for the public good.

2. '*not as a proprietor, but a steward.*'

This is the whole sermon in a nut-shell.

3. Wesley is eminently sane and balanced. He plainly teaches that it is a moral duty to keep oneself and one's family in health

and decency. Money spent in this way is given to God. He would not have a man with family responsibilities rush into voluntary poverty, through fancied religious devotion.

### QUESTIONS

1. Wesley told his preachers: 'You have nothing to do but to save souls.' (*Twelve Rules of a Helper.*) Is he then inconsistent in preaching on 'The Use of Money'?

2. Increase of wealth commonly occasions a decrease of grace. Does a decrease of wealth often occasion an increase of grace?

3. Is it in accord with the spirit of Christ to spend millions on a noble Cathedral, when there may be many short of food and housing in the city? (Mark xiv. 3, 8.)

4. Are there any exceptional occasions when a man ought to fling himself, his wife, and his children, into want at the call of Christ? What may we learn from the example of Jesus?

5. Should a Christian with money to bestow give first to the Church, and to the Christian poor, and only after that to the outside world?

6. In the light of this sermon, what are the ethics of smoking?

7. A Christian Minister professes to have given his whole life to the service of God, and yet requires a measure of modest comfort. Is there anything inconsistent in this?

8. Comprehensive 'social insurance' would minimize the scope of 'charity'. Would this morally be a loss or a gain to society?

9. What are the ethics of gambling?

10. What is the Christian attitude toward necessary tasks which may be dangerous to health, limbs, or life?

11. Is it right for a Christian to spend liberally upon the education of his children? Is it right to consider the social prestige of a school, as well as the quality of the education?

12. Is money spent on good pictures, music, &c., thus supporting the arts, to be regarded as given to God?

# INDEXES

# I. INDEX OF THEOLOGICAL SUBJECTS

NOTE. 4.i.1 represents a reference to the *text of Wesley's Forty-four Sermons:* Sermon 4, section i, paragraph 1, etc.
The figures in *italics* denote *pages in this book* of Notes.

'ABBA': *p. 78*
ADOPTION: 4.i.1, 9.1,2, 18.ii.7; *p. 78*
ANGELS: 21.iii.9, 29.i.1,2, ii.6, iii.10, 31.ii.3; *p. 186*
ANTINOMIANISM: 1.iii.4, 10.ii.7, 20.iii.7,8, 22.1, 29.iv.3,8, 30.4-6, i.1, 2, ii.1,2,5,7, iii.1,4, 31.1, iii.5, 42.i.1, iii.1,2; *pp. xxv-xxvi, 8, 65, 76, 95, 104, 154-5, 184, 189, 191, 256-7*
ASSURANCE of salvation (joy, peace): 3.iii.6, 4.i.2-4, 7.i.10-11, ii.11, 8.ii.2,3,7,10,13, iii.4-6, 11.16,17, 14.i.7, ii.1,2, 16.i.13, 23.5, 29.iv.10, 36.2, 37.i.6,7, 40.i.1,3,4, iii.12, 41.iii.9, v.1,2; *pp. 4, 5, 20-1, 28, 63-4, 70-1, 72-4, 93-4, 247-8.* See also *Witness of the Spirit, Witness of one's own spirit*
ATONEMENT: 1.ii.3, 5.i.7,8, ii.5, iv.5, 12.ii.4, 30.1; *pp. 42, 44-6, 47-8, 50-4, 57, 64.* See also *Christ, Saving Work of; Reconciliation*

BAPTISM: 9.iii.8, 13.3, 39.ii.3; *pp. 70, 84, 115-19, 121-2, 212, 242-4, 244*
BAPTISMAL REGENERATION: 3.i.2, 14.1, iv.2-5, 39.iv.1,2,4; *pp. 115-17, 121-2, 241, 243-4*
BIBLE
*Exposition of:* see *Exegesis*
*Inspiration, authority of:* 12.iii.8-10, 15.ii.3, 21.iii.7, 24.2, 32.8; *pp. 107, 221-2*
*Study of:* 32.27; *p. 221*

CALVINISM: see *Grace*
CHRIST
*Divine claims:* 16.i.9; *pp. 132-3*
*Divine nature:* 44.1
*Foreknowledge:* 16.3; *p. 132*
*'in Christ':* 8.1,3; i.1; *p. 68*
*Saving work of:* 1.i.5, 7.ii.8, 20.i.4, 31.i.6, iii.3; *pp. 42, 153.* See also *Atonement*
CHRISTIAN HOPE, the: 4.iii.1-6, 21.iii.10, 44.2; *p. 30.* See also: *Eschatological expectation*
CHURCH, the
*Allegiance to:* 27.iii.9; *p. 103*

CHURCH, the (cont.)
  *Authority of:* pp. 99, 211-12
  *Catholicity:* 34.4, i.3,6,11-18, ii.1-8, iii.1-6; *pp. 212-14*
  *Divisions of:* 17.iii.18, 33.ii.2-6, 34.3, i.8; *pp. 203-4, 206, 210-11*
  *founded by Christ: p. 26*
  *nature of: pp. 25-6*
  *necessity of:* 34.i.10, iii.2,3; *pp. 88, 103-4, 210*
  *Primitive:* 4.i.10, ii.1-9; *p. 31*
  *Unity:* 33.ii.1-2; *pp. 201, 203-4*
  See also *Ministry, the*
CONVERSION: 3.ii.11, 4.i.1, 9.4, 15.1, 16.ii.1, 24.13, 33.i.13-14, 35.i.8, 37.2, 39.ii.4, 40.1,2; *pp. 72-3, 92-3, 94, 123, 246-7*
CREATION-story: 5.i.1-4; *pp. 38-40*

DEATH: 5.i.5, 9.ii.4, 39.i.3, *pp. 40, 79*

ENTIRE DEPRAVITY: see *Man*
EPISCOPACY: see *Ministry*
ESCHATOLOGICAL EXPECTATION: 3.iii.13-15, 6.3; *pp. 22, 26*. See also *Christian hope; Judgement*
EXEGESIS: see Sermons (Index II)
EXPERIENCE: 10.i.11.; *p. 94*

FAITH
  *and Works:* 1.iii.1,2, 2.ii.4, 5.iii.5,6, 13.i.8, ii.4, 14.i.6, 19.iii.1-3, 22.2, 24.4, 28.iii.5, 30.ii.5,6, *pp. 37-8*. See also *Antinomianism*
  *Divine gift of:* 1.iii.3, 3.ii.2, 5.iv.5,6, 6.i.8, 9.iii.3, 15.iii.3, 28.iii.5; *pp. 7-8, 218-19*
  'naked' ('dark night of the soul'): 40.ii.(ii.)1,2, iii.7-12, 41.iii.7; *pp. 248-9*
  *nature of:* 1.i.1-5, 2.ii.4-6, 5.iv. 2-3, 7.i.6-7, ii.10, 8.ii.3, 11.8, 12.iii.6, 13.i.6,7, ii.2, 14.i.2,3, 15.iii.2-3, 20.iii.9, 24.4, 28.ii.1,3,4, iii.4,5, 31.ii.3,5,6, 37.i.8, ii.1,5; *pp. 3-4, 6, 7-8, 52, 58, 68, 89, 91-2, 182-3, 193-4, 220-1*
  *Salvation by:* 1.iii.8, 5.iv.1, 6.i.6-11, 7.ii.9, 14.i.1,4, 25.27, 38.iii.3; *pp. 133-4, 182-3, 258-60*
  *'Stillness':* see *Means of Grace*
FALL, the: see *Sin*

GOD
  *the Father:* 21.iii.5
  *goodness of:* 25.20, 28.ii.2, 40.ii.10

GOD (cont.)
  *holiness (majesty):* 5.iv.7, 6.ii.7, 21.iii.6,7,16, 29.iii.6, iv.9, 34.i.12, 35.i.2,3; *p. 51*
  *moral attributes:* 5.ii.2, 9.i.2, ii.1, 29.i.2,3, ii.3,4, iii.4, 37.i.2, 38.i.3, 39.i.1; *pp. 57, 63, 95, 152, 186, 188*
  *Righteousness of:* 5.ii.5, 6.ii.7, 17.i.12, 18.iii.5; *pp. 46, 47-8, 106*
  *sovereignty of:* 18.iii.5,6, 29.iii.7,8, 42.i.2, 44.iii.2; *pp. 142-3, 257*
  *Wrath of:* 5.1, 6.ii.6, 7.ii.5,7, 9.iii.4; *p. 38*
GODS, heathen: 22.i.2
GOSPEL-call, the: 1.iii.6,7,9, 2.ii.7-11, 3.ii.1-13, iii.1-5, 4.ii.3,4, 6.iii.1-6, 7.ii.13, 8.iii.1-6, 9.iv.1,4, 16.i.12, 18.iv, 20.iv.12,13, 23.19, 24.14,15, 28, 26.iii.4-6, 28.iii.12, 30.i.3-12, 37.ii.3,8, 40.iii.14; *pp. 8-9, 57, 231*
GOSPELS, composition of: *p. 140*
GRACE,
  *divine:* 9.iii.2, 11.14,15, 12.ii.3,6, v.4, 18.ii.6, 19.iii.7, 20.ii.3, 21.iii.4,11-13, 22.ii.7, 29.iv.2, 30.ii.3,4, 37.ii.2,7, 41.v.3; *pp. xxiv, 45, 106, 160*
  *Calvinism:* 1.ii.4, 42.i.1; *pp. 4-5, 7, 88, 256-7*
  *Election:* 5.iv.7; *pp. 51-2*
  *Final perseverance:* 1.ii.4; *pp. 4-5*
  *free:* 1.1, ii.3, iii.3, 5.iv.7, 6.ii.8, 14.iv.4, 29.iii.10
  *Prevenient:* 11.6, 12.ii.1, 15.i.6, 29.i.4-6, 38.i.4,5, ii.9; *pp. 82, 105, 124, 235, 236*
  *universal:* 1.ii.2, 21.iii.5, 29.iii.10, 40.ii.1
  *Predestination:* 42.i.1; *pp. 81-2, 256-7*
  See also *Means of Grace*

HEAVEN: 21.iii.8, 37.ii.4
HELL: 7.ii.4, 17.i.11, 26.i.5, iii.4, 39.iii.2; *pp. 15, 20, 137, 175-6, 242-3*
HOLY COMMUNION
  *doctrine of:* 12.iii.12, 27.iii.8; *pp. 27, 180-1*
  *obligation to:* 12.iii.11-12, 20.iv.8, 21.iii.11; *p. 160*
  *use of:* 12.iii.11; *pp. 107-8*

INSPIRATION, of man: 32.19,25; *p.198*

JESUS
  *the historical: pp. 96, 154*
  *and Judaism:* 27.iii.6; *p. 180.* See also *Law*
  *teaching of:* 24.23, 25.15; *pp. 44, 80-1, 171, 173*
JUDGEMENT
  *Last, the:* 5.ii.5, 25.4, 30.i.10

# INDEX

JUDGEMENT (cont.)
*present:* 3.iii.13-15, 7.ii.4

JUSTIFICATION (forgiveness): 1.ii.3,4,7, 5.1-3, ii.1-5, iii.1,2, iv.5,6, 6.i.13-14, 8.2, ii.1, iii.1, 9.iii.4, 15.1-3, 21.iii.13, 22.2, 24.21, 29.iv.4, 30.1, ii.5-7, 31.2, 35.ii.28, 37.i.2,3, ii.2, 39.1, 41.iii.9; *pp. 43-5, 46, 123-4, 162*

KINGDOM OF GOD: 7.i.1,12-13, 17.i.13, iii.18, 21.iii.8, 37.2; *pp. 60-1, 160*

LAW
*fulfilled by Christ:* 20.1,2, i.3, ii.1,2,4, iii.1,2; *pp. 6-7, 152-4*
*Moral:* 29.1,2,3, i.1-4, ii.1-3,5-6, iii.1-12, iv.1-10, 30.2-5
*Moral and Ceremonial Law:* 20.i.1-2, 29.2, 30.3; *pp. 151-2, 171, 185*
*Mosaic:* 29.1, i.5, ii.1,2, iv.4,10; *pp. 46, 48, 80-1, 186-7*

LEGAL RELIGION: 1.iii.8, 2.i.4-13, 3.i.5-7, ii.12, 6.2-4, i.1-5, ii.1-5, iii.1, 7.i.1-5, ii.5, 9.2,5, ii.9-10, 22.iv.2,3, 24.12,21,22, 26.i.5, ii.2, 28.i.1-6, iii.1-4,9, 29.2, 30.iii.2,3,7, 31.i.4,5, 32.16,17, 39.iii.2, iv.4; *pp. 61-2, 79, 83, 155-6, 190-1, 193, 206*

LORD'S PRAYER
*expounded:* 21.iii.1-16
*paraphrase of:* 21.iii.16

LOVE of God: 14.iii.1,2, 24.5, 28.ii.1,2, 31.ii.1,2,3,6, iii.3, 34.i.14, 40.i.1, 41.iv.4

MAN
*'collective personality':* p. 41
*conscience:* 11.1-6, 25.22; *pp. 98-9*
*constitution of:* 8.i.2, 36.ii.3-9, iii.5, iv.3-5,7; *pp. 69, 227-8, 252*
*'Covenant of Works':* 5.i.2,4, 6.1, i.1-5,11-14, 11.20, 30.ii.3; *pp. 55-6*
*creation of:* 1.1, 5.i.1, 39.i.1; *pp. 38-40*
*Entire Depravity:* 1.2, 3.iii.10-12, 5.iii.3, 6.i.11, ii.5,6, iii.1,2, 7.ii.1-3, 9.3, i.7, 11.10, 13.i.2, ii.1, 16.i.4,5, 25.7, 26.i.3-6, 28.iii.6,7, 29.i.4, iii.4, 31.i.3, 33.i.3-12, 35.ii.10, 36.i.2,3, 38.i.1-5, ii.1, iii.1-3, 39.i.4, 42.i.3-5; *pp. 233-5, 238.* See also *the Natural Man*
*the Flesh:* 8.i.2, *pp. 69, 84*
*guilt of:* p. 40. See also MAN, *Entire Depravity; Repentance; Sin*
*moral bondage and Free Will:* 7.ii.6, 9.i.4, ii.7-10, 13.i.3, 21.iii.13, 35.ii.14; *pp. 81-2, 222-3, 234.* See also MAN, *Entire Depravity*
*the Natural:* 2.i.1-3, 3.i.2-11, 4.ii.5, iv.1,3,5-10, 9.5, i.1-8, iii.8, iv.2, 10.ii.2, 11.6,19, 13.2, 15.i.7, 16.ii.6,7, 18.iii.4,8, 24.10, 25.20, 26.ii.4-8, 27.1, 29.i.6, 35.i.8, 36.ii.1,2, 38.ii.1-8, 39.ii.4; *pp. 3, 99*

# INDEX

**MAN** (cont.)
*and Nature:* pp. *38-40*
*need of salvation:* **16**.i.6,10, **28**.iii.6, **38**.iii.4,5; pp. *130, 239, 265-6*
*original state:* **5**.i.1-4, **29**.i.3, **31**.ii.4,5, **39**.i.1,2; pp. *39-40, 241-2*

**MEANS OF GRACE**
*Bible study:* **12**.iii.7-10. See also *Bible*
*fasting:* **20**.iv.8, **22**.4, i.1-6, ii.1-12, iii.1-7, iv.1-6; pp. *162-3*
*fellowship:* **19**.i.1-2,5, **34**.2, ii.3,4, **43**.iii.5; pp. *88, 125-6, 261*
*images:* pp. *205-6*
*necessity and use of:* **4**.i.8, **7**.i.4, **12**.i.1-3, ii.7,8, iii.1-12, iv.1-5, v.1-4, **15**.i.8, iii.2-3, **18**.i.8, **19**.i.1, iii.4-6, **20**.iv.8,12, **21**.1,2, **22**.3-4, ii.7, iii.2,3,4, iv.1, **23**.28, **28**.i.3, iii.3, **30**.iii.8, **32**.39, **34**.ii.2, iii.3, **40**.ii.4, **42**.ii.1,6; pp. *62, 87, 102-4, 108, 124, 127*
*prayer:* **12**.iii.1-6, **21**.ii.1-5, **22**.ii.6, iv.6, **25**.18,19, **34**.ii.2; pp. *158-9*
*'stillness':* **12**.i.6, **19**.3,4; pp. *87, 102-3*
*work of Spirit in:* **12**.ii.3
See also *Baptism; Holy Communion*

**MINISTRY**
*Call to preach:* **33**.iii.6-10; pp. *206-7*
*conduct of:* **4**.iv.7,8
*Episcopacy:* **34**.ii.2; p. *213*
*Orders:* **33**.iii.10.
*unworthy Ministers:* **20**.iii.4-8, **27**.2-4, i.4-7, ii.1-5, iii.5-14; pp. *179-181*
*work of:* **4**.iv.8, **27**.i.2,3, iii.1-4; p. *34*

**MORALITY**, need of; see *Antinomianism*


**NATURAL RELIGION:** **38**.ii.4; p. *237*
**NEW BIRTH**, the: **1**.ii.7, **14**.1,2, iv.1-5, **15**.1-3, i.1-10, **39**.1,2, i.4, ii.1-5, iii.1-3, iv.3,4; pp. *123-4, 243-4*


**ORDERS:** see *Ministry*


**PERFECTION**, Christian: **1**.ii.6, **6**.ii.9, **8**.ii.4-13, iii.4, **13**.ii.10, **14**.i.5 **16**.5,6, **17**.i.10, ii.6, **18**.iii.13, **31**.iii.6, **35**.1-4, i.1-9, ii.1-2, 21-30. **36**.1, iii.1-7, iv.1,2,5-8, **37**.2-5, i.5,10,11, ii.3; pp. *5-6, 70-1, 74-5, 100-1 119-20, 132, 215-20, 222-5, 226, 228, 229, 230-1*
**PROPHECY:** **27**.i.2; pp. *178-9*
**PROPITIATION:** pp. *45-6*
**PROVIDENCE**, divine: **18**.i.7,11, iii.5-6, **21**.ii.5, **23**.21, **24**.17,18,23,24,25, 29, **32**.28-29, **36**.iii.1; pp. *171, 199*
**PURGATORY:** p. *175*

# INDEX

REASON, place in religion: 10.i.2, 13.ii.2,3, 32.24-25, 38, 34.i.3-5, 38.ii.3; pp. 90, 112-13, 197-9, 214, 236-7

RECONCILIATION: 5.i.8-9, 6.ii.7-8, 14.iii.1, 29.i.4; pp. 42, 186

REGENERATION, see *New Birth*

REPENTANCE: 1.iii.4-6, 7.ii.1,6,7, 8.iii.2,4,6, 9.i.3, 10.ii.4, 16.i.13, 26.iii.6, 40.iii.1-6, 42.ii.2-4; pp. 64, 82, 94-5, 162. See also: *Sin, conviction of*

REVELATION
*Biblical:* **Pref.** 5, 11.6, 31.i.5, 32.22, 35.i.5, ii.2; pp. 99, 107, 214
*divine:* 29.i.2-5, ii.3-6, 38.ii.3; pp. 197-8, 237
*in Christ:* 16.3
*progressive:* p. 99

SALVATION, present: 1.ii.1, 7.i.13; pp. 4, 111-12

SANCTIFICATION (holiness): 1.ii.5,6, 2.ii.2, 4.i.5,7,9, 7.i.8,9, ii.12, 8.i.3-6, ii.4, 9.iii,5-7, 10.ii.5,6,8, 11.11,12,18,20, 13.i.1,2,11-13, ii.9, 14.i.4,5, iii.3-5, 15.iii.2, 17.ii.2-6, 18.i.1-3,6, 23.2-4, 24.6,7,20, 28.ii.1, iii.8,10-12, 29.iv.10, 30.ii.6,7, iii.3, 31.ii.1, iii.2-4, 35.ii.3,4, 39.iii.1, iv.3, 40.i.5, iii.14, 41.iv.5; pp. 45, 70-1, 74-5, 137, 145, 218, 244. See also *Love of God*

SATAN (evil spirits): 4.ii.9, 5.ii.2, 9.ii.6, 10.ii.13, 17.i.11, 21.iii.15, 28.ii.4, 33.i.1-6, 36.ii.9, iv.6, 37.1, 38.ii.8,9, 41.iii.6; pp. 43, 83, 201-2, 238

SECOND COMING: see *Eschatological expectation*

SIN
*in believers:* 15.ii.4-10, iii.1-4, 16.ii.1-2, 19.i.9, 40.ii.(i)2-10, ii.(iii.)1,2
*conviction of:* 5.iii.4, iv.8, 6.iii.3-6, 8.iii.2,3, 9.ii.1-8, 10.ii.4, 13.i.2-5, 14.i.3, 16.i.4,5,7,8, 22.ii.2, iv.5,6, 25.7, 26.iii.5, 28.ii.1, 29.iii.4, iv.1,2,4-6, 30.i.3,8,12, iii.4-7, 37.ii.1,2, 41.iii.9; pp. 83, 84, 188, 192
*nature of:* 8.ii.8-9, 11-13, 15.ii.2, 20.iii.2, 21.iii.13, 23.6-8, 26.i.2, 34.i.5, 35.ii.21, 36.iii.1-6, 44.ii.5; pp. 73-5, 125-7, 227-8, 232-3
*origin of (The Fall):* 3.i.1,8-9, 5.i.5,6, 29.i.4, 31.ii.5, 38.4, 39.i.2-4; pp. 223-4, 235, 241-2
*Original:* 16.i.4,10, 38.iii.2,5, 39.i.4; pp. 225, 232-4, 236, 239
see also: *Death*

SPIRIT, gifts of: 4.1-5, 32.18,38; pp. 25-6

TEMPTATION:
15.ii.7-10, iii.1, 19.i.5, 21.iii.15, 24.27, 35.i.8, 36.iii.4-6, 37.i.1-14, 41.iii.6, iv.2-3. See also *Satan*

TRINITY, Holy: 21.iii.7; pp. 159-60

WITNESS of the SPIRIT: 3.i.11-12, ii.8,9, iii.6-9, 7.i.11, 8.2, ii.2,3, 10.1-3, i.7-12, ii.1-14, 13.i.9, ii.5, 14.ii.3-5, iv.1-2, 40.i.3; *pp. 81-9, 91-4, 95-6, 111-12, 195*

WITNESS of one's OWN SPIRIT: 10.i.2-6,8-11, ii.12,13, 11.7, 15-20, 13.i.9; *p.90*

WORKS, Salvation by: see *Legal Religion*

## II. INDEX OF HISTORICAL SUBJECTS

Addison, Joseph: **17**.iii.8; *p. 138*
ANGLICAN CHURCH
  *Clergy of:* **4**.iv.8, **33**.iii.9; *pp. 154, 179, 207*
  *contemporary services:* **2**.i.7, *p. 12*
  *Homilies quoted:* **1**.iii.8, **2**.ii.4,5, **5**.iv.3, **14**.i.3, **22**.ii.2, **39**.ii.4; *pp. 9, 15, 48, 119, 242*
  *Prayer Book quoted:* **3**.iii.9, **4**.iv.8, **5**.i.7, iii.5, **7**.ii.9, **10**.ii.4, **12**.ii.1, **13**.ii.1, **21**.iii.8, **39**.iv.1; *pp. 21, 34, 42, 46, 48, 62, 95, 105, 112, 125, 132, 160*
  *Wesley's relation to:* **3**.iii.9, **5**.iii.5, iv.3, **12**.ii.1, **20**.iv.8, **22**.i.4,6, ii.2, **27**.iii.6,8-9, **28**.iii.1, **33**.ii.4, iii.9-10, **34**.i.10, **39**.iv.2; *pp. 11, 15, 21, 48-50, 87, 105, 115-6, 156, 163, 180, 205, 207, 211, 243*
Aristotle: *p. 12*
Arminius: **5**.iv.7; *pp. 51-2*
Augustine, S.: **3**.ii.5, **32**.28; *pp. 20, 200*

Band Meeting: *p. 261*
Baptismal Office, Methodist: *pp. 118-19*
Baptists: **33**.ii.4; *pp. 205, 212*
Bell, George: *p. 65*
Blackstone, William: *pp. 25, 35*
Böhler, Peter: **13**.9; *pp. 87, 111-12, 183*
Book Room: *p. 270*

Calvin, John: **5**.iv.7, **33**.iv.6; *pp. 51-2, 208*
Catechism, Shorter: **28**.ii.2; *p. 182*
Chrysostom: **35**.ii.16
Church of England: see *Anglican Church*
Church, Thomas: *p. 197*
Cicero: **38**.ii.11, *p. 239*
Circumcision; *pp. 110-11*
Class Meeting: *p. 261*
Cudworth: **13**.ii.5; *p. 113*
Cyprian: **35**.ii.16

Davies, Sir John: **31**.ii.4; *p. 194*
'Deed of Declaration': *p. xix*
Deism: **33**.iv.4; *p. 208*

Dion Cassius: 33.i.8
discipline, of the Society: 43.iii.1,2; *p. 263*
Dodd, C. H.: *p. 53*
Donne, John: 16.ii.3; *p. 134*

Edward VI: 18.iii.5; *p. 143*
'enthusiasm', charges of: 3.iii.6,10, 7.ii.13, 32.1-39; *pp. 21, 22, 65, 195, 197, 200, 238*
Epicurus, Epicureanism: 2.i.9, 9.i.2, 38.ii.6; *pp. 13, 80*
Epiphanius: 22.i.6; *p. 163*
exorcism: 33.2; *pp. 201-2*

Felix: 25.16; *p. 174*
Flew, R. N.: *p. 61*
'Foundery', the: *p. 103*

Gamaliel: 20.iv.2; *p. 100*
Glas, John: 7.ii.10; *p. 65*
grammar: see *Sermons*
Green, Richard: *p. xxi*
Guyon, Madame: 41.iii.8,9; *p. 253*

Hobbes, Thomas: 38.iii.4; *p. 239*
'Holy Club': 4.i.8-9, 22.i.6; *pp. 25-6, 28, 163, 271*
Homer: 32.9
Horace: 2.i.9, 23.18, 38.iii.1, 44.2; *pp. 13, 167, 239, 267*
Humanism: *pp. 9-10*
Huntingdon, Countess of: *p. 11*
Hutcheson, Francis: 11.5; *p. 98*

Jerome: 35.ii.16
Judaism: 20.iv.4,5, 22.i.6, 31.i.3, 35.ii.7-8,13, 39.ii.3; *pp. 155-6, 193, 222, 242*. See also *Law*
Julian, Emperor: 43.iii.5; *p. 263*
Juvenal: 39.iii.3, 41.iii.3; *pp. 243, 253*

Kennicott, Benjamin: 4.iv.9; *pp. 25, 31-2, 34*
Kimchi, Rabbi David: 31.i.3; *p. 193*

'Large Minutes': *p. xix*
Latitudinarianism: 34.iii.1-3; *p. 214*

Law, William: **13**.i.2, ii.8, **19**.iii.1-8, **23**.1,23,24, **39**.iv.3; *pp. 105, 111, 113, 148, 165, 168, 244*
Local Preachers: **33**.iii.5-12; *pp. 206-7*
Luther, Martin: **1**.iii.9; *pp. 56, 74*

Marx, Karl: *p. 129*
Maxfield, Thomas: *pp. 65, 206*
METHODISM
   *persecution of:* **1**.iii.9, **18**.iii.1-3,6-7,11; *pp. 26, 143*
   *prejudice against:* **16**.ii.7, **18**.iii.3,8, **25**.6, **26**.ii.9-10, **27**.ii.5, **31**.i.5, **32**.1-4,11,16-17, **35**.1,2, **37**.i.14, **39**.iv.4, **40**.iii.1, **43**.iii.5; *pp. 144, 173, 176, 179, 195-7, 249, 263*. See also *'Enthusiasm'*, charges of
'Methodist', name: **43**.iii.5; *p. 263*
Milton, John: **41**.iii.1; *p. 251*
'Model Deed': *pp. xix-xxi*
Moravians: **12**.ii.4, iv.1-6, **19**.iv.3, **42**.i.1, iii.2; *pp. 87, 93, 102-3, 105-6, 108, 148, 150, 155, 259*
Mysticism (Mystics): **10**.i.2, **12**.i.4,5, **13**.ii.10, **40**.ii.(*ii.*)1,2, **41**.iii.8-9, **42**.4; *pp. 86, 90, 104-5, 113, 247, 249, 253-4, 255-6*

national situation: **3**.iii.13-15; *p. 22*
Newton, Sir Isaac: **44**.i.2; *p. 268*
Nonconformists: **39**.iv.1; *pp. 24, 243*

Paul, S., education of: **11**.14; *p. 100*
Pharisees: **20**.iv.2-11; *pp. 155-6*
Plato: **29**.ii.4, **38**.iii.3; *pp. 187, 195, 239*
Pope, Alexander: **14**.i.7; *p. 120*
Presbyterians: **34**.i.11; *p. 212*
Pretender, Young: **3**.iii.15; *pp. 22, 266*
Prior, Matthew: **23**.20, **31**.ii.1, **38**.ii.10; *pp. 168, 194, 239*
Protestants: **17**.iii.18, **26**.i.4, **31**.1.4; *p. 220*. See also *Reformation*

Quakers: **12**.i.4, **18**.i.10, **33**.ii.4; *pp. 105, 141, 205*

Rabbinical tradition; *p. 155*
'Ranters': **42**.i.1; *p. 257*
Reformation: **18**.iii.5, **34**.i.10; *pp. 143-4, 211*
Ritschl, A.: *p. 60*
Roman Catholicism: **1**.iii.8, **16**.i.3, **17**.iii.18, **21**.ii.4, **31**.i.4, **33**.ii.5; *pp. 86, 104-5, 106, 139, 144, 205-6, 249*

# INDEX

Sadducees; *p. 155*
Salmon, Matthew: *p. 181*
Sandeman, Robert: **7**.ii.10; *p. 65*
Scribes: **20**.iv.1,2; *p. 155*
Seneca: **17**.iii.6, **25**.13; *pp. 138, 173*
SERMONS, WESLEY'S
  Charles Wesley's: *pp. 17-19*
  Exegesis of: **2**.1; *p. 11*  **3**.i.7, ii.10,11; *pp. 19-21*  **4**.3; *p. 27*  **5**; *pp. 37-8*
    **5**.ii.5, iv.1; *pp. 46-8*  **5**.iv.5,7; *pp. 50-2*  **6**.1, i.1,7; *pp. 55-6*  **7**.i.11, ii.4;
    *pp. 64-5*  **8**.i.2; *p. 69*  **8**.ii.1,4; *pp. 72-3*  **9**.ii.9; *p. 84*;  **10**.i.1; *p. 90*
    **11**.8,11; *p. 100*  **12**.iii.7,8, iv.4-6; *pp. 107-8*  **13**.ii.9; *p. 113*  **14**.i.5, ii.4;
    *pp. 119-20*  **15**.i.4; *p. 125*  **16**.i.2, ii.5; *pp. 133-4*  **17**.i.11, iii.11,18;
    *pp. 137-9*  **18**.i.4; *p. 140*  **18**.iii.13; *pp. 144-5*  **20**.ii.1; *p. 153*  **20**.iv.5;
    *p. 156*  **21**.i.3, iii.6,7-14; *pp. 158-61*  **23**.2-8; *p. 165*  **24**.4, 21; *p. 170*
    **26**.iii.1,2; *p. 176*  **27**.i.2; *p. 178*  **31**.i.1; *p. 193*, **33**.iii.7; *pp. 206-7*
    **35**.ii; *pp. 221-2*  **35**.ii.18; *p. 223*  **37**.i.13; *p. 231*  **38**; *pp. 234-5*  **43**.iii.3;
    *p. 263*  **44**.1; *p. 267*
  number of: *pp. xx-xxi*
  occasions of preaching: *pp.1, 11, 18, 24-5, 37, 60, 110, 259, 261, 266*
  purpose of: **Pref.** 6, 7; *pp. xxiii, 17-18*
  style and character of: **Pref.** 2, 3, **2**.ii.6, **4**.iv.1-11, **10**.1-3, **15**.i.3-10,
    **19**.iii.5, **23**.16, **27**.i.1, **34**.i.4; *pp. xv, 1-3, 6, 15, 31-2, 37, 67-8, 90,
    102, 124, 129-31, 149, 167, 195, 210, 217-18, 246-7*
  Vocabulary and Grammar of: **1**.1; *p.2*  **1**.ii.3; *p. 7*  **2**.i.1-3; *p. 12*  **3**.iii.10;
    *p. 22*  **4**.ii.2; *p. 28*  **7**.i.4; *p. 62*  **7**.ii.4; *p. 65*  **8**.i.2; *p. 69*  **8**.i.5; *p. 72*
    **9**.1, i.2; *pp. 79-80*  **11**.3,4; *p. 98*  **13**.1, i.7; *p. 111*  **14**.iii.2; *p. 121*
    **15**.iii.3; *p. 127*  **16**.8; *p.132*  **17**.i.2; *p. 135*  **19**.5, i.6; *p. 148*  **20**.iv.7;
    *p. 156*  **22**.2, ii.6; *p. 163*  **25**.17; *p. 174*  **26**.ii.1; *p. 176*  **29**.iii.6,9, iv.4;
    *pp. 188-9*  **32**.7,14; *pp. 196-7*  **33**.i.6; *p. 202*  **35**.ii.8; *p. 222*  **35**.ii.26;
    *p. 227*  **36**.ii, iii.4; *p. 227*  **37**.5; *p. 230*  **41**.ii.2, iii.1; *p. 251*
  University Sermons: *pp. 1-2, 11, 18-19, 24, 110*
Severus, Alexander: **25**.22; *p. 174*
Shaftesbury, Lord: **11**.5, **32**.9; *pp. 98, 195-6*
Shakespeare, William: **23**.18; *pp. 167, 269*
Stoics: **17**.i.2; *p. 135*
Sundar Singh, Sadhu: *p. 256*
Superstition: **38**.ii.6; *p. 238*

Taylor, John: **38**.2; *p. 236*
Tertullian: **22**.i.3, **35**.ii.16; *pp. 163, 263*

Unitarians: **33**.iv.4; *p. 207*

Vocabulary; see *Sermons*

Watts, Isaac: *p. 47*
WESLEY, JOHN
   *character:* **Pref.** 8, 9, 2.i.12-13, 23.12, 24.26, 41.iii.3-4, 44.i.2; *pp. xxvi, 14-15, 67, 93, 130, 167, 171, 176, 252, 255, 264-5, 268*
   *relation to Anglican Church;* see *Anglican Church*
   *relation to Oxford:* 4.iv.2-11; *pp.11, 31-5*
   *Standard Sermons:* see *Sermons*
Westminster Confession: *pp. 81-2*
Williams, Joseph: *p. 18*

Young, Dinsdale T.: *p. 1*

Zinzendorf, Count von: 42.iii.2; *pp. 259-60*

## III. INDEX OF PRACTICAL AND ETHICAL SUBJECTS

almsgiving: 20.iv.9, 21.i.1-4, 22.iv.7, 23.23,24,26-28, 25.26, 44.iii.1,3,6; *pp. 266, 270-2*
anger: 17.i.8-10, 35.ii.26, 40.ii.7
apostasy: 19.i.9; *p. 148*
asceticism: 16.i.3, 17.i.2,3,5, 41.iii.4, 42.i.14; *pp. 133, 135, 220, 228, 253, 258*

banking: 44.iii.1; *p. 270*
breeding, good: 17.iii.8; *p. 138*

charity in judgement: 17.iii.6,11,15, 25.8-14, 25, 32, 34
Communism; *p. 257*
covetousness: 16.i.3, 23.13-16, 22

diligence: 24.16, 30.iii.6, 44.i.7,8
divorce: 18.i.5; *pp. 140-1*

economic system, the: 23.26; *pp. 168, 264-5, 271-2*
envy: 37.ii.6
ethical religion: 19.2; *p. 147*
evangelistic calling, the: 16.ii.8, 18.ii.6, 19.i.7,8, ii.1-7, iii,7,8, iv.1-4, 24.26, 25.15-18, 33.iii.11,12, 40.i.2, 41.iii.5, 43.iii.3; *pp. 149-50, 171, 246-7, 248*
evil speaking: 17.iii.14, 43.1-5, i.6,7, iii.4,5; *pp. 261-2*
example, force of: 20.iii.3, 41.iv.7
extortion: 20.iv.7, 23.25, 44.i.3

forgiveness: 21.iii.14

gambling: 44.i.3; *p. 268*
guidance, divine: 32.20-26,38, 44.iii.5; *pp. 197-8*

happiness: 39.iii.3
health, preservation of: 22.iv.4
homiletics, points of: Pref. 3, 2.ii.6, 25.16, 30.i.12, 37.ii.14; *pp. xxiv, 3, 6, 15, 44, 69-70, 173-4, 231*
humility: 13.i.2, ii.1, 16.i.4,7-9; *pp. 111, 134*

infirmity, bodily: 8.ii.9, 36.ii.3, iii.4-5, iv.3-4, **41**.ii.3, iii.1-2; *pp. 75, 251-2*
inheritance, of wealth: 44.ii.6-8; *p. 270*
invincible ignorance: 34.i.5; *p. 210*

Just Price, the: **20**.iv.7, **44**.i.3; *pp. 156, 269*

language, use of: 32.26; *pp. 198-9*
liquor traffic: 44.i.4; *p. 269*
love: **17**.iii.1-17, **18**.ii.4-7, iii.13, 25.22-26, 34.1,2,4, i.17-18, ii.3,4. See also *Sanctification* (Index I)

master of a house: 2.i.4; *p.12*
meekness: 17.i.1-7
money, use of: 18.iii.12, 19.iv.4, 23.9-12,23-24,26-28, 30.iii.5-6, **44**.2,3; ii.1-7, iii.1-7; *pp. 144, 167-8, 265, 267, 270-1, 272-3*. See also *Economic System*

oaths, legal: 18.i.10; *p. 141*

patriotism: 33.i.10; *pp. 30, 203*
pawnbroking: 44.i.3; *p. 268*
peace-making: 18.ii.2,3
perjury: 4.iv.9; *p. 34*
persecution: **18**.iii.2-12, **42**.4; *pp. 143-4*
poverty: **41**.iii.3; *p. 252*
poverty, religious: **16**.i.3; *p. 133*
praise, desire for: 30.iii.6, 38.ii.11, 44.ii.4
pride: 32.30-32, 38.ii.7, 40.ii.6
primitive races: 23.9, 33.i.9; *pp. 165-6, 203*
purity, sexual: 18.i.4,5, 38.ii.9; *pp. 141, 238*

resignation: 21.iii.9, 42.i.11,12
reproof, duty of: 43.i.1-5, ii.1-4, iii.1-2
riches: 23.17-21,25; *pp. 266-7*
riches, trust in: 24.8,9; *p. 133*

self-denial: **13**.i.10, ii.6-8, **16**.ii.4, **18**.i.4, **19**.iv.4, **22**.ii.3,4,5, iii.5,6, **30**.iii.4-5, **42**.1-4, i.1-14, ii.1-7, iii.1-4; *pp. 257-8*
self-righteousness: 14.iv.4
self-will: 38.ii.8, 42.i.5
sermon preparation: 32.27

smuggling: **44**.i.2; *p. 268*
Social Gospel, the: **17**.18, **19**.2,5, iii.7; *pp. 129-30, 139, 145, 149, 264*
social order, the: **23**.26; *pp. 168, 264-5*
Socialism: *pp. 264-5*
solitary religion: **19**.5, i.1-6
sorrow, ('heaviness'): **41**.1, i.1-6, ii.1-4, iii.1-5, iv.1-2, v.1-4; *pp. 251, 253*
sublimation: **17**.5; *p. 136*
sympathy: **41**.iii.3-5; *p. 252*

theatre: **44**.i.6; *p. 269*
toleration: **Pref.** 9, 10, **17**.iii.12-13, **32**.36, **33**.iii.4,11,12, iv.1-6, **34**.i.6 9-11; *pp. 138, 205, 207-8*

usury: **44**.i.3; *pp. 264, 268*

wandering thoughts: **36**.i.1-4, ii.1-9, iii.1-7, iv.1-8; *pp. 226-7*
war: **4**.iii.3, **17**.iii.18, **36**.i.4; *pp. 30, 227*
work: **23**.1, **44**.i.1-8; *pp. 267-8, 269*

www.ingramcontent.com/pod-product-compliance
Lightning Source LLC
Chambersburg PA
CBHW050623300426
44112CB00012B/1626